READING THE WEB

Solving Problems in the Teaching of Literacy

Cathy Collins Block, Series Editor

Reading the Web

STRATEGIES *for* INTERNET INQUIRY

Maya B. Eagleton and **Elizabeth Dobler**

FOREWORD by Donald J. Leu

THE GUILFORD PRESS
New York   London

© 2007 The Guilford Press
A Division of Guilford Publications, Inc.
72 Spring Street, New York, NY 10012
www.guilford.com

Printed in the United States of America

This book is printed on acid-free paper.

Last digit is print number: 9   8   7   6   5   4   3   2   1

Library of Congress Cataloging-in-Publication Data

Eagleton, Maya B.
   Reading the Web : strategies for Internet inquiry / by Maya B. Eagleton and
Elizabeth Dobler ; foreword by Donald J. Leu.
      p.   cm. — (Solving problems in the teaching of literacy)
   Includes bibliographical references and index.
   ISBN-13: 978-1-59385-217-7 (pbk.)   ISBN-10: 1-59385-217-7 (pbk.)
   ISBN-13: 978-1-59385-361-7 (hardcover)   ISBN-10: 1-59385-361-0 (hardcover)
   1. Internet in education.   2. Computers and literacy.   I. Dobler,
Elizabeth.   II. Title.
LC149.5.E16 2007
371.33′44678—dc22
                                                                    2006032712

To my daughter, Emily, who inspires and amazes me daily
—M. B. E.

To my mother, who instilled in me a love of reading and writing
—E. D.

ABOUT THE AUTHORS

Maya B. Eagleton, PhD, is an Adjunct Assistant Professor in Language, Reading, and Culture at The University of Arizona. She teaches courses in traditional literacies, digital literacies, and qualitative research methods. She also works as a Senior Research Scientist for CAST (Center for Applied Special Technology), where she researches and designs literacy software prototypes for students with learning disabilities. Dr. Eagleton has extensive K–12 classroom experience as a Title I coordinator and a Reading Recovery teacher.

Elizabeth Dobler, PhD, was a classroom teacher for 13 years before assuming her current position as an Assistant Professor of Reading and Language Arts at Emporia State University. In this capacity, she teaches preservice and experienced teachers in both face-to-face and online formats. Dr. Dobler has been a primary researcher for studies involving Internet reading, in which she has worked closely with classroom teachers, library media specialists, and instructional technology specialists.

FOREWORD

This important new book, *Reading the Web: Strategies for Internet Inquiry*, takes on a difficult question: How do we best integrate the Internet into our classrooms? It also explains things clearly, with both feet planted firmly in the classroom context. Finally, it pushes us to reconceptualize reading.

Maya B. Eagleton and Elizabeth Dobler have crafted an exceptional book with many useful suggestions for integrating the Internet into your classroom through an inquiry model. New literacies of online reading comprehension are increasingly required in the 21st century; this book will provide essential guidance for teachers seeking to prepare their students for those challenges. Preparing students for the new dimensions of reading that many already encounter at home will be one of the greatest challenges our schools will face in the years ahead.

The nature of reading has changed. Over one billion readers are now reading on the Internet, and this number is expanding rapidly. New information and communication technologies such as the Internet itself, search engines, e-mail, instant messaging, wikis, blogs, and online gaming worlds require new literacies and have become important new contexts for literacy, learning, and life. Few of these new literacies, however, have found their way into the classroom. The logistics of providing instruction in these new literacies have proven to be daunting to the educational community, especially when educators are less conversant with digital literacies than the students they teach. This delay in getting up to speed is unfortunate, given the widespread recognition of how important the Internet has become in our daily lives and the data showing that new skills and strategies are required for reading online.

Today, literacy educators are under enormous pressure to increase reading test scores on assessments that have not incorporated the new literacies of online reading comprehension. No state currently assesses students' ability to read search engine results, to critically evaluate information on the Internet, to read a blog, or to read and write e-mail and instant messages. The focus of current policies on testing students' skills and strategies for offline reading comprehension are missing the mark if what students really need is support in developing the new literacies of online reading comprehension. This is especially true for those students who require our support the most—those who do not have access to the Internet at home. Economically challenged school districts which are already under the greatest pressure to raise offline reading test scores face difficult choices for how to allocate resources for literacy instruction.

The authors of this practical volume are to be commended for challenging us to expand our conception of what it means to be a reader today and for providing teachers with the tools to prepare students for an online world. Each chapter is clearly written and contains numerous examples for classroom instruction. A thorough collection of handouts and overheads is also included.

I expect this volume will increase the number of us who understand that the challenge of the Internet has less to do with technology, and more to do with reading, and that to meet this challenge we will need many new skills and strategies. Thus, the material in this book will make an important difference in the lives of our students, helping us to prepare them for new forms of reading and writing in the 21st century.

DONALD J. LEU, PhD
Johan and Maria Neag Endowed Chair
  of Literacy and Technology
The New Literacies Research Team
University of Connecticut

PREFACE

One afternoon, as Beth was busily trying to clean the house, her 4-year-old son was bored. In order to get her work done, she enticed him to sit at the computer to look at the Lego website at *www.lego.com*. He had very little experience with computers, except for perhaps a game or two he had played at his day care center. This was his first time encountering the Internet. As Beth returned to her cleaning, she noticed how adeptly he navigated around the website, easily finding icons and links of interest. She became so engrossed in watching him that the cleaning was forgotten. Although Beth knew he could not read the links, she could clearly see that he was able to meet his personal needs for information and entertainment. How did he know what to do next? She began to think about the different reading strategies he might need to make his browsing of the site even more purposeful. Beth also began to wonder about all the skills he would eventually need to learn in order to more effectively use the Web.

Thus began the formation of a kernel of an idea. From that point on, Beth has had a growing interest in better understanding how we find, understand, and use information from the Web. This interest led to a dissertation, multiple research studies, and coauthoring this book with Maya. It is ironic to recall a conversation in the teachers' lounge several years back in which Beth remarked that she could not see herself using computers because typewriters were so much easier! In some ways, Beth came to the field of technology through the back door. Maybe it's the same door through which you have come. Or perhaps you have entered through the front door, like Maya, who began to wonder about the potential for technology to motivate and support struggling readers and writers back in the early 1990s. Wherever you are on the continuum of technology use, whether for personal or instructional purposes, we welcome you.

Actually, this book is about more than technology, although we do address hardware, software, websites, search engines, and a host of other technology topics. First, and foremost, this book is about learning. Technology, specifically the Internet, can be a powerful tool for learning; in fact, this tool may be the most influential communication and learning device we have ever encountered. In our classrooms, across the grade levels and across the content areas, we recognize the need to teach students how to use computers through instruction in keyboarding, word processing, and creating electronic presentations. We have spent time teaching students how to turn on computers, log in, type in Web addresses, and click on links. However, have we also spent time teaching students how to critically read once they locate a website? Have we prepared them with strategies for finding the most important or useful information within a website? Have we taught them ways to harvest information from a website and to then display this information in their own words? You may be familiar with the term "digital divide," which acknowledges that people without computers have limited access to electronic resources, but educators also talk about a "second level digital divide," which recognizes that even when children have access to computers, they will be disadvantaged if they are not taught how to use them (Hargittai, 2002). Not teaching children how to use computers is like giving them books but not teaching them how to read.

The heart and soul of this book stems from our belief in the importance of providing our students with the skills and strategies needed to be successful in their current role as students as well as in their future role as productive citizens. Since the Internet is the most comprehensive resource for authentic student research, one goal of this book is to apply what we already know about effective instruction to teach strategies for negotiating this potent but disorganized information space. Another of our purposes is to draw from what we already know about literacy processes in print in order to understand the benefits and challenges of reading on the Web. Throughout this book and on our companion website (*www.ReadingTheWeb. net*) we explore the similarities and differences between technology and print in order to build connections to new ideas and information. Finally, this book provides a research-based, classroom-tested model for the cycle of Internet inquiry that we call "QUEST." Though Maya is currently a university professor and educational researcher, she served as a reading specialist for many years; therefore, she has a passionate interest in promoting literacy for all types of students. To that end, this book also offers suggestions for adapting and extending curricular activities for diverse learners.

Using the Web to answer our personal questions, whether for school, work, or entertainment, relies on the belief that the Web will meet our informational needs. Beth's son is now a fifth grader, and he has mastered many of the basic skills for locating information on the Web. In fact, the Web has become his resource of choice for everything from a recipe for peanut butter cookies to directions for a magic trick. He has grown up with this tool as an integral part of his daily life, as have many of our students. Sometimes we feel as though we are playing catch-up with our students. However, keep in mind that your experience and knowledge of learning and reading, whether just budding or in full bloom, is the connection that will help students be effective Web readers now and in their future. We sincerely hope that you find this book useful, whether you are a teacher, library media specialist, instructional technologist, university professor, or researcher, and that you will share your stories with us as we continue to investigate this fascinating new phenomenon of searching for meaning on the Web.

ACKNOWLEDGMENTS

We owe a special debt of gratitude to the students and teachers who have shared their thoughts and experiences with us. Without their openness, we would have a very different view of the classroom world. Each one has taught us something about reading, learning, and Internet inquiry. To our spouses and children, we thank you for your patience, understanding, and support when the dishes did not get washed or the laundry was not folded because we were too busy writing! A special thank you goes to our friend and colleague Kathleen Guinee, for her careful research and insights. Another special thank you goes to our friend and colleague Julie Coiro, who provided ideas, information, and inspiration throughout the writing process. We thank CAST, Inc., and the U.S. Department of Education for funding the research that informed much of this work. To Chris Jennison at The Guilford Press, we appreciate your belief in us as writers, and to Craig Thomas, William Meyer, and everyone else at Guilford, we couldn't have asked for more friendly and supportive guides to shepherd us through the publication process.

CONTENTS

I UNDERSTANDING PRINT AND WEB LITERACIES

Most educators would agree that the Internet has tremendous potential to enhance student learning across all content areas; however, most educators would also agree that it is difficult to use the Web for answering compelling questions. This is because, quite simply, *finding information on the Web is hard.* This is true for both children and adults, especially if they are computer novices. For years, finding information in traditional venues like the library has proven challenging for young learners, but locating and comprehending information on the Web is even more challenging. At a minimum, students need to be able to identify an information need, figure out which resources to use to address that need, evaluate the information they find, read and synthesize information from multiple sources, and perhaps even transform all those stray pieces of information into something original. This is a highly complex process, one that many learners of all ages find difficult.

> Ironically, many Web-based environments introduce a new set of cognitive barriers that can cause competent readers of conventional text to be cognitively overloaded and emotionally frustrated. . . . Teachers need to be aware of these new cognitive challenges posed by Internet environments before we unnecessarily confuse our competent readers or overwhelm the struggling ones.   —Coiro (2003, p. 462)

Fortunately, we can teach students strategies for managing information on the Web. Moreover, we can address multiple learning objectives and meet numerous learning standards across the content areas at the same time. *The primary goal of this book is to explain the complexity of reading and learning on the Web and then to offer practical instructional ideas and tools for your classroom.* Our fundamental approach to understanding the strategies readers need in order to find informa-

1

tion on the Web is to build on what we already know about learning, the reading process, and effective teaching practices. Applying this knowledge to digital texts, classrooms, and learning on the Web helps us get a handle on what is involved in online inquiry. Once we've established this understanding (Part I), we'll embed ready-to-use Web activities in the context of authentic (student-generated and purposeful) Internet inquiry, using an acronym—QUEST—that serves as an apt metaphor for the recursive process of finding and comprehending information on the Web (Part II).

There is so much information available to us today that no one can possibly retain it all. Therefore, it is crucial to have knowledge of available resources and to have flexible strategies for finding information using the most efficient methods possible. In the Information Age, knowledge is a form of power; however, since no one person can "own" all the knowledge in the world, the most valuable asset is the ability to find information expediently (Leu, Kinzer, Coiro, & Cammack, 2004). Although textbooks, encyclopedias, and other traditional forms of information media are still highly useful resources, there is no doubt that the Internet has far exceeded every previous information technology in breadth, depth, and immediacy (de Argaez, 2006). The Internet has become an integral part of gaining information in schools, at home, and in the workplace; however, researchers have found that people of all ages are surprisingly inefficient at finding information using this unique resource (e.g., Bilal, 2002; Broch, 2000; Dennis, Bruza, & McArthur, 2002; Gibson & Mazur, 2000; Guinee, Eagleton, & Hall, 2003; Hargittai, 2002; Hill & Hannafin, 1997; Jansen & Pooch, 2001; McEneaney, 2000; Nachmias & Gilad, 2002; Palmquist & Kim, 2000; Rouet, 2003; Wallace, Kupperman, Krajcik, & Soloway, 2000).

Unlike traditional texts, which can be easily obtained by a quick trip to the library, useful online texts can be more difficult to find. Students who know how to locate resources, when to use them, what to do with them, and which resources are best for the job at hand will have significant advantages over those who lack this understanding. Interestingly, as many as 73% of American teens aged 12 to 17 are teaching themselves how to search for information on the Internet at home by using a trial and error approach (Gunn & Hepburn, 2003). Students also rely on friends and classmates more frequently than teachers to show them how to locate information on the Internet for school assignments (Gunn & Hepburn, 2003; Lubans, 1999). A danger of having students teach one another about using the Internet is that they can proliferate misinformation about this critical literacy. To counteract this tendency, Internet literacies must be systematically incorporated throughout K–12 curricula (Castek & Bevans-Mangleson, 2006; Leu, Leu, & Coiro, 2004; Wallace, et al., 2000). It is imperative that schools take on the task of teaching strategies for understanding today's information resources so that students develop systematic rather than haphazard research habits. However, we can't leave all this instruction up to computer teachers and media specialists, because they rarely have sufficient time to work with individual students in the context of authentic inquiry. Classroom teachers also need to step up to the plate, because the Internet is here to stay, as the following statistics clearly indicate.

Internet Usage in Schools

According to the National Center for Education Statistics (NCES), 100% of all U.S. public schools have Internet access and 93% of all U.S. public schools have Internet access in instructional areas (NCES, 2005). The incredible rate of computer adoption over the past decade has been "unprecedented in schools for any previous technology including televisions, radios, telephones, VCRs, and even books" (Leu, Kinzer, Coiro, & Cammack, 2004, p. 1578). The quality of this access is also on the rise. In 2003, 95% of U.S. public schools reported having broadband connections (NCES, 2005), which allows students faster Internet access as well as the ability to experience memory-intensive multimedia such as audio and video. Many school districts in the United States are also moving toward newer, more portable technologies such as laptops and handheld devices that have the same speed and portability as laptops but are much smaller and more durable in the hands of students.

Teenage Life Online, a Pew Internet and American Life Project in 2001, reported that 94% of American online teens use the Internet for research purposes for school and that 71% relied mostly on the Internet as the source of information for their last big school project, as compared to 24% who cited library sources (Lenhart, Simon, & Graziano, 2001). Electronic resources have become the primary tools for information gathering, particularly among high school students and undergraduates (Hafner, 2004), and we know that elementary and middle school students are also using the Internet more frequently for school research projects (Eagleton, Guinee, & Langlais, 2003). Though standardized assessments have yet to catch up, most states in the United States are now including online literacies in their core learning standards (International ICT Literacy Panel, 2001).

Internet Usage in Homes

Nearly 75% of all households in the United States reported that they had Internet access in 2004 (Nielsen/NET Ratings, 2004). Among those who had not previously used the Internet, 47% stated that they are somewhat likely or very likely to go online soon (Lebo, 2003). The percentage of U.S. households with broadband Internet access doubled every year between 1998 to 2001, "an adoption rate in households exceeding that of any previous technology including telephones, color televisions, VCRs, cell phones, and pagers" (Leu, Kinzer, Coiro, & Cammack, 2004, p. 1578).

Our students are spending a lot of time on the Internet at home, including 99% of Canadian youth who report using the Internet frequently and nearly 50% of Canadian students who report using the Internet daily (Gunn & Hepburn, 2003). These youngsters and their first world peers, dubbed "millenials," engage in media use for an average of 6.5 *hours per day* outside of school (Hagood, Stevens, & Reinking, 2002). Although much of this use can probably be attributed to gaming and various forms of chatting, those who use a computer regularly for any purpose are gaining valuable operational and navigational skills that will benefit them when they engage in online reading and inquiry.

Internet Usage in the Workplace

In the United States, there have been massive increases in Internet use in the workplace. In just one year, between 2000 and 2001, the use of the Internet at work among all employed adults 25 and older increased by nearly 60%, from 26% of the workforce to 42% (Leu, Kinzer, Coiro, & Cammack, 2004). If this rate increase continues, almost everyone will be using the Internet at work within just a few more years. If we want to prepare today's students to excel in tomorrow's workplace, we had better start teaching them to be Web literate. Web literacy requires familiarity and fluency with all the ways information is presented on the Internet; for example, web pages (the focus of this book), e-mail (Tao & Reinking, 2000), instant messaging (Jacobs, in press), blogs (Mortensen, in press), and wikis (Thomas, in press).

About This Book

In Part I of this book, we draw from reputable theory and research on literacy and learning to establish a framework for understanding the skills, strategies, and knowledge that are necessary in order for students to learn on the Web. Throughout the book, we also share our own observations of the complex process of Web reading, having worked with hundreds of students who were engaged in online inquiry. We are eager to share what we've learned and sincerely hope that these ideas will enhance your instruction. Many of the key ideas, graphics, and reproducibles are also available on our companion website (*www.ReadingTheWeb.net*).

In Chapter 1, "Learning How to Learn," we seek to answer the questions "What is learning?" and "What are some effective ways to promote learning?" Toward that end, we outline three time-tested theories of learning—constructivism (learning by doing), socioculturalism (learning with others), and semiotics (learning through symbols)—that guide our work in the classroom and help us interpret the research data we collect. We also discuss a specific curricular approach (inquiry-based learning) that is compatible with all three theories of learning and that has direct application to learning on the Web. Next, we describe four elements of instruction—modeling, scaffolding, practice, and feedback—that serve as a robust model for effective teaching in any subject. Finally, we describe some of the challenges faced by teachers with the convergence of learning, curriculum, and technology. The overriding message in this chapter is that *teaching students transferable strategies for learning how to learn* will serve students not only while learning on the Web, but throughout their school careers, personal lives, and beyond.

In Chapter 2, "Becoming Literate," we provide some commonly agreed-upon answers to the questions "What does it mean to become literate?" and "What are Web literacies?" We begin with applying two influential reading theories—Cueing

Systems Theory and Transactional Theory—to the reading process, both in print and on the Web, noting that digital texts are similar to but more complex than print texts. Next we describe how reading comprehension strategies and foundational reading skills are challenged when applied to online reading. Then we describe three theories of Web literacies, supporting the increasingly prevalent view that the current definition of literacy must be expanded to include digital literacies. Finally, we investigate features of informational text structures found in print and on the Web. The overarching theme for this chapter is that *reading is a very complex cognitive and metacognitive process.* Therefore, although some students become proficient readers without adult guidance, many others benefit from reading strategy instruction, both in print and on the Web.

The first two chapters serve as a solid, research-based foundation for exploring what it means to be "Web literate," which is the central aim of this book. Literacy gives individuals access to power, and people who are not fluent with culturally valued literacy practices are disadvantaged. This has consequences for what constitutes literacy and how literacy is taught in schools. Part II of this book focuses on classroom instructional practices that can promote and nourish Web literacy, or the ability to locate, understand, and use information found on the Web.

Before we get started, we'd like to point out some logistics that govern the style and organization of this book. First, we alternate gender pronouns throughout the chapters. Second, whenever we give examples of keywords, we place them in brackets because quotation marks have a specific purpose in keyword construction. For example, we might suggest keyword combinations such as <baskeball + history> or <hurricane + "disaster relief">; however, when you are searching the Web, the brackets should not be included. Third, although we have provided numerous activities and handouts for your use, you should not attempt to use all of them in one lesson, unit, or semester. Finally, we provide some definitions for terms that are used in this book (below).

Although the Internet and the Web (World Wide Web, or WWW) are technically different, they have merged to the point where the terms are often used interchangeably. The *Internet*, which is a global network of computers that includes features such as e-mail, chat rooms, bulletin boards, newsgroups, and websites, is accessed via an *Internet Service Provider* such as AOL or Comcast, using a phone line, cable, or wireless connection. The *Web*, which is actually a subset of the Internet, is accessed through *Web browser* software such as *Internet Explorer* or *Netscape Navigator,* and is a massive interconnected set of *websites* that use standardized coding languages (html, XML, flash, etc.) so that everyone's computer can interpret them. People locate webpages either by typing the *URL* (Uniform Resource Locator) directly into the address field or by using a *search engine* such as Google or Yahoo. At this point in time, most features offered by the Internet can be accessed via the Web (such as Web-based e-mail and newsgroups), so the two entities have essentially become one.

Hypertext is nonlinear text that can be read by selecting hyperlinks, an idea linked to another idea that can be accessed by clicking on a word, phrase, or symbol. *Hypermedia* refers to computer technology that combines text, graphics, animation, audio and/or video in a nonlinear format, such as computer games, electronic encyclopedias, and Internet websites. The term *multimedia* refers to computer technology that may incorporate all of these same media forms but is generally linear in its presentation, such as electronic storybooks and multimedia slide shows.

We define *literacy* as "the ability to encode or decode meaning in any of the forms of representation used in a culture to convey or express meaning" (Eisner, 1994, p. x), which includes being able to create and interpret print, but also being somewhat fluent with art, dance, music, multimedia, and other areas of expressive language. We are particularly interested in defining what it means to be *Web literate*, that is, making meaning out of texts typically found on the Web.

Finally, references to the word *text* should be broadly interpreted as "any chunk of meaning that has unity and can be shared with others" (Short, Kauffman, & Kahn, 2000, p. 161). Therefore, when we talk about *Internet texts*, *Web texts*, or *webpages*, we mean hypermedia documents found on the Web that may contain several different features, including print, images, links, icons, multimedia, and so on. Similarly, a *reader* is someone who is actively constructing meaning from any of these media forms, not just from print.

We earnestly hope you find this information easy to understand and immediately applicable to your teaching situation, whether you are a preservice teaching candidate, an English language arts teacher, a science teacher, a library media specialist, or a university professor. More and more of us are using the Internet to satisfy our information needs at home, in school, and in the workplace; however, we cannot assume that our students automatically know how to effectively locate, evaluate, and synthesize online information. It is our job as educators to help students become more strategic and flexible readers on the Web.

1 LEARNING HOW TO LEARN

KEY IDEAS

▷ Since there is no single method of teaching that works with all learners, it is important that students *learn how to learn*.

▷ Constructivism, socioculturalism, and semiotics are three compatible theories that guide our understanding of the learning process.

▷ Inquiry-based learning is a curricular approach that is highly congruent with learning on the Web.

▷ Four elements of effective instruction in any content area are modeling, scaffolding, practice, and feedback.

▷ Factors such as time, teacher expertise, and technical glitches can pose challenges for Web learning.

> **If we want children to be deeply engaged in conversations about issues of great significance in books, we must not only teach them how to read, but show them how to reason.**
> **—Keene and Zimmermann (1997, p. 80)**

The questions that guide this chapter are "What is learning?" and "What are some effective ways to promote learning?" While it may be tempting to skip this chapter and jump straight to the teaching ideas and lesson plans in Part II, it is important to understand the underlying beliefs that have shaped the concepts presented in this book. Beliefs provide the framework for our decisions and actions in the classroom.

Whether we can articulate it clearly or not, every teacher has a theory, or set of beliefs about how people learn. Most teachers collect bits and pieces of theories to form a personal philosophy of education. This philosophy guides the daily decisions we make in our classrooms, about everything from conducting science experiments, to discussing poems, to deciding how to arrange the classroom furniture, to using the Web to find information. Instructional decisions, large and small, are guided by our own set of beliefs.

Since we believe that there is no single method of teaching that will reach all learners at all times in all places, it is imperative that we help children *learn how to learn* so that they can adapt and extend their knowledge and strategies when they encounter new tasks in new contexts. Based on this stance, our philosophy of learning merges three highly compatible theories (Figure 1.1): constructivism (learning by doing), socioculturalism (learning with others), and semiotics (learning through symbols). This combination leads to a definition of learning that reads, "Humans construct and deconstruct meaning in socially situated contexts using multiple sign systems." Put simply, we try to make sense of the world by communicating with others for authentic purposes. In this way, babies learn to talk, children learn to read, and people learn to navigate and comprehend on the Web.

 The only competitive skill in the long run is skill at learning.
        —Papert (1996, p. 166)

In this chapter, a brief description of each theory is followed by an example of how it is typically applied in the classroom and the ways in which reading on the Web impacts teaching from each of these perspectives. We use inquiry-based learning as an example of an instructional approach that draws from all three theories of learning. Next, we present four elements of effective instruction that are consistent with these theories and easily applicable to learning in any context, but especially on the Web. Finally, we will discuss several of the challenges teachers face when using a Web-based context for learning.

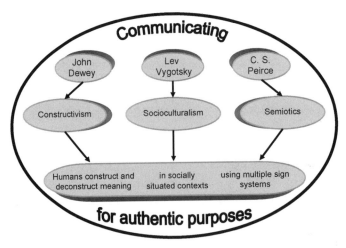

FIGURE 1.1. Holistic view of learning theories.

How People Learn

Understanding how people learn has been an issue of great interest for theorists and researchers from such diverse fields as education, linguistics, psychology, sociology, anthropology, and neuroscience. Many theories have been popularized over the years, but three stand out as being particularly relevant to our work with the newer literacies required for reading and learning on the Web. We present each theory as concisely as possible, using examples to illustrate how it is applied in classroom contexts and on the Web.

Learning by Doing: Constructivism

Constructivism's basic premise is that learning is an active process in which students construct new ideas or concepts based on their current knowledge (Bruner, 1986). In constructivist classrooms, teachers encourage students to make their own discoveries rather than always relying on the teacher to tell them what to think. The constructivist teacher is often described as the "guide on the side" rather than the "sage on a stage," as in more traditional classrooms where the teacher is viewed as an authority figure whose primary job is to dispense knowledge.

> **Classrooms that encourage the active construction of meaning focus on big understandings and powerful ideas rather than facts, and they encourage students to ask their own questions, follow their own interests, make their own connections, reformulate ideas, and reach unique conclusions.**
> **—Wilhelm and Friedemann (1998, p. 30)**

Teachers who are guided by constructivist principles view the cup as being half full rather than half empty; in other words, our job is not to transmit knowledge by pouring information into our students' heads but rather to set up active learning opportunities that allow students to create their own personal meanings and associations. From this stance, many aspects of the curriculum are negotiated between the students and the teachers, so that students are empowered and engaged in the learning process (Harste, 1994; Short et al., 1996). As we discuss later, this pedagogical perspective is particularly well suited to Web-based inquiry.

Strategy Instruction

A classic example of a teaching approach used by constructivist-oriented teachers is cognitive strategy instruction, or teaching students to become aware of the patterns of thinking they use to learn and read. Strategies are the in-the-head processes students use to develop an understanding of a concept. Although some students develop flexible strategies on their own, many benefit from explicit instruction in this area. Strategy instruction often starts

> **"During read-alouds, I stop frequently to allow the kids to make predictions, ask questions, confirm or restructure predictions, make connections, etc. We stop and discuss and write down several things for each chapter."   —Cheryl, fourth-grade teacher**

with an expert, perhaps a reading teacher, modeling the strategies that she uses when she reads texts.

After students are given multiple opportunities to practice certain strategies—for example, predicting what will happen next in a storybook—it is hoped that they will not only be able to apply those strategies independently in similar contexts, but to generalize and transfer them to other texts or new learning situations. Ideally, the strategies that are used by proficient learners are assimilated by novices and eventually become automatic, unconscious habits. Strategy instruction and modeling are major frameworks for the ideas and teaching activities presented in this book, subjects to which we return frequently.

Constructivism and Technology

In constructivist classrooms, the Internet can be used as a powerful tool for exploration and discovery. Although it is a complex learning environment (Eagleton, 2002; McEneaney, 2000), it allows learners to engage in authentic, meaningful experiences that they might otherwise be unable to access, such as virtual field trips to museums, zoos, and parks in other states or countries (Kinzer, Gabella, & Rieth, 1994). Expanding on Dewey's (1938) belief that "a philosophy of education [should be] based upon a philosophy of experience" (p. 29), one of the most promising applications of the Web in the classroom is that it can help students visualize and understand concepts they have never directly experienced, such as the Doppler effect or the water cycle. Websites that use multimedia (images, audio, video, and animation) to illustrate complex ideas can help activate children's prior knowledge, promote new knowledge, and highlight connections between difficult concepts. As Eisner (1994) affirms, "Through imagination—the creation of mental images—we are able to conceive what we have never experienced in the empirical world" (p. 25).

> In cyberspace we will be able to see virtual reality worlds. ... We will be able to hear all frequencies, from the echoes of earthquakes and the songs of whales and insects, to the resonances of crystals. We will be telepresent with probes on Mars and on the deep-ocean floor, we will be able to walk the Martian plains, kick lunar dust, sound with the whales. We will be able to float above the earth at any elevation, seeing in any spectrum, observing cities or rainforests in real-time or watching the changes of days or years go by in minutes, or seconds. We can live at the pace of a tree or a forest, a hurricane or a glacier, a cell or a molecule. We will do all this as children. We will not develop along the same cultural paths as in the past.
>
> —Lemke (1993, online)

Further, multimedia technology has the potential to level the playing field between learners with high prior knowledge and those with low prior knowledge through the use of anchored instruction (Sharp et al., 1995). Anchored instruction uses multimedia technology to provide a group of learners with a common experience at the outset of a lesson or unit. This type of input is helpful for young children, English language learners, and students with disabilities because it gives everyone an opportunity to discuss what they observe using similar language (Kinzer et al., 1994). For example, the popular website for children *How Stuff Works* (*www.howstuffworks.com*) explains and demonstrates how things work, from cell phones to car engines. These multimedia demonstrations provide a common experience and a common vocabulary for all students to draw upon as they embark on a unit of study.

A combination of constructivist theory and technology naturally leads many teachers across all content areas to plan hypermedia design projects (websites, slide shows) in their classrooms. The students with whom we've worked have published slide shows and websites on incredibly diverse topics, everything from Arnold Schwarzenegger to wheelchair-accessible vacations. Although some children have dabbled in hypermedia design outside of school, most still benefit from instruction. Fortunately for educators, with today's software, composing with hypermedia has become as easy as word processing. In preparation for a design project, students engage in critiques of previous students' projects in order to discover desirable design features. Students are quick to identify webpages that have confusing navigation, crowded layouts, and slow loading times and can determine when a slide show has too much text, not enough information, or too many distracting "bells and whistles." It is also advisable for students to design a storyboard (a sketch on paper) in advance and to practice creating simple projects before attempting complex ones.

Learning with Others: Socioculturalism

While constructivism emphasizes the individual learner's construction of meaning through active learning experiences, socioculturalism is primarily focused on the social benefits of learning with others. However, the two theories are not incompatible. Each offers a slightly different lens to understand how people learn, and each helps us create effective curricula and make instructional decisions in our classrooms.

 The Zone of Proximal Development is . . . the distance between the actual developmental level as determined by independent problem solving and the level of potential development as determined through problem solving under adult guidance or in collaboration with more capable peers.
—Vygotsky (1978, p. 86)

Current understanding of the sociocultural perspective on learning is based on the assumption that "human learning presupposes a specific social nature and a process by which children grow into the intellectual life of those around them" (Vygotsky, 1978, p. 88). From this perspective, a primary aim of schooling is for students to be able to communicate their understandings effectively with others, and for teachers to provide experiences for students that promote purposeful interactions with others. As Dewey (1938) states, "all human experience is ultimately social . . . it involves contact and communication" (p. 38).

A sociocultural perspective views all learning as socially situated; that is, it takes place in a certain setting at a certain time, whether it is school sanctioned or outside of school. This means that the context that surrounds the learning activity should not be overlooked. All learners filter new ideas through their own personal

To learn a mediational tool, including talk or writing, children need other people who not only model and guide the appropriate processes but also respond to their efforts (their spoken words, written texts, drawings and paintings) in situationally and culturally appropriate ways. It is those responses that imbue the child's symbolic acts with social meaning, and it is, in turn, the sense of a functional goal that organizes and drives the symbolic process.

—Dyson (1993, p. 29)

stances or views of the world based on sociocultural influences, such as culture, religion, family, and community.

Collaborative Learning

A classroom teacher with a sociocultural perspective is generally inclined to offer students multiple opportunities to collaborate. Collaboration is not easy and does not come naturally to all learners, so the mediating role of the teacher remains important. Most students need to be taught how to collaborate productively. There are numerous educational benefits of collaboration. According to Eisner (1994), "The process of collaboration gives birth to new ideas and develops social skills that matter in a democracy" (p. 9). The old adage "two heads are better than one" is certainly applicable in the classroom. In fact, working in groups of three or four can help children improve their communication skills, design more creative solutions to problems, and gain a sense of what it is like to manage real problems in the workplace (Figure 1.2). As society becomes more complex, finding ways to share our knowledge and skills is essential.

Socioculturalism and Technology

Despite concerns that computers might promote social isolation in the classroom (it is interesting to recall that there were once critics who feared that books would hamper children's social development because they were considered to be an isolationist medium!), in many classrooms the computer center can more accurately be described as a "social center" that expands communication close to home and far away. It has been noted by several researchers that open-ended software, such as draw/paint programs, word processing, music-making programs, problem-solving software, and simulation games, invites purposeful communication among students

FIGURE 1.2. Student collaboration.

and can promote collaborative efforts to solve problems (Kinzer & Leu, 1997). Students come to rely on the collaborative expertise of classmates to figure out how to use software. When Dickson (1985) reviewed the influence of different types of media on learning, he found "significantly more collaboration between children when they worked with computers when compared with other classroom tasks" (p. 37). According to Downes and Fatouros (1995), "researchers have consistently found that small groups using a computer often generate much more oral language, of higher quality, than groups involved in more traditional learning experiences" (p. 27).

> Multimedia environments, because they are both powerful and complex, often require us to communicate with others in order to make meaning from them. Thus, learning is frequently constructed through social interactions in these contexts, perhaps even more naturally and frequently than in traditional print environments.
> —Kinzer and Leu (1997, p. 133)

In addition to the social interactions inside the classroom, technology promotes social interaction with students in other cities, states, and countries. Through keypal projects and other online collaborative projects, students can share information and resources with children and adults in other localities. Internet technology can be a venue for children from different countries to come closer together through personal communication, which might serve to "break down classroom walls" and lessen community isolation as students from different geographic regions, with different worldviews and resources, communicate with each other. In addition to e-mail and webpage design, it is feasible in some schools to arrange for computer conferencing and live chat sessions with people in distant locales. While it is possible to utilize more traditional forms of communication (such as pen pals) for these kinds of exchanges, the Internet is more immediate and can provide a wider range of audiences and purposes for reading, writing, talking, listening, and researching.

> The mission of the school is decidedly not to bring everyone to the same place but rather to increase the variance in performance among students while escalating the mean for all.   —Eisner (1997, p. 352)

Internet technologies are also powerful tools for children with special needs to engage in meaningful communication with others. For example, multilingual students can make contact with children in other locations with a shared first language; children in a cultural minority group can communicate with people from the same cultural group in other communities; and students with physical disabilities can interact with other students who may be unaware of their disabilities and can respond without any preconceived images of disability (Garner & Gillingham, 1998; Reinking, 1997).

Learning through Symbols: Semiotics

We have defined constructivist learning theory as learning by doing and socio-culturalism as learning with others. Now we add just one more lens through which to view the learning process and guide our classroom decisions: semiotics (learning through symbols). Semiotic theory is highly compatible with the previous two theories because it describes the symbolic forms we use to communicate with others in our efforts to construct meaning.

Humans use signs (defined as anything we use to convey meaning, such as pictures, letters, words, gestures, and/or objects) to describe the world. Our capacity to create and interpret signs, symbols, and sign systems is a major distinguishing feature between humans and animals (Gardner, 1983; Siegel, 1995; Suhor, 1984). While signs can have significance to just one person (such as a personal shorthand style), symbols are conventionalized (such as the fairly universal symbols for women's or men's restrooms). A sign system is a conventionalized set of symbols that is commonly understood by people versed in certain disciplines, such as art, music, dance, language, science, and mathematics. The phrase "forms of representation" refers to how we symbolically communicate our private conceptions about the world and is often used interchangeably with the phrase "sign systems."

It is important to expose children to different sign systems because each is uniquely capable of addressing different aspects of the world around them (Labbo, 1996; Kozma, 1991; Salomon, 1997). Certain sign systems are better suited for representing specific concepts or ideas; therefore, one aim of education is to teach students which symbols to apply at which times. For example, an algebraic concept is best represented using mathematical symbols, and while a poetic concept might be well represented using art, song, dance, or writing, it would be hard to express through a mathematical equation.

 The forms we use to represent what we think—literal language, visual images, number, poetry—have an impact on how we think and what we can think about. If different forms of representation performed identical cognitive functions, then there would be no need to dance, compute, or draw.
—Eisner (1997, p. 349)

Multiple Literacies

From a semiotic perspective, the goal of instruction is to teach children how to understand and orchestrate a variety of sign systems. Many semioticians recommend a "multiple literacies" approach to learning, in which students are taught to move freely between sign systems. The following is an example of a multiple literacies approach: A social studies teacher invites her students to conduct a cross-curricular inquiry project on a critical social issue, and one student chooses air pollution. This student might search the Internet (information literacy), interview experts (oral literacy), read books and articles (print literacy), analyze images taken from space (visual literacy), develop a time line (historical inquiry), and explore the current and future impact of pollution on the environment (scientific inquiry). Toward the end of the inquiry project, students may use a variety of sign systems, or formats, to demonstrate what they've learned, such as poems, reports, posters, or websites.

A multiple literacies approach is relatively easy to accomplish in the lower grades, where the separations between content areas are more easily blurred; however, even secondary teachers can team up to help students explore issues from multiple perspectives, which is much closer to how inquiry is carried out in the real world outside the classroom.

Semiotics and Technology

Technology is a satisfying fit for educators with a semiotic viewpoint because multimedia has the unique capacity to combine multiple sign systems into one medium

In our lives outside school, we naturally move continuously between visual image, music, movement, mathematics, drama, and language as ways of thinking about our world. . . . It is only in school that students are restricted to using one sign system at a time to work at understandings.
—Short, Kauffman, and Kahn (2000, p. 60)

(i.e., the computer). No other communicative medium can combine so many semiotic systems in one place at one time; for example, a website may contain print, graphics, audio, video, and animation—all on one page. According to Kinzer and Leu (1997), "constructing meaning from multiple perspectives, using multiple media sources, provides a richer understanding of complex information, especially if one lacks prior knowledge about a topic" (p. 130). When multiple sign systems are presented together, they can complement and extend the intended meaning of the message. For example, when text about the rain forest is accompanied by photographs and a multimedia clip, the information can be accessed in a variety of ways to support the reader's knowledge acquisition. The clichéd phrase "a picture is worth a thousand words" comes to mind because pictures can transmit so much information instantly whereas language is constrained in a linear sequence of ideas. Communicating with several sign systems at once can enhance the power of the message (Glasgow, 1997; Reinking, 1994); however, the juxtaposition of too many sign systems can also serve to confuse and distract a reader.

One of the most promising aspects of combining multiple sign systems through technology is that it provides alternate methods for communicating complex concepts and ideas other than by the use of print alone. The inclusion of icons, graphics, visuals, and multimedia conveys information in a variety of ways, which provides greater educational equity for children who struggle with language-based delivery systems such as lectures and books (Rose & Meyer, 2002). We mentioned earlier the capacity for multimedia to "level the playing field" in terms of students' prior knowledge, but it can also level the playing field in terms of learning exclusively through language. For years, print has been the dominant sign system for learning in just about every core content area in schools, from language arts to social studies to science. While we still value print, we recognize the importance of offering alternative, supportive learning experiences to students who find print

Language is not the only important communicational system. Today images, symbols, graphs, diagrams, artifacts, and many other visual symbols are particularly significant.
—Gee (2003, p. 13)

difficult to manage, such as struggling readers or learners of English as a second language. Some of these same students who encounter difficulty with linguistic tasks excel in other sign systems, or forms of intelligence, such as musical, logical/mathematical, spatial, bodily/kinesthetic, and interpersonal intelligences (Gardner, 1983).

How We Create Curriculum

We have presented a view of computers in the classroom as socially valued (sociocultural stance) symbolic tools (semiotic stance) for making meaning (constructivist stance). This philosophy of education is what drives our teaching decisions at the curricular level as well as at the lesson plan level. Here we use inquiry-based learning as an example of a curricular approach that is highly congruent with all three of the learning theories just presented.

Inquiry is the essence of active learning, a direct application of constructivist theory (Bruner, 1986). From a constructivist stance, inquiry learning is a powerful method for students to construct meaning through purposeful exploration. It is nearly impossible to conduct authentic (student-generated) inquiry in a classroom that is not constructivist oriented because inquiry requires that teachers let go of a traditional teaching model based on transmission. Through inquiry projects, learners ask questions, think critically, and construct knowledge. Teachers encourage students to discover new information by themselves while engaging in an active dialogue (Short et al., 1996).

From a sociocultural perspective, inquiry projects can convert classrooms and schools into communities of practice "where students pursue personally relevant inquiry and create socially significant artifacts with other students, teachers, and members of the community" (Wilhelm & Friedemann, 1998, p. 2). For example, one group of middle school students designed and carried out an inquiry project on Russian orphans, a topic about which they were very passionate. After reading news articles, viewing a disturbing video documentary, and discussing the topic in class, they wrote persuasive letters to politicians and celebrities and eventually designed a website that alerted the community to the issue.

Another example of a group inquiry project that benefited others was carried out by a group of high school students with learning disabilities. They chose to do an inquiry project on cars, a topic about which this age group is extremely interested. Each student chose a favorite car, then designed a website that described the car's "specs" (specifications) in addition to one other focus area about the car, such as its history, off-road capability, or modification options. The goal of the project was to provide useful information so that other students their age could make informed car-buying decisions. Because these students struggled with traditional literacies, they received help as needed from the special education teacher, the school librarian, and an outside researcher. In this case, the classroom was not teacher centered or student centered but *learning centered*, with teachers and students working collaboratively to support each other's learning and inquiry (Short & Burke, 1991). As we have discovered for ourselves, a learning-centered classroom often means adults are learning as much as the students.

> There is, I think, no point in the philosophy of progressive education which is sounder than its emphasis upon the importance of the participation of the learner in the formation of the purposes which direct his activities in the learning process.
> —Dewey (1938, p. 67)

An inquiry-based approach is also congruent with semiotic theory because inquiry projects allow students to experiment with multiple forms of representation in their efforts to gain and demonstrate emerging understandings. Including technology in an inquiry project immerses students in a "multimedia symbol bath" (Mackey, 2003, p. 403) that allows them to explore ideas using different sign systems. For example, one group of elementary students did an inquiry project on the history of cartoons (Figure 1.3). They conducted interviews and surveys (speaking, listening), consulted books (reading, notemaking), created a hilarious script that depicted Wiley Coyote suing the ACME Corporation for selling him defective products (collaborative writing), and posted everything on a website, using colorful animations to illustrate cartoon characters, cartoon artists, and how cartoons are made (hypermedia design). We've also worked with whole classes of elementary and middle school students who have designed inquiry projects about famous people or interesting animals, representing their findings using PowerPoint slide shows and websites that combined print, audio, video, and/or animation. One eighth-grade student's use of video clips in PowerPoint to illustrate skateboarding techniques and a third-grade student's inclusion of whale sounds on a website were particularly memorable. Many educators and researchers agree that "the successful use of [technology] within an instructional setting is tied directly to a pedagogical approach that promotes inquiry-based learning" (Jakes, Pennington, & Knodle, 2002, online).

Neither the cookie cutter nor the assembly line is an apt model for education. The studio is a much more congenial image.
—Eisner (1991, p. 127)

How We Design Lessons

Once teachers are able to identify and articulate their own theories of learning and their comfort with particular curricular approaches, such as inquiry learning, they can begin thinking about lesson planning. Theory and research drive curriculum, and curriculum drives daily practice. As beginning teachers, while trying to comply with learning standards and preparing our students for high-stakes testing, we often rely on textbooks and random lesson plans found on the Internet simply

FIGURE 1.3. Cartoon inquiry project.

in order to survive. However, as we mature as teachers, we begin to figure out what works and what doesn't work, through experience and a better understanding and application of research. What works for me might not work for you if we don't share the same theory of learning; however, there are four key research-based instructional elements that are consistently found in the classrooms of effective teachers, which also apply to learning on the Web. These four techniques are (1) modeling; (2) scaffolding; (3) practice; and (4) feedback (Figure 1.4), all of which depend on effective, ongoing assessment. The target outcome of this cycle of instruction is independent, metacognitive, self-regulated learners, a goal that is shared by many educators, particularly those who subscribe to a Universal Design for Learning (UDL) theory of curriculum development (Rose & Meyer, 2002).

UDL is based on recent advances in brain research with respect to learning and individual differences, and is analogous to work in the field of architecture with universal design. In universally designed architecture, structures are designed to accommodate the widest spectrum of users, including those with disabilities. Just as universally designed buildings provide options that accommodate a broader spectrum of users, universally designed curricula offer a range of options for accessing and engaging with learning materials that accommodate a broader spectrum of students (Rose & Meyer, 2002). With UDL, learning experiences are designed to be flexible from the outset, rather than retrofitted for each new learner.

Modeling

Anyone who has taught a young child a new skill has most likely used modeling to demonstrate proficient use of the skill, such as tying a shoe. "Let me show you" is an

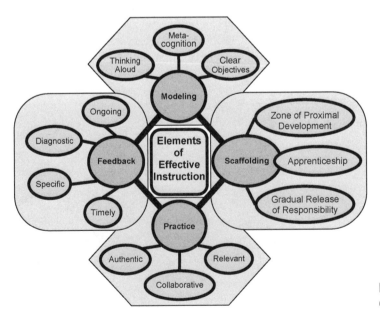

FIGURE 1.4. Elements of effective instruction.

oft-heard refrain in this context. Similarly, after assessing learners' needs, effective teachers show students how to perform an unfamiliar set of skills or strategies before expecting them to execute these independently. An extremely powerful use of modeling is the teacher think-aloud. For example, when modeling the use of a new computer strategy, the teacher narrates his thinking as he performs the task. He might say, "First, I'm going to choose a search engine. Since I already have a lot of background knowledge about my topic, I'll try Google. I'm typing *www.google.com* in the URL field. While I'm waiting for it to load, I'm thinking about my keywords."

> In schools, effective teachers are those who engage in continued prompts to get children to plan and monitor their own activities. Effective teachers model many forms of critical thinking. . . .
> —Brown, Palincsar, and Armbruster (2004, p. 784)

Thinking aloud provides a natural opportunity for teachers to model key vocabulary appropriate to the task (Kymes, 2005); even more important, it sets up an occasion to develop a common *metalanguage*—a language for talking about language, images, texts, and meaning-making interactions (New London Group, 1996). Talking about the learning process with others stimulates students to be more metacognitive about their own learning processes, that is, to think about their own thinking. Successful teachers continually prompt learners to become more metacognitive so that students begin to monitor their own learning, adjusting and extending strategies as needed.

Teachers who are effective at modeling clearly articulate the purpose of the learning objective so that students not only know *what* the strategy, process, or product looks like, but *how* to apply it, *when* and *where* to apply it, and *why* it can be useful. For example, after modeling a new notemaking strategy, the teacher may say something like "This strategy can be used when you're reading a textbook, when you're listening to a lecture, or when searching the Web. You can use this strategy in all your other classes, not just in this one. You may even use this note-

> "As I have grown as a teacher, I realize the importance of showing kids how to do things instead of telling them. Of course, this type of teaching takes a great deal more time and effort, but I feel it will be worth it in the end."
> —Darcy, fifth-grade teacher

making technique outside of school. This strategy will help you *remember important ideas*, which will not only help you do well on tests, but will help you write papers and remember important things in your daily life." Describing the purpose and rationale for a new learning task engages all parts of the brain as currently understood by cognitive neuroscientists—the recognition, strategic, and affective networks (Meyer & Rose, 1998; Rose & Meyer, 2002).

Scaffolding

Another extremely effective element of instruction is scaffolding. This is analogous to Vygotsky's use of the zone of proximal development (ZPD), in which a more experienced child or adult helps a learner do a task that is slightly beyond her ability to do independently. Nudging learners along their individual ZPDs helps them extend their current levels of knowledge and ability in incremental steps.

In all forms of scaffolding, there is a gradual release of responsibility from the expert to the novice. Think of the metaphor of a house painter's temporary scaffold—it is never intended to adhere to the house permanently, but is dismantled piece by piece until the painter can reach the walls without the use of the scaffolding that was needed when she first started the project.

When young children and novice computer users first start to use the Web, they need a lot of teacher scaffolding. This may be as formal as students' following a set of oral and written instructions prepared by the teacher in advance or as casual as the teacher's looking over students' shoulders while they are on the computer and providing hints for what to do next. Experienced teachers are masters at providing just the right amount of scaffolding so each learner can perform the task with confidence and awareness.

Interestingly, well-designed computer software can also be used to scaffold learners. Although no computer program has yet to match the sensitive and nuanced learner support provided by an experienced teacher, students can develop "intellectual partnerships" with software programs that embed models of expert performance, strategy prompts, feedback systems, and tools to reduce cognitive load. A premiere example of this type of software is Tom Snyder's *Thinking Reader* (*www.tomsnyder.com*), an award-winning, research-based program that scaffolds readers by embedding individualized comprehension strategy prompts (questioning, clarifying, predicting, summarizing, visualizing, connecting, and reflecting) and metacognitive think-alouds within high-quality, high-interest juvenile novels.

 Appropriate scaffolding is essential to teaching in the ZPD. Too much scaffolding undermines a student's sense of accomplishment; too little means frustration and discouragement. The right amount helps engage students in the learning process, building interest and enjoyment. The right blend of challenge, support, and meaningful feedback can put even beginning students in the state of flow described [by Csikszentmihalyi], fully engaged in the learning process.
—Meyer and Rose (1998, p. 60)

Practice

Another linchpin of effective instruction is providing adequate time for students to practice the skills and strategies being presented. In addition to the power of collaboration, individual guided and independent practice is also important so that learners can confidently implement strategies on their own. Some students may need very little practice to master a new skill, while others may need to revisit a learning task repeatedly—in different contexts and at different times.

Whenever feasible, practice activities need to be authentic. By this we mean that students should be engaged in activities that have a real purpose rather than a contrived one. For example, synthesizing ideas from multiple websites assigned by the teacher is not nearly as potent a practice as having students practice synthesizing information gleaned from sites of their choosing to be used in an inquiry project. Similarly, creating a product that is never shared with others, such as a website that is never actually published on the Web, is not an authentic activity. An audience of one (i.e., the teacher) is not really an audience at all. Research has repeatedly shown that students produce higher-quality work when writing for an authentic audience (Cohen & Riel, 1989; Eagleton, 1999). In a similar vein, inquiry topics that are chosen by the teacher are much less engaging for students than those that are driven by authentic learner questions. Giving students an opportunity to select their own inquiry topics builds a sense of ownership and empowerment. Many of our students have the capacity to design creative solutions to real-world problems if we allow them to take on the "mantle of the expert" (Wilhelm & Friedemann, 1998).

Related to the concept of authenticity is that of relevance. Unless they are highly motivated by grades and/or instructor approval, students need to perceive school-related tasks as relevant to their lives. The understanding that children have an intrinsic need to make connections with what they are learning in school has been noted throughout history by educational theorists such as Dewey (1938) and Vygotsky (1978), who both believed that teaching should involve tasks that students see as connected and relevant to their lives rather than tasks that seem isolated from the real world.

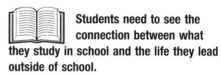

Students need to see the connection between what they study in school and the life they lead outside of school.
—Eisner (1994, p. 84)

Technology is a natural point of reference for today's children because they are already immersed in and familiar with media. According to Smith (1997), "For children, computers can be interesting things to work on and to think, talk, read, and write about, even when the children's particular interests are as diverse as art, music, science, or sports" (p. 149). It is fascinating to observe that the "novelty" of computers has not worn off, as many educators predicted. Clearly, many of today's students view computers as an "our generation kind of thing" (Eagleton, 2002) and feel impoverished if they are not proficient in new technologies. One of the best ways to help students become skilled at learning on the Web is to have them practice reading lots and lots of webpages and then reflect on their experiences together. This authentic, relevant activity can familiarize students with the features commonly found on webpages and eventually lead to independent, self-regulated learning.

Feedback

Another element of effective instruction is feedback. Children need to know how they are doing on a task so they can modify their approach if necessary and develop the confidence to continue with the task. Feedback can be given in a variety of forms, but it is imperative that it be specific and timely. Anyone who's taken a basic teacher education course knows that generic praise such as "good job" or "great" does not offer adequate specificity to impact student performance in the future. Experienced teachers recognize that feedback must be timely in order to make a difference. There is a point of diminishing returns as feedback is delivered farther and farther away from the original act. We have all met teachers who are so slow to grade tests or review their students' work that the papers end up in the "circular file" (aka the trash can) because it is no longer useful for improving student learning.

Feedback should also be ongoing, not just at the end of a chapter, unit, or semester. When students receive constructive feedback—whether it's enthusiastically positive or gently negative—on their understanding of a topic or their performance on a task *right at the moment of need*, there is a much greater chance of retention and transfer. When a teacher recognizes a student's location of useful information within a website, the student not only develops confidence in his Internet reading abilities, but he is more likely to look for information about other topics and for other purposes. The ideal time to give feedback to students is when they are immersed in a task and open to suggestion; this is often referred to as the "teachable moment."

Feedback is not only useful for students, but serves as a primary diagnostic tool for teachers. Although it can be difficult with large class sizes and caseloads, effective teachers are aware of their students' learning processes and can modify and adapt instruction as needed in order to reach as many learners as possible. True diagnostic instruction guides teachers toward what needs to be taught (or retaught) next, thus initiating a new cycle of modeling, scaffolding, practice, and feedback. Teacher–student conferencing is a handy technique for individually assessing and providing private feedback to learners.

There are many instances in which teacher feedback is crucial during the process of learning on the Web, since the Web itself does not provide feedback to learners. Teachers can prescreen students' research questions and keywords before they even get on the computers, and while students are online, teachers should "hover," providing specific feedback regarding students' choices of search engines, alternative keywords, links to follow, and webpages to skim quickly or read more deeply.

Challenges with Web Learning

Even when a strong theoretical framework is used to make curricular decisions and plan lessons, teachers and learners on the Web still face a variety of challenges, from gaining access to the Internet in a busy computer lab to locating a website that was there just yesterday. Many of these challenges are faced by learners *before* they can even reach a webpage. There is no doubt that "new technologies for networked information and communication are complex and require many new strategies for their effective use" (Leu, Kinzer, Coiro, & Cammack, 2004, p. 1596). In keeping with our view that technology is not a silver bullet for all the ailments in education, in this section we describe some of the challenges that we have experienced in our work with computers in the classroom so that you can be better prepared when lesson plans go awry.

The Nature of the Web

The sheer volume of information on the Web can quickly lead to cognitive overload, or too much information for the brain to handle at once. Because of the vast amount of available information on the Web, readers rarely have a sense of where they are in the "book." Readers

Finding information on the World Wide Web [is like] getting a drink of water from a fire hose.
—Grisham (2001, online)

don't know whether there are hundreds of screens yet to read or just a few (Bolter, 1991). This can cause anxiety, frustration, and difficulty with time management.

Another challenging issue in reading on the Web for students is that most websites are not designed or written with young readers in mind (Kafai & Bates, 1997). In fact, some researchers have discovered that when reading in hypertext, even proficient readers of print text can exhibit characteristics more associated with individuals with reading disabilities, such as "field dependence, poor visualization and spatial ability, external locus of control, and use of less active learning strategies" (McEneaney, 1998, online).

Search Engine Technologies

Unlike a traditional search for information in a library, in which a live person can assist with the search process for young inquirers, searching for information on the Internet today relies exclusively on search engine technologies. Search engines are used by about 85% of users to locate information, and several search engines consistently rank among the top 10 sites accessed on the Web (McNabb, Hassel, & Steiner, 2002). Not only do students need to know which search engines to use for certain type of searches (Eagleton & Guinee, 2002), but they need to be able

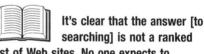

It's clear that the answer [to searching] is not a ranked list of Web sites. No one expects to approach a librarian, ask a question about the Panama Canal, and get 50 book titles in response.   —Roush (2004, online)

to negotiate various search engine interfaces, most of which require perfect spelling, flexible keyword strategies, and the ability to interpret the results of a search. Clearly, search engines are not learning tools. They do not provide any of the elements of effective instruction previously discussed, such as modeling, scaffolding, guided practice, or feedback. We share some strategies for becoming more adept with search engines in Chapter 5.

Further, although a broad search query can return more websites than anyone could possibly peruse in a lifetime, search engines still access only a very thin layer of the Web. Some estimates put the number of webpages that are hidden from

Search engines as they now exist represent a primitive, first cut at efficient information access on the Internet.
—Berghel (1997, p. 20)

the view of most search engines at 500 billion (Hafner, 2004). As Kajder (2003) notes, "you cannot literally search the Web. You can only search a snapshot taken by a search engine" (p. 55). The so-called Deep Web is qualitatively different from the surface Web, and some would say it contains more valuable, credible information. The problem is that Deep Web sources, such as libraries, museums, and government institutions, store their content in databases that cannot be accessed by many of today's search engines.

Technical Issues

Because we are interested in Web activities in the context of actual classrooms, technical issues loom large. Here is just a short list of the technical roadblocks that we personally have encountered in our work with computers in school settings:

- School network is down.
- Internet connection is down.
- Computers are too old.
- Computers are too slow.
- Software isn't working.
- Screen is frozen.
- Mouse won't work.
- Keyboard won't work.
- Monitor looks weird.
- Printer won't print.
- Disk drive doesn't work.
- Sound doesn't work.
- LCD projector is overheating.
- Headphone cord is too short.
- Cables are unplugged or missing.
- Malicious tampering.

There is no need to belabor this point, other than to emphasize that it is unwise to overlook the role of technical issues when planning technology-mediated learning activities. Teachers must always be ready to launch a backup plan when technical problems arise, unless they or their students are sufficiently tech-savvy to troubleshoot technical glitches on their own. We discuss the role of teachers' computer expertise shortly.

Time Constraints

As with technical issues, time constraints must be considered in the context of school environments. Deep learning takes time, authentic inquiry takes time, and technology exploration takes time. Unfortunately, school schedules, curricular obligations, transitions between activities, student behavior problems, and constant classroom interruptions reduce the time available for learning, retention, and transfer.

Researcher's Log: "Well, there was a power outage over the weekend, so all the computers on the school network are down. Unfortunately, the district network people don't arrive at work until 8:30 A.M., so we can't do any Web searching during first period today. Arrgh!"

Just as no one would expect a student to become a master reader, mathematician, or dancer after one or two lessons, semesters, or years, it is unrealistic to expect learners to become instantly proficient with all the complexities of finding and using information on the Internet. This is why we advocate an Internet inquiry curriculum that spans all the years of schooling. "Becoming a self-reflective learner, developing awareness of one's cognitive resources and regulating them, is a process that occurs over much time" (Baker & Brown, 1984, p. 4). Learners need time to discover, make mistakes, self-regulate, and integrate new knowledge with what they already know.

> Both teachers and students need time to explore, to collaborate with others, to present their understandings to others, to reflect on and monitor their inquiry, and to create new questions.
>
> —Short and Burke (1991, p. 68)

Finding a balance between completing tasks and the time needed to engage in the process of learning is not easily accomplished in this age of increasing time pressures and accountability (Carroll, 2004). Fortunately, as discussed in the introduction to Part I, activities such as Internet inquiry have the potential to address multiple learning objectives across several content areas (Eagleton, 1999, 2002; Eagleton & Hamilton, 2002), so the time is well spent. Further, we believe that many strategies for reading on the Internet carry over to strategies for reading in print, and vice versa.

Teacher's Role

Without a doubt, the teacher's role is a significant factor in students' ability to learn about, with, and from technology. As mentioned earlier, it has been repeatedly noted by researchers that the teacher's stance must shift away from a transmission-oriented philosophy toward a more constructivist approach if effective learning is going to take place on the Web. If there is a mismatch between the teacher's philosophical beliefs and an instructional activity such as Internet inquiry, students are not likely to be successful.

A common assumption teachers make in the context of technology-mediated learning is that today's children know more about computers than do adults. This is true in some respects (which makes some teachers uncomfortable), but faulty in others. Many of today's young learners do indeed know how to troubleshoot computers, play computer games, send and receive e-mail, and instant message multiple friends while simultaneously listening to music, watching TV, and doing their homework. These are the students whose technical expertise is a precious asset in classrooms in which distributed expertise is valued. However, there are several important exceptions to this widespread view of today's students. First, not all students are comfortable with computers, especially those whose families don't own computers. Second, children who have learning disabilities often experience difficulty in learning with computers. Finally, numerous studies have shown that middle school and even high school students have surprisingly low levels of success using the Web as a search tool (e.g., Bilal, 2002; Broch, 2000; Guinee et al., 2003; Jansen & Pooch, 2001; Kuiper, Volman, & Terwel, 2004; Wallace et al., 2000). Therefore, the teacher still has a significant role to play in technology-mediated learning (Figure 1.5).

Clearly, a teacher's level of computer expertise is an influential factor in students' success with technology. Just as search engines are not designed to be teaching tools, neither are most websites. It is up to the teacher to "provide support to stu-

FIGURE 1.5. Teacher–student collaboration.

dents as they attempt to make sense of information in an environment that does not foster the construction of understanding but merely provides information" (Hoffman, Wu, Krajcik, & Soloway, 2003, p. 343). Although bold teachers can, and do, learn alongside their students, it is certainly conducive to students' learning on the Web if teachers have a minimal level of comfort with hardware, operating systems, the Internet, search engines, and search strategies. The availability of experts, the amount of professional development opportunities, and sheer time spent online can greatly enhance teachers' computer expertise. However, as with students, this type of learning takes time, so teachers who have not yet ventured into technology-mediated learning need to get started soon. It is a fallacy that new teachers entering the profession will automatically be proficient with new literacies; further, new teachers will not intuitively know how to effectively integrate technology into the curriculum unless this has been repeatedly modeled for them in preservice education.

 [Not teaching students to be savvy Internet users] leaves them to navigate the information superhighway without a map, a tank of gas, and a spare in the trunk.
—Kajder (2003, p. 49)

Although this is not an exhaustive list, we have addressed several of the most urgent concerns teachers face as they strive to create a classroom environment in which learning and technology come together.

Summary

Because we believe that there is no single method of teaching that works with all learners all the time, a more practical and far-reaching instructional objective is to teach learners how to learn. In this chapter we described three well-established theories of learning: constructivism, socioculturalism, and semiotics. Each theory was followed by examples of common classroom applications of the theory and the ways in which technology supports teaching from each perspective. We discussed strategy instruction as an application of constructivist thinking, collaborative learning as an application of a sociocultural perspective, and multiple literacies as an example of putting semiotic theory into practice. We also foreshadowed a major theme of this book by suggesting that inquiry-based learning is a powerful curricular approach that is driven by all three theories of learning.

Later in the chapter, we presented four elements of effective instruction that can serve as a framework for the learning strategies and classroom activities presented in this book: modeling, scaffolding, practice, and feedback. Examples of modeling include teacher-think alouds, fostering metacognition, and clearly articulated objectives. Scaffolding was discussed with respect to the zone of proximal development and the gradual release of responsibility. Guided and independent practice activities were presented as being most effective when they are authentic and relevant and include peer collaboration. Feedback was described as making the greatest impact on student learning when it is specific, timely, ongoing, and used for diagnostic purposes. Finally, we described several of the factors that pose challenges to using the Internet as a learning tool in the classroom.

In the next chapter we turn our attention from learning in general to literacy in particular. While reading on the Web is similar in many ways to reading in print, when we apply Cueing Systems Theory and Transactional Theory to the process, we find that Web reading involves more complexity. We discuss the similarities and differences between print reading and Web reading with respect to comprehension strategies and foundational reading skills, while promoting the idea that current definitions of literacy must include digital texts such as those found on the Web. Some of those definitions can be found by investigating contemporary literacy theories such as New Literacy Studies, New Literacies Perspectives, and Hypermedia Cueing Systems Theory. Finally, we posit that knowledge of informational text structures can aid readers with making meaning on the Web.

2 BECOMING LITERATE

KEY IDEAS

▶ Reading on the Web is similar to reading in print, but when viewed from both cueing systems and transactional perspectives, is it clear that Web reading is more complex than print reading.

▶ Decades of reading research have consistently revealed comprehension strategies used by proficient readers that are necessary for both print and electronic texts.

▶ In order to gain automaticity and comprehension, readers need to be proficient with foundational skills such as decoding, fluency, and vocabulary.

▶ Current definitions of literacy must include digital texts such as those found on the Web.

▶ Contemporary literacy theories include New Literacy Studies, New Literacies Perspectives, and Hypermedia Cueing Systems Theory.

▶ Knowledge of informational text structures can aid readers in making meaning on the Web.

Just because our students are able to cruise through the Internet with speed and what looks like skill doesn't mean they know what they are doing.

—Kajder (2003, p. 49)

In this chapter, we seek to answer the questions "What does it mean to become literate?" and "What are Web literacies?" by building on what we already know about the reading process and applying it to reading on the Web. We strive to paint a vivid picture of the ways we make meaning from text, both print and digital. First, we begin by describing two well-established views of the reading process—Cueing Systems Theory and Transactional Theory—and then apply them to reading on the Web. Then we summarize six major reading comprehension strategies used by proficient readers of both print and Web texts. We follow with a description of the role that foundational skills, such as decoding, fluency, and vocabulary knowledge, play in comprehending any type of text. Next we describe contemporary theories of what it means to be literate and how this impacts literacy teaching and learning. Finally, we investigate the features of informational text structures that are ubiquitous on the Web. Along the way, we acknowledge that reading is a very complex cognitive and metacognitive process, and while some digital texts offer supports for novices and struggling readers, in many cases there are additional challenges to be overcome on the road to understanding.

Our primary approach in this book is to build a bridge between traditional literacy and new literacies. This concept of connecting the old with the new is important because teaching Web literacies is not about teaching totally new concepts or adding on to the currently overloaded curriculum. We view Web literacies as an extension of our traditional view of literacy, incorporating the technologies that so strongly influence the ways we access information. The main ideas in this chapter, in conjunction with the focus in Chapter 1 on the ways we learn, serve as a solid foundation for exploring what it means to be "Web literate."

Web literacy is not yet very well understood, and only a few theorists have even attempted to explain what it means. Similarly, only a few educators have attempted to create a Web literacy curriculum or design a cohesive set of instructional practices to enhance students' ability to read on the Web. This makes sense, given that the Internet is only a few decades old, and large institutions such as schools tend to be slow to change. However, with 16% of the total world population now using the Internet (de Argaez, 2006), we cannot afford to ignore this information resource. This is the primary reason that we are interested in understanding contemporary literacies and how to teach them to our students.

 Nam et ipsa scientia potestas est [Knowledge is power].
—Sir Francis Bacon (1597)

Views of the Reading Process

The act of making meaning, or comprehending, is a complex process, whether we are making that meaning from print text or Web text. Fortunately, teachers benefit from years of research on print text that focuses on defining comprehension and identifying effective instructional strategies (National Institute of Child Health and Human Development, NICHD, 2000; Rand Reading Study Group, RRSG, 2002, 2004). When it comes to reading Web text, we are still in the early stages of developing our understanding of the comprehension process. Research in this field faces the challenge of trying to keep pace with the changes occurring in technology, although we have begun to study the ways readers comprehend Internet text (Coiro & Dobler, in press), the strategies readers use to search for information (Guinee et al., 2003; Lawless, Brown, Mills, & Mayall, 2003), and the navigational paths readers follow when reading on the Internet (McEneaney, 2003). An understanding of the Internet reading process is beginning to take shape, based on the work of teachers and researchers who seek to link literacy and technology.

Cueing Systems Theory and Transactional Theory are two influential views of the reading process that provide a solid foundation for understanding how readers make sense of both print and digital texts. Though reading print and reading on the Web have many similarities, the use of additional cueing systems and the reliance on navigation for making meaning add layers of complexity to Web reading.

Cueing Systems Theory

In Chapter 1 we discussed sign systems from a semiotic perspective. Every major symbol system, such as dance, music, art, math, and print, uses a common set of cues or "cueing systems" to help the learner understand and create meaning in that form of representation. For example, in musical notation, there are cues for melody, rhythm, harmony, texture, form, dynamics, and timbre. A widely accepted view of the reading process suggests that there are at least three major cueing systems used by readers to make sense of text: graphophonic (letter–sound relationships), syntactic (grammar), and semantic (meaning) (Goodman, 1996; Clay, 1991). This three-cueing-systems perspective is often depicted as a Venn diagram (Figure 2.1), which provides a visual display of the ways each cueing system interacts with and relies on

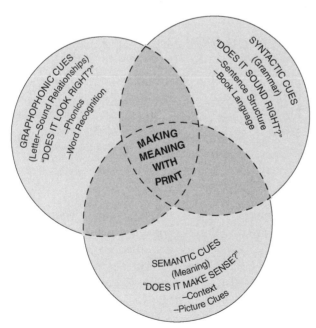

FIGURE 2.1. Three-cueing-systems model.

the others to promote the making of meaning. The three-cueing-systems model has guided reading teachers for several decades, and while some educators have suggested that readers actually utilize additional cueing systems, such as lexical (word knowledge), schematic (prior knowledge), and pragmatic (knowledge of audience/purpose) (Keene & Zimmermann, 1997), the three-systems model has provided a useful starting point for understanding the cognitive complexity of making meaning from print.

Effective readers simultaneously apply the cueing systems through the use of complex connections. An understanding of a single word or phrase may be acquired by applying various combinations of cues. For instance, in order to understand the word "forelimbs" in a text on whales, a reader would likely consider his knowledge of compound words (syntactic), letter–sound combinations (graphophonic), and an illustration with labeled parts (semantic), all within a matter of seconds. Effortless application of cueing systems is a complex task requiring a high level of thinking, which many children find difficult. Reading is clearly not a passive process; rather, it is a very active process, involving multiple parts of the brain as connections are made between the various cues provided by the text.

Cueing Systems on the Web

When literacy researchers talk about cueing systems in texts, they are typically referring to primary-level narratives with simple text and static images. However, when readers enter the upper elementary grades, they more frequently encounter multifaceted texts such as magazines, textbooks, and encyclopedias. These expository genres include additional text features that must be negotiated, such as tables of contents, heads, subheads, indexes, and so on. Such is also the case for the Web reader. Not only does the Web reader need to apply the three traditional cueing systems attributed to print, but she has a host of other cueing systems available because of the unique characteristics of Web text. Comprehension on the Web requires the orchestration of a daunting number of additional cueing systems, such as operational, organizational, and multimedia cues, plus knowledge of informational text structures and the inclination/ability to access text supports, thereby placing an even heavier cognitive load on learners (Figure 2.2). It's one thing to have three or four cues working together to help determine meaning, but now the Web reader may encounter at least a dozen. Reading on the Web is truly a cognitively complex endeavor.

> "I have a terrible time reading. So you know, the Internet's not really the best place for me to go because it's like reading a giant book."
>
> —Kevin, middle school student

Transactional Theory

Many educators believe that the act of understanding or comprehending occurs in the transaction between the reader and the text (Kucer, 2001; Rosenblatt, 1978). The transactional view of literacy is attributed to American literary critic Louise

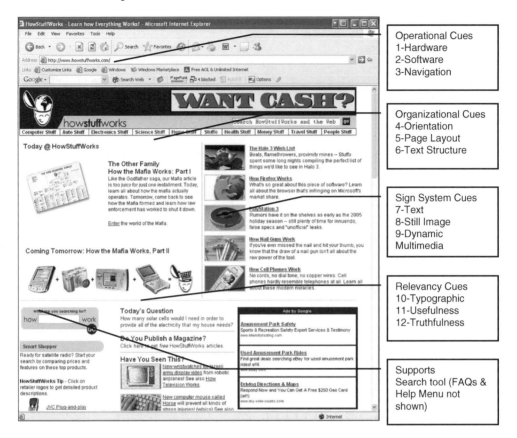

FIGURE 2.2. Website cueing systems. (*Source: How Stuff Works*, available at *www.howstuffworks.com.*)

Rosenblatt, who first advanced the theory in 1938. The prevailing view at that time was that the texts themselves were central to determining meaning and that teachers were supposed to teach the skills of close, concise, attentive analysis while discouraging expression of differences in students' own individual responses. The meaning of the text was seen to lie with the author, while the teacher served to interpret the author's intent for the students. Many adults experienced this view in high school literature classes and may recall learning a prescribed interpretation for a Shakespeare play or an English sonnet. Rosenblatt advanced a revolutionary view of the reading process that is quite influential today, which is characterized by concepts such as "locus of meaning" and "reader response," described next.

Rosenblatt (1985) theorized that the meaning of the text does not merely lie within the words on the page, but is created when each individual reader interacts with the text. The meaning becomes a new entity—a virtual text in one's mind—each time the text is read, based on a combination of what the reader brings and what the author created. The Transactional Theory of reading focuses on "the reading act as an event involving a particular individual and a particular text, happening at a particular time, under particular circumstances, in a particular social and cultural setting, and as part of the ongoing life of the individual and the group" (Rosenblatt, 1985, p. 100). What is significant about this interpretation of the reading process is that it is impossible to find "a single absolute meaning for a text because the same text can take on different meanings in transactions with different readers or even with the same reader in different contexts or times" (Rosenblatt, 1994, p. 1078). The Transactional Theory honors the unique perspective and interpretation each reader has to offer while emphasizing the process of meaning making.

Another key idea in Transactional Theory, also known as Reader Response Theory, is that the reader's "stance" has a significant influence on how he approaches the text and on what he takes away from the text. The concept of reader stance refers to the unique combination of a reader's perspective and purpose for reading. An aesthetic stance focuses on a reader's sense of enjoyment and personal connections made with the text. An efferent stance focuses on the information or the details gathered from the text. Efferent and aesthetic stances are not mutually exclusive, but rather form a continuum on which the reader moves seamlessly throughout the reading process. Rosenblatt describes this flow as a continuous, unconscious fluctuation between the two stances.

The skilled reader effortlessly moves between both stances, blending inforation and emotions, facts and personal connections, as he progresses through the reading process. In contrast, the novice or struggling reader is less able to move effortlessly between stances and is often less aware of his purpose for reading in the first place. With Internet texts, this challenge can be magnified.

> Texts are constructed by authors to be comprehended by readers. The meaning is in the author and the reader. The text has the potential to evoke meaning but has no meaning in itself; meaning is not a characteristic of texts . . . meaning does not pass between writer and reader. It is represented by a writer in a text and constructed from a text by a reader.
>
> —Goodman (1994, p. 1103)

Transacting on the Web

Like the reader of print text, the reader of Web text also brings prior knowledge and purpose to the reading task as she fluctuates between the efferent (informational) and the aesthetic (personal) stance. Her view, or perspective, guides her transaction with the text as she moves through the uniquely individual process of making meaning. However, a printed text cannot literally change its characteristics as a result of being read, nor is there a direct interaction between the reader and the author of the text, so this transactional exchange is purely metaphorical.

In contrast, electronic texts can actually change the fundamental relationship between the reader, the author, and the text by permitting a literal transaction between the reader and the text (Murray, 1999; Reinking, 1994). Not only can an electronic text be programmed to adapt and respond to an individual reader's needs and interests during reading, hypertext documents allow the reader to select her own path through extensive networks of textual and multimedia information. Therefore, the idea of the act of reading being an "active process" takes on new and more literal meaning when we describe Web reading, where the process involves engaged readers' constantly making choices about what to read and then taking physical action by clicking on links or scrolling up or down the page (Figure 2.3). The Web reading process can continue only when the reader navigates, that is, when the reader reads, makes a decision, clicks or scrolls, and reads again.

> We shall all be closer through electronic technology, whether we want to be or not. Readers will be closer to authors, writers to editors, learners to practitioners.
>
> —Smith (1997, p. 150)

In their book, *Teaching with the Internet K–12: New Literacies for New Times*, Leu, Leu, and Coiro (2004) recognize the role navigation plays in the active process of comprehension. They write, "We see the act of deciding which path to follow on the Internet as very tightly woven within a complex process of reading and meaning making. . . . It is not simply about how quickly students can move through this online world, but more about how they decide which information is most accurate, relevant, appropriate, and useful for their purposes" (p. 37). Researchers are taking a closer look at the interconnection between comprehension and navigation (Coiro, 2003; Leu, Kinzer, Coiro, & Cammack, 2004; Schmar-Dobler, 2003; Smolin & Lawless, 2003; Sutherland-Smith, 2002). In our work with Web readers, we have observed, and readers have described for us, a mental process of moving between making reading decisions and developing an understanding (Coiro & Dobler, in press). By sharing their thought processes aloud, the readers we study demonstrate the complex, high-level thinking that occurs as they mentally crisscross back and forth between comprehension and navigation until the lines are blurred between these processes. In the Web reading process, navigation becomes the action that facilitates the transaction between the reader and the text. However, for reading to make sense in any context, readers must have a toolbox of reading comprehension strategies from which to draw.

FIGURE 2.3. Web reading is an active process.

Reading Comprehension Strategies

Throughout the reading process, proficient readers orchestrate a number of strategies to support their construction of meaning (Pearson, Roehler, Dole, & Duffy, 1992). Strategies are those in-the-head processes a reader uses to make sense of what is being read. Since these internal processes are not easily observable and can be hard to gauge based solely on having readers retell a story or answer comprehension questions, we frequently must guess whether our students are using strategies. Listening to students work through texts by reading aloud gives us a "window on the reading process" (Goodman, 1982). Within the last 30 years, a strong body of research has been developed to describe what good readers do when they read (see Pressley & Afflerbach, 1995; Block & Pressley, 2002, for review). Good readers are active participants with a clear goal or purpose in mind for their reading. They continually evaluate whether the text and their reading are helping to meet this goal. Researchers have found that explicit instruction in specific strategies such as asking questions (Raphael & Pearson, 1985), determining important ideas (Afflerbach & Johnston, 1986), and making inferences (Hansen, 1981) can improve

 Thinking about how we use strategies with adult literature provides the best foundation for understanding how to teach comprehension.
—Harvey and Goudvis (2000, p. 7)

students' overall comprehension of text. Even more effective comprehension occurs when a reader knows when, why, and how to use a strategy (Paris, Lipson, & Wixson, 1983).

Teachers recognize the need for quality, explicit instruction of strategies as a way to provide students with tools for their mental reading toolbox (Figure 2.4). A clear description of each strategy is needed, along with the teacher or classmates modeling the strategy in action. As mentioned in Chapter 1, many educators (e.g., Palincsar & Brown, 1984; Pearson & Gallagher, 1983) recommend a gradual release of responsibility for strategy instruction whereby, at first, the instruction and model-

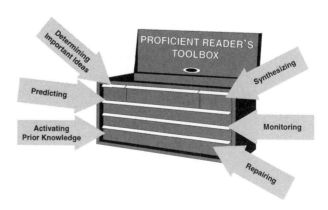

FIGURE 2.4. Proficient reader's strategy toolbox.

ing are done primarily by the teacher. Then the lesson moves into guided practice and scaffolding, which involves shared responsibility between the teacher and the students. Eventually the students take on more responsibility through independent strategy use, while the teacher plays more of a supportive role. Because of the complexities of Web reading, consider introducing and practicing comprehension strategies with print text first. When students are confident and comfortable with the use of reading strategies, then instruction in and application of these strategies to Web text will help the students ease into the additional complexities and distractions encountered on the Web. What follows is a brief description of a few key comprehension strategies and their application to both print and Web-based reading: activating prior knowledge, predicting, determining important ideas, synthesizing, monitoring, and repairing.

> **Explicit teaching uses "strategy" to mean a technique that readers learn to control as a means to better comprehend.**
> —Duffy (2002, p. 30)

Activating Prior Knowledge

Good readers use prior knowledge to check whether their construction of meaning matches what they know about the topic and structure of the text (Duke & Pearson, 2002) by developing connections between the text and themselves, the text and other texts, and the text and the world. These connections help build a bridge between new information and what is already known. Readers with greater prior knowledge can remember more, determine the important information in the text, and draw conclusions from what they read. Prior knowledge of the topic and the structure of the text provides a starting point from which to move forward through the comprehension process.

> **We build up our store of knowledge not so much for its own sake but in order to develop insight. With insight, we think more deeply and critically. We question, interpret, and evaluate what we read. In this way, reading can change thinking.**
> —Harvey and Goudvis (2000, p. 9)

Web readers must also rely on their prior knowledge to form connections and make meaning. In addition, they draw from their experiences of navigating websites and search engines. These additional sources of prior knowledge add another layer to the complexity of the Internet reading process, so that students who struggle with prior knowledge of the topic or the text structure often find themselves making random choices as they read on the Internet. Without enough information from which to draw, these readers may feel as if they are looking for a needle in a haystack. Moreover, one must not assume that because a reader has strong prior knowledge of the topic or the text structure he will necessarily be skilled at reading on the Internet. Without having the experiences of navigating through websites or knowing the nuances of various search engines, a skilled reader of print text may be at a loss when encountering the Internet. Thus, our description of the skilled Internet reader must include a strong level of prior knowledge in the areas of topic, text structure, website organization, and search engine formats.

Predicting

Making predictions is one way to draw a reader into the text. Good readers make predictions before, during, and after reading. Accurate predictions rely on a sensitive balance of prior knowledge of the topic, other experiences with similar types of text, and a sense of wonderment or curiosity (Pressley, 2002). A prediction is special kind of inference in which the reader draws from her prior knowledge to make an informed guess about what information will come next (Keatley, 1999). The strategy of predicting involves three steps: making the prediction, gathering information to confirm or disconfirm the prediction, then making a judgment about the accuracy of the prediction. When accurate predictions are made, a reader feels a connection with the text and a sense of understanding, perhaps thinking, "I thought this information would be presented, and it was, so I must be understanding this text." When predictions are made that are not confirmed in the text, a reader begins to feel disconnected or lost, which can break down meaning if this occurs too often and is not corrected (Beers, 2004).

Readers of Web texts rely on a similar process of making, confirming, and adjusting predictions. However, not only do Web readers make predictions about what is to come in the text (and within other multimedia elements), they also make predictions about how to move through the text in order to find information. When a reader who wants to know more about how to do an olley on a skateboard and clicks on the hyperlink "olley," she is mentally making a prediction that this link will lead her to learn more about this skateboarding trick. Making and confirming predictions is a major goal of efficient Web reading. Randomly clicking on links without thoughtful predictions may be interesting when browsing a website, but this strategy is not only frustrating but a waste of time when searching for information.

Determining Important Ideas

Strong readers mentally reduce the text into manageable chunks of key ideas by sifting out the important from the unimportant. They determine which important ideas on which to focus their attention during the reading process and which unimportant details deserve little or no attention (Afflerbach & Johnston, 1986). Before reading, the reader makes predictions regarding the main idea through interpretation of the title, and illustrations and a scanning of the text for key words or headings that can be linked to the reader's schema, or mental representation of the text. These predictions are verified during the reading process. After reading, the

Given that accomplished readers regularly assess their knowledge, their strategies, and their progress toward goals, we need to specify the means for helping less able readers develop self-assessment mind-sets and strategies.   —Afflerbach (2002, p. 99)

reader combines the mental chunks of key ideas into one overall main idea or several key ideas representing the text in general. This process of determining important ideas differs according to a reader's purpose for reading, but is especially crucial when reading informational text. Here the reader must both decide and remember what is important if he is going to learn something from the text or find the answer to his question(s). Text features often provide clues to the reader about what is important through the use of the title, headings, and captions.

Determining important ideas when reading Internet text is very similar to the process used for reading print text. One difference in Internet text is the variation of cues that provide hints about what is most important. Headings and captions may be available, but a reader might also draw information from icons, hyperlinks of keywords, bright colors used for highlighting text, and interactive graphics. Meanwhile, commercial pop-ups and banners are intentionally used to attract the reader's attention. With all of these visuals, in addition to the text itself, the reader may feel overwhelmed with the amount of information encountered on a webpage. This feeling of being overwhelmed may make it difficult for a reader to determine exactly what is and is not important. Experienced Web readers learn which visuals are merely meant to be distractors and which typically provide important information. These readers are able to determine what is most important by relying on their prior knowledge of the structure of websites. As with many of the reading strategies for both print and Internet text, we can see an overlapping or intertwining when the task of determining important ideas and prior knowledge come together.

Synthesizing

Synthesizing is thought to be the most challenging of the comprehension strategies because it requires the reader to bring together an awareness of the reading process and an understanding of the text (Dole, Duffy, Roehler, & Pearson, 1991; Harvey & Goudvis, 2000). Skilled readers learn to stop every so often in their reading and summarize by thinking about what is being read and how this information enhances their understanding and supports the construction of meaning. Strong readers not only sort and summarize the most important ideas from within single texts, but also between texts in order to synthesize ideas to help create an understanding of what is being read. At the highest level, synthesizing goes beyond determining meaning and moves into the development of a new perspective or viewpoint, also known as transformation. A reader's thinking changes based on her transaction with texts, as she comes to "own" her new ideas. Personal responses, whether written or oral, give the reader a chance to work through this new thinking and to share it with others.

Synthesis of Web texts provides a chance for a reader to formulate a new idea or understanding in a similar way as with print text. Information is gathered from one website or by combining ideas from several websites. Still, a reader must determine what is most important and hold those ideas in her memory (if not on a notepad) as she navigates within and between websites. One difference in the synthesis process is that skilled Web readers *expect* to read in more than one place within a website or to read more than one website to locate the answer to a question. They understand that the answer will likely not jump out at them but rather will require the making of inferences and the summarizing and bringing together of ideas from separate locations. We return to the topic of synthesizing in Chapter 7.

Monitoring

Strong readers tend to be careful in their reading and spend more time on difficult parts of the text. These readers possess the metacognitive ability to mentally summarize chunks of the text during and after reading to monitor their process of making meaning. They are more aware of their level of understanding or lack of understanding and can skillfully maneuver between skimming, scanning, and slow, careful reading. Skilled readers use skimming by initially glancing over the text to determine the topic and type of text and so decide if these ideas match their purpose for reading. Scanning is used to quickly read a text, noting headings, bold words, dates, numbers, or other details that stand out for the reader. Careful reading requires moving through the text at a pace slow enough to notice, understand, and remember details. Not only can skilled readers adjust their reading rate, but they can also adjust their use of reading strategies in order to better understand a text. When the text structure or vocabulary is difficult, good readers use various strategies, such as rereading, to repair meaning (Pressley, 2002). The opposite is true for poor readers, who are typically less careful with their reading and often do not recognize the loss of meaning when new words or concepts are unknown. When problems do arise with comprehension, these readers have few strategies for getting their comprehension back on track.

Good readers know when they need to exert more effort to make sense of a text.
—Pressley (2001, online)

Web readers must also monitor their comprehension throughout the reading process by combining the use of traditional monitoring strategies with an understanding that the information in Web text may be hidden below the screen or beneath several layers of links on a website. The homepage of a website may contain information the reader is seeking, but often desired information is gained only through navigating several links, taking the reader within the depths of the website. Monitoring comprehension through these various layers is a more complex process than merely checking whether the text is making sense to the reader. The reader must also check to make sure he knows where he is within the text and have a fairly good idea of how to find the information he needs.

Repairing

Good readers know what to do when they discover that meaning has been lost. They anticipate problems and take action to solve problems as soon as they arise. Using what are often called "fix-up" strategies, skilled readers select an appropriate mental tool or strategy to repair confusion (Garner, 1987). The strategies may include rereading, skipping ahead, or searching for context clues. Skilled readers are also more flexible in their use of strategies, displaying an ability to change strategies to meet different reading situations.

All of the reading strategies described in this chapter can serve as effective fix-up strategies for a skilled reader. In fact, a reader may use two or more of these strategies simultaneously as a bundle of strategies to be accessed as needed. When comprehension is occurring, the reader is often unaware of how the text is being processed. Yet when a reader becomes stuck and comprehension is lost, she shifts into a metacognitive mode in order to draw upon effective strategies. We recognize a loss of comprehension when we pause in reading and say to ourselves, "What did I just read? I am not sure, so I better go back and read again."

> **It is through the application of these strategies at various moments throughout the interaction that meaning emerges.**
>
> **—Pardo (2004, p. 277)**

When reading within search engines and across websites, Internet readers also reread to gain meaning or scan a webpage to search for context clues. In order for these readers to use fix-up strategies, they must be adept at navigating within and between websites. A reader who wants to reread a text must know how to return to that text, whether this is done through the use of the back button, following the links back to the webpage, or finding the webpage listed on the drop-down menu or history list. Several paths will take the reader back to the same information, although some paths are more efficient than others. Less-skilled readers may lose sight of what they are looking for or even forget the information they already understood. Again, the interweaving of navigation and comprehension clearly impacts the Web reader.

The strategies used by proficient readers represent a collection of those habits or thought processes necessary for making meaning from text. These strategies are often used simultaneously when reading; for example, we might ask a question, make a prediction, and monitor our comprehension, all within a few seconds. While some readers may not need explicit instruction in comprehension strategies to use when reading print, we know that many less-skilled readers do—and that all readers must be prepared to read on the Web, which is a more complex activity than reading printed texts.

> **If reading is about mind journeys, teaching reading is about outfitting the travelers, modeling how to use the map, demonstrating the key and the legend, supporting the travelers as they lose their way and take circuitous routes, until, ultimately, it's the child and the map together and they are off on their own.**
>
> **—Keene and Zimmermann (1997, p. 28)**

Foundational Reading Skills

In addition to orchestrating cueing systems, alternating stances, and flexibly applying comprehension strategies, being a skilled reader involves adeptness with foundational, or "gatekeeper," skills. When use of these foundational skills becomes automatic or an unconscious habit, cognitive energy is available for comprehension. Skills that must be in place for readers to achieve automaticity include decoding, fluency, and vocabulary knowledge. Although important for reading print text, automaticity is especially crucial for reading Web text, because the reader can encounter massive amounts of information and must make reading decisions quickly so as to effectively understand and use the information encountered. If a student is weak in one or more of these areas, he will need appropriate scaffolding in order to comprehend effectively.

Decoding

The ability to decode, or sound out, unfamiliar words is an important complementary, or foundational, skill for comprehension. Students must be able to read texts with a reasonable degree of accuracy before they can make much sense of them. If readers cannot recognize a substantial number of sight words and easily decode unfamiliar words, they will not be able to extract meaning from the text. Decoding on the Web remains equally important to the reading process because today's Web texts still contain heavy amounts of print. To balance this, unique features of Web texts are available to support decoding. Determining meaning can be greatly aided by interactive graphics, multimedia, hyperlinks to definitions, helpful icons, and text-to-speech software, which reads digital texts aloud.

Fluency

Fluency is another foundational skill for effective reading comprehension. If readers are laboriously slogging through texts, either silently or orally, the cognitive load of remembering what was read will overcome their ability to make sense of the text. Clearly, fluency relies on decoding ability, but being able to decode accurately is insufficient. Readers must be able to decode quickly and with ease in order to be considered fluent (Pikulski & Chard, 2005), and they must have adequate syntactic awareness to attend to punctuation cues. The key is automaticity—being able to effortlessly use the skills of phrasing, tone, and pacing to read in a way that enhances understanding.

Fluency on the Web is equally important to the comprehension process. In one way, fluency may be more important for Web readers, who must constantly adjust their rate of reading as a variety of information is encountered. As mentioned previously, in order to effectively and efficiently deal with the incredible amount of information available on the Web, people must decide how to adjust their rate of reading, which can vary from (1) a quick visual scan for a particular word, phrase, or concept; to (2) skimming through the text; to (3) a careful reading of a Web page. Overreliance on any one of these reading rates is problematic. Habitual scanning or skimming may cause readers to miss useful information; conversely, slow, careful reading of every website is unnecessary and inefficient. Fluent Web readers adjust their reading rate depending on their purpose and the Web texts they encounter.

Vocabulary

Also essential to reading are vocabulary skills, as affirmed by the National Reading Panel (NICHD, 2000). Like those with decoding and fluency deficits, readers with weak vocabulary skills will most likely struggle with comprehension (Blachowicz & Fisher, 2003). Perhaps you have known readers who can decode just about any word they encounter and can even read fluently, but cannot truly understand what they read. Unless there is a significant language or learning disability, vocabulary is usually the culprit. Second-language learners often have difficulty in this area, as do any of us when reading in unfamiliar genres with unusual terminology, such as medical texts or legal contracts.

Vocabulary on the Web represents additional layers of complexity in the reading process. As with print text, a reader encountering Web text must have a good working knowledge of key vocabulary and concepts related to the topic of the website. Some websites support vocabulary development by providing hyperlinks to a picture or word definition. These supports individualize the text and encourage the reader to use the text based on her own vocabulary needs. However, many websites do not provide this assistance. An additional challenge in the area of vocabulary development lies in the need for the reader to also be proficient with the vocabulary of the Web itself. An understanding of terms such as *search engine*, *back button*, *scroll*, *drop-down menu*, *hyperlink*, and *icon* supports the reader as she locates and understands information.

Another complexity arises when the reader is determining a keyword for use in a search engine. The selection of an accurate keyword or combination of keywords hinges on the reader's ability to identify vocabulary to match her topic and purpose. Overly broad keywords yield an overwhelming number of search results. Unduly narrow keyword combinations can yield few or no search results. Selecting just the right keyword or phrase allows the search engine to provide adequate results so that the reader has choices as to where to locate information but does not feel overwhelmed. We return to the topic of keyword strategies in Chapter 5.

The foundational skills of decoding, fluency, and vocabulary play a powerful role in the ultimate success of a reader, whether reading print text or Web text. One theme has emerged from our description of foundational skills. Those skills needed to read Web text are the same foundational skills needed to read print text; however, additional layers of complexities develop when reading on the Web. Notice that this theme echoes our earlier comparison of reading comprehension strategies in print and on the Web—an apt catch phrase might be "similar, but more complex." In the next sections, we dig a little deeper into current understandings of what it means to be Web literate.

Web Literacies

In the past, reading was strictly defined as decoding and comprehending printed text, and literacy was defined as proficiency in reading and writing with print. With the advent of new technologies, this is no longer the prevailing view. It has been widely argued that the traditional definition of literacy must be expanded to include the multiple, semiotic ways in which humans communicate, including music, dance, math, reading, multimedia, and so on. In fact, the International Reading Association's (IRA, 2001) position statement on literacy and technology suggests that "traditional definitions of reading, writing and viewing, and traditional definitions of best practice instruction—derived from a long tradition of book and other print media—will be insufficient" and that therefore, "literacy educators have a responsibility to effectively integrate these technologies into the literacy curriculum in order to prepare students for the literacy future they deserve." As literacy educators ourselves, we agree with this view, but add that the monumental job of helping our students become Web literate is everyone's responsibility, not just the responsibility of language arts teachers or library media specialists (Figure 2.5).

The position taken by IRA supports the view that what it means to be literate is changing. With time and new technological advances, the expectations for being literate have evolved from writing one's name, to reading a bible, to reading a ballot, to our present-day expectations that to be successful in many endeavors and fields, one must be skilled at accessing, understanding, using, and creating information through technology. Some would say that the Internet is the most influential advancement in modern times because a seemingly limitless amount of information is available to all who have access to the technology. Others might say that the Internet is still in its infancy and it is too early to determine the long-term impacts of instant access to information. However, few can deny that the use of hypertext on the Internet affects how we read and write, how we teach reading and writing, and how we define literacy practices (Snyder, 1996).

> Any definition of literacy adopted must be broad enough to encompass the existing multiple literacies without being either so broad as to be meaningless, or indistinguishable from educational outcomes in general.
> —Lonsdale and McCurry (2004, online)

Fortunately, we are not left to our own devices to understand these new ways of being literate. Although the idea of contemporary literacies may be new to some, theorists have been focusing on ways to help us to sharpen our understanding of what it takes to become literate. A brief discussion of three of these theories follows.

FIGURE 2.5. Teaching students to become Web literate.

New Literacy Studies

New Literacy Studies have emerged in English-speaking countries other than the United States, such as England, Australia, and New Zealand. Jim Gee (2001) and Brian Street (1993) have had a strong influence on this field of thought. Lankshear and Knobel (2003) characterize this primarily sociocultural theoretical stance as "paradigmatic," indicating a major paradigm shift from literacy as an isolated social practice that takes place in schools to literacy as socially situated within communities.

This group of theorists is interested in literacies that are not just associated with new technologies but are also involved in the multiple linguistic and cultural differences that have an effect on how students negotiate their public and private lives. According to Gee (2003), "reading and writing should be viewed not only as mental achievements going on inside people's heads but also as social and cultural practices with economic, historical, and political implications" (p. 8). New Literacy Studies theorists are primarily concerned with how schools regulate access to contemporary forms of representation, so that graduates can more easily obtain employment, political power, and cultural recognition (New London Group, 1996).

New Literacies Perspectives

The New Literacies Perspective can be attributed to the work of Donald Leu and his colleagues (Coiro, 2003; Leu, 2000, 2002; Leu, Kinzer, Coiro, & Cammack, 2004). This group of researchers, guided by cognitive constructivist theory, is primarily concerned with understanding and teaching the new reading, writing, and communication strategies required for students to maximize the potential of information and communication technologies (ICTs) such as the Internet. Toward that end, they recommend four effective instructional models: Internet workshop, Internet project, WebQuest, and Internet inquiry, the focus of this book (Leu, Leu, & Coiro, 2004).

> The new literacies of the Internet include the skills, strategies, and dispositions necessary to successfully exploit the rapidly changing information and communication technologies continuously emerging in our world for personal growth, pleasure, and work.
> —Leu, Kinzer, Coiro, and Cammack (2004, p. 1572)

As a result of rapidly evolving new technologies, Leu (2000) suggests that literacy is becoming increasingly "deictic," meaning that it is changing so fast that it has become a moving target. This has a significant impact on classroom teachers, who must avoid spending valuable time teaching one particular type of technology and instead focus on helping students learn how to learn strategies for managing new technologies as they emerge.

The New Literacies Perspective has identified five "functions" of new literacies: (1) generating important questions or problems to be solved; (2) locating relevant information; (3) critically evaluating the usefulness of that information; (4) synthesizing information to address those questions or problems; and (5) communicating possible solutions to others (Leu, Kinzer, Coiro, & Cammack, 2004). From a New Literacies Perspective, it is imperative that we seek to gain a better understanding of what these new literacies entail so that we can teach students to be more strategic learners in digital contexts.

Hypermedia Cueing Systems

Hypermedia Cueing Systems Theory, first proposed by Eagleton in 2002, is strongly influenced by semiotic theory. From this perspective, literacy is defined as the skillful orchestration of the cues typically found within prevalent sign systems, and therefore being literate requires producing and understanding others' creations in a given sign system. Humans have created, and continue to create, many distinctive communicative formats in order to entertain, inform, and interact with others, so it is important to expose students to a variety of genres.

Hypermedia is obviously the most historically recent sign system, but it is already a complex language form that encompasses a number of different genres that fulfill a variety of communicative purposes. Many educational theorists suggest that we situate computer-based literacies within a historical context, placing electronic texts alongside such pivotal inventions as the ancient papyrus roll, the medieval manuscript, and the printed book (Bolter, 1991). If it is true, as Kozma (1991) suggests, that "media can be defined by its technology, symbol systems, and processing capabilities" (p. 180), then hypermedia, with its flexible use of text, image, audio, video, animation, and virtual reality, represents a revolutionary new form of human discourse. In the same way that print and sign language are not considered "simulations" of oral language, but as language forms in their own right, electronic text is a distinct language form that can either help or hinder literacy learning (Bolter, 1991; Eagleton, 1999; Reinking, 1998).

 I think that computer-related technologies have the potential to affect human thinking and communication as much as the technology of written language has.
—Teale (1997, p. 81)

It is important to explore how modern views of literacy impact teaching and learning. We know that proficiency in traditional forms of reading and writing is necessary, but not adequate, for our students to be successful. We also know that with the use of technology, our students must read and create a wider variety of texts in order to attain a higher level of literacy. The shifts in expectations for what it means to be literate are in response to the changes that have occurred in the texts we encounter. When Gutenberg invented the printing press and bibles were mass produced, people had access to text and needed to be sufficiently literate to read a bible. In today's world, the advent of the computer, the World Wide Web, and, most specifically, hypertext itself, has caused our expectations for being literate to change to include proficiency in locating, understanding, and using information on the Web. Comprehension strategies and foundational reading skills can get us started, but are not enough for us to make sense of the large amount of information available from just one webpage.

Though not the primary focus of this book, it is important to note that changes in literacy brought about by technology are acutely felt in the literacy function of writing. Technology has drastically changed the ways we compose, revise, and edit through the use of word processing software. In addition, even novice writers have opportunities to publish their thoughts and works through such venues as blogs (Web journals), wikis (Web encyclopedias), zines (Web magazines), and the creation of their own websites. Daily activities and calendars are recorded on personal handheld devices such as Palm Pilots and Blackberries, and textual, numerical, and visual messages can be sent instantly to family, friends, and colleagues through cell phones, e-mail, instant messaging, chat rooms, and text messages. Technology has clearly changed the ways we write, nearly rendering obsolete the adage "get your ideas down on paper." Although the changes in written communication are fascinating and important, in this book we have chosen to focus our attention on the process of reading and, more specifically, on the ways we locate, understand, and use information from the Web. We end this chapter with a discussion of informational text structures because they play such an important role in negotiating Internet texts.

Informational Text Structures

Throughout history, as texts have changed, we have adapted our literacy goals from reading bibles, to reading textbooks and novels, to reading websites. Throughout these "modernizations" of texts, we have adjusted our view of what it means to be a successful reader or to be literate. In each case, the way the text is structured, or organized, influences what a person needs to know to be able to read the text. Knowing how to identify a verse is important when reading a bible, while identifying structures such as cause–effect or compare–contrast is important when reading a textbook. Similarly, when reading a narrative, it is important to be able to identify common story elements such as characters, setting, and plot. In other words, our literacy instruction responds to the types of texts we are expected to read in order to be considered productive, successful members of society. This premise is the same today with Web texts, specifically, informational text found on webpages. Since an estimated 96% of the text found on the Internet is expositive rather than narrative (Kamil & Lane, 1998), it behooves us to teach students about informational text structures.

Informational Text Structures in Print

Skilled readers use a text's structure, or organizational model, to develop a mental organization system to help sort and store important ideas from the text. Readers who can identify, understand, and use text structures can recall more textual information than those who aren't as knowledgeable (Harvey, 1998) and can more easily predict the types of information and potential challenges to be found within the text.

Informational texts are usually read when a person is seeking an answer to a question or is interested in learning more about a topic by reading a textbook, encyclopedia, article, or expository picture book or chapter book. When encountering an informational text, skilled readers use navigational tools to locate information, such as the table of contents, index, and glossary (Armbruster, 1984). These tools can provide the reader with an organizational structure or framework for the text and suggest a place to begin looking for information. With the exception of picture books and chapter books, informational text is typically not read from beginning to end in the same way one would read a narrative. Because the reader's purpose is to locate information, he often uses strategic, selective reading by skimming and scanning to rapidly locate information that meets his needs. The organizational aspects of the text can make this type of reading move more quickly and be more productive. Text features, such as headings and captions, provide a reader with explicit clues about what is important in the text while also emphasizing the overall structure.

> In general, research suggests that almost any approach to teaching the structure of informational text improves both comprehension and recall of key text information.
> —Duke and Pearson (2002, p. 217)

> Once students become familiar with the basic organizational structures, they can more easily predict challenges in text, identify language features, and incorporate critical attributes to their own writing. Knowledge of these core structures and signal words provide support to readers so they can better anticipate language and features of each structure during reading.
> —Hoyt and Therriault (2003, p. 53)

Teachers can prepare students for the variety of text structures encountered in informational text. Explicit instruction in common informational text structures prepares students to activate their prior knowledge about such structures while they're reading. Students can be taught to recognize signal words such as first/last, although, same/different, however, if/then, and so on, which serve as cues that alert the reader to the type of text structure being used. Common informational text structures include the following:

- Descriptive—Presents facts that describe the characteristics of persons, places, things, and events; may include persuasive details.
- Sequential—Arranges information and events in order, often chronologically.
- Compare/contrast—Organizes information about two or more topics according to their similarities and differences.
- Cause/effect—Provides reasons or explanations for an event or occurrence.
- Problem/solution—Poses a problem and its potential solution(s).

Within all but the most simple informational texts, bits of text will be presented in a number of forms. For example, an informational book about owls may follow a descriptive structure, focusing on describing the habitat and behaviors of owls, while also including a sequential description of an owl's growth from birth and a persuasive section about the need to protect the habitats of owls.

Informational Text Structures on the Web

Although many of the same informational text structures that are found in print are also found on the Web, one of the challenges the Internet reader faces is being prepared to switch between various text structures quickly. Within one website or even one webpage, a reader may encounter description, sequence, and comparison. Then, when the reader clicks on a hyperlink to another website, the text structure may switch. Because online reading often occurs at a fast pace, readers must become skilled at quickly determining the text structure and adjusting expectations about content accordingly.

Text features such as headings, captions, and labels can be found in both printed texts and in digital texts. Unfortunately, webpages are inconsistent in their use of these features and conventions are still in flux. For example, one research study showed that of 30 random webpages, no two pages had the same text features (Dobler, 2003). Now, more than ever, a reader must be skilled at adapting to changes in both the structure and features every time a new website is encountered.

Navigation cues provide Web readers with hints (both words and images) for finding information. Books primarily use page numbers to guide the reader in a linear fashion from beginning to end. Hypertexts such as encyclopedias, textbooks, and magazines rely on tables of contents and page numbers to help readers locate desired information. In contrast, hypermedia documents such as webpages use hyperlinks in the form of buttons, tabs, image links, image maps, icons, scroll bars, and text links to help the reader navigate within and across websites. These varied navigational cues can serve to either orient or disorient learners, depending on their ability, experience, and attitude.

Today, particularly on homepages, almost every visible feature on the page is a hyperlink to somewhere else. In some ways, reading on the Web can best be described as a series of "comings and goings," since there is so much horizontal and vertical traversal between texts. The active verbs that we use to describe movement on the Web illustrate this dynamic spatial metaphor—for example, "browsing," "surfing," "visiting," "navigating," and "exploring" in "cyberspace." Many of today's students perceive the Web as a virtual "place," "space," or "meeting ground" rather than an inert object such as a book or stand alone desktop computer.

In addition to classic text structures such as comparison and description, the Web has spawned an unbelievably huge variety of new text genres in the form of e-mail, bulletin boards, chat rooms, blogs, multiuser gaming, and instant messaging. Not only does each of these contemporary genres have its own set of cues and features, but each has developed its own set of grammatical structures, such as using all lowercase letters, defying spelling conventions, and using abbreviations (LOL, FYI, BTW, etc.). New text genres have even generated new vocabulary, like "emoticons" (smiley faces to represent mood in text messages), "flaming" (sending rude messages), "spam" (junk e-mail), "netizens" (citizens, or people who frequent the Internet), and "netiquette" (courteous Internet behavior, such as not typing in all capital letters). Although the focus of this book is on webpages, these other Internet genres are also reshaping the way we think of literacy and literary structures.

Summary

In this chapter we connected traditional and contemporary understandings of what it means to be literate. Toward that end, we applied both Cueing Systems Theory and Transactional Theory to reading on the Web. We also investigated the reading comprehension strategies and foundational skills utilized by proficient readers of both print and Web-based texts, noting that digital texts can be more challenging because of their additional complexity. We supported the view that current definitions of literacy must include technology and summarized three modern views of literacy: New Literacy Studies, New Literacies Perspectives, and Hypermedia Cueing Systems Theory. Finally, we highlighted the importance of informational text structures in print and on the Web.

In Part II of the book, we apply the theory and research presented in Part I by presenting the QUEST model, an acronym that stands for the five phases of Internet inquiry: Questioning, Understanding Resources, Evaluating, Synthesizing, and Transforming. Each QUEST chapter begins by explaining the importance of each phase, gives a description of the strategies required in each phase, tells when the strategies should be applied and, finally, how strategies for each phase can be taught. Each chapter closes with a large variety of reproducibles that can be adapted for your classroom and your particular students.

II THE QUEST MODEL OF INTERNET INQUIRY

Since we believe that children learn best when they practice skills and strategies within the context of authentic learning activities rather than artificial ones, we have designed a model of Internet inquiry—QUEST—that engages and supports students as they tackle the complexities of reading on the Web. QUEST also serves as an ideal metaphor for the active *quest* for information that characterizes our daily lives, whether at home, in school, or in the workplace. Our QUEST model should not be confused with the term *WebQuest* (*webquest.sdsu.edu*), a lesson plan format for web-based learning, or *ThinkQuest* (*www.thinkquest.org*), a web design competition for children.

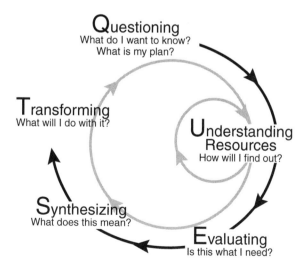

The QUEST Model of Internet Inquiry

51

The QUEST model illustrates the cyclical nature of Internet inquiry. The QUEST model visually reminds students that Internet inquiry is a multistep *process*, not a one-time *event*, much like our predecessors in writing instruction (Calkins, 1994; Graves, 1983) have shown. We like to point out to students that the word "research" is composed of the prefix "re-" and the root word "search," thus emphasizing the notion that the process is recursive. For example, as readers move through the Understanding Resources phase, they may find that they need more practice with using search engines or selecting keywords before continuing on to the Evaluating phase. Learners cycle through the Evaluating phase repeatedly as they encounter new websites and new information and must decide if what they find meets their information needs.

Note that there are several preparatory steps that must be taken before students actually start reading and Synthesizing information; this is analogous to the prewriting activities that good writers use and the prereading activities that proficient readers use. These preparatory activities are time well spent because they help activate prior knowledge and set the stage for strategic, reflective learning. In schools where resources are scarce, it is especially prudent to engage students in presearch activities before they actually sit down in front of the computer to begin searching for information.

The QUEST model is based on our observations of hundreds of learners and is consistent with existing models of information literacy, most of which do not differ significantly in concept but use diverse terminology (e.g., Eisenberg & Berkowitz, 2001, *Big6*; Macrorie, 1988, *I-Search*; Kuhlthau, 1993, *ISP*; McKenzie, 1999, *Research Cycle*; Pappas & Tepe, 1997, *Pathways to Knowledge*). Having used several of these models in the classroom, we have found that a visual model with a memorable acronym is optimal for students and teachers.

> **"I think your graphic of the Internet search process is outstanding. It's a graphic that all of us are using on the seventh grade team now. There are different ways of viewing the research process, but I think that the cyclical nature of this one is really great."**
> **—Deborah, special education teacher**

The teacher's role during Internet inquiry is to scaffold all aspects of the process until learners are able to self-reflect and self-regulate. This may take the form of frequent metacognitive reminders, such as "What are you trying to find out?," "Is this the best search engine for your question?," "Why did you click on that link?," "Does this webpage have the information you're looking for?," or "How do you know this information is reliable?" This will also take the form of frequent teacher modeling of both the process and, if applicable, the final product. We strongly suggest that teachers conduct authentic inquiry alongside their students so the learners can observe what an expert inquirer thinks and does.

Part II of this book is separated into seven chapters. Chapter 3 provides logistical tips and assessment tools from which to choose when preparing for a QUEST. Chapter 4 provides teaching ideas and activities for the Questioning phase. Chapter 5 focuses on Understanding Resources. Chapter 6 emphasizes the Evaluating phase. Chapter 7 covers the Synthesizing step. Chapter 8 offers strategies for helping students through the Transforming phase. Finally, Chapter 9 presents ideas for reflecting on the entire process. We use a traditional framework for our discussion of each phase of the QUEST model—that is, WHY we use it, WHAT it is, WHEN we use it, and finally, HOW strategies for each phase can be taught. Each chapter includes numerous classroom-ready reproducibles that are easily identified by upper case letters and numbers; for example, Handout Q-1 is the first form in Chapter 4 on Questioning. Many of these resources are also freely available for downloading from our companion website (*www.ReadingTheWeb.net*).

As you read, please keep in mind that internalizing complex strategies and skills takes a long time, so you can't teach the entire QUEST model in one brief lesson. Internet inquiry strategies must be taught recursively throughout the K–12 curriculum (Leu, Leu, & Coiro, 2004; Wallace et al., 2000). Our approach has been to focus on one strategy at a time; for example, we have done 6-week Internet inquiry units focusing just on keyword selection strategies and 4-week units emphasizing notemaking techniques. While focusing on one strategy, remember to provide scaffolds (models, templates, etc.) for the other strategies so that students are not overwhelmed with too many challenges at once. Please note that although we have provided numerous handouts for each phase of the QUEST, these reproducibles and lesson plans should be treated as a menu of possibilities rather than a prescription for using them all.

[It is helpful to have] goals specifying which aspects of instruction and assessment are central (and therefore, must be held constant) and which aspects are not central (and therefore, can be varied).
—Rose and Meyer (2002, p. 104)

Happily, Internet inquiry is an effective way for students to develop and apply traditional literacy skills, as well as newly emerging electronic literacy skills *while practicing generative metacognitive strategies that lead to more self-regulated learning*. The teachers with whom we've worked value Internet inquiry because it fulfills multiple instructional objectives necessary for success in all subject areas. To demonstrate this, we include examples of pertinent learning standards across several diverse content areas applicable to grades 3–8: language arts, science, math, library media, and social studies. The standards were collected by our friend and colleague Julie Coiro and drawn from state and local standards applicable to the Windsor Public School District in Connecticut, USA (Connecticut State Department of Education, 1998, 2005; Windsor Public Schools, 2001, 2002a, 2002b, 2004). Because the standards are representative of typical learning standards across the country, we have elected not to clutter the text with citations for each standard.

"Inquiry accomplishes about 20 things I feel I need to do as a language arts teacher. . . . It supports writing, nonfiction reading, putting text into your own words, and documentation."
—Tracey, eighth-grade English teacher

3 PREPARING FOR THE QUEST

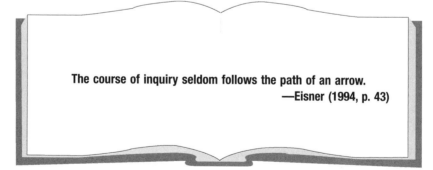

The course of inquiry seldom follows the path of an arrow.
—Eisner (1994, p. 43)

In this chapter we provide ideas and materials that will help you determine how well prepared you and your students are for Internet inquiry. First, we cover technical preparation by suggesting minimal requirements for school networking and file storage options, and by recommending essential hardware and software. Then, we discuss conceptual preparation by providing some basic information and vocabulary related to the Internet, such as URLs and domain names, search engines, keywords, and Boolean operators. Finally, we offer several types of assessment tools from which to choose so that you can determine your students' level of preparedness to engage in Internet inquiry as well as gauge their level of progress after instruction in Web reading strategies.

Am I Technically Prepared?

So you're thinking about trying out some Web inquiry with your students? That's great! Let's make sure you have all the technical requirements in place and that you and your students know how to use them. After reading the following three sections on networking and file storage, hardware, and software, you can use the *Technical Preparation Checklist* (Handout P-1) to ensure that you are technically prepared to launch a Web project. Most schools already have an Acceptable Use Policy (AUP) in place, but if yours doesn't, you can find plenty of samples online by searching for <school + AUP>. The AUP is a signed agreement between students, parents, and school district personnel. Among other things, it may state that students will not visit inappropriate websites, use offensive language, plagiarize, or harm the computers. In return, the district agrees to keep the network in working order and protect students by using software filters and disallowing personal information exchanges.

An ideal situation for Web inquiry is a school with a stable computer network, high-speed Internet service, modern multimedia computers for every student, and friendly technical support personnel at your beck and call. If this dream vision is not descriptive of your school, you're not alone. Not to worry, you can still teach Web reading strategies with a larger student-to-computer ratio and older stand-alone (non-networked) machines—just be forewarned that it may be frustrating at times. We have found that students are generally forgiving of unreliable computer systems, but teachers sometimes have difficulty going with the flow. We understand your pain. There's nothing more aggravating than shepherding all your students to a computer lab and having the whole system crash right in the middle of a lesson or project. Remind your students to SAVE EARLY and SAVE OFTEN. Remind yourself to always have Plan B ready to roll.

It is beyond the scope of this book to explain how to use and troubleshoot every computer program. Know that there are plenty of great books, hardware manuals, software help menus, and online tutorials available to help you and your students. To find an online tutorial, search for <NameofProgram + tutorial>. Here are two pieces of sage advice: (1) Never assume that everything will work as it should, and (2) encourage your tech-savvy students to help. It's best to try everything out yourself in advance of

Most system crashes are caused by temporary software problems. Restarting the computer clears the computer's memory and usually solves the problem. Unplugging the computer from its power source should be used only as a last resort.

teaching a computer-mediated lesson, especially if you are new to computers and the Internet.

When troubleshooting hardware, check all the cable connections first, since they are often the culprit. When troubleshooting software, try closing programs and starting them up again. With a frozen PC, try the "three-fingered-salute," which means pressing the <Ctrl+Alt+Delete> keys all at once to shut down programs and/ or restart the machine. On a frozen Mac, you can shut down a program by pressing <Command+Option+Escape> and then restarting the computer by pressing the Power key or choosing Shut Down from the Special menu. If that doesn't work, press <Command+Option+Shift+Power> to restart the machine.

Networking and File Storage

Your school may have a Local Area Network (LAN) already in place. This means that you can access the school network, the Internet, and peripherals such as printers and scanners from any computer in your school. If this is the case, you and your students only need to know how to log on to the school network and how to save, move, and access files in their proper location. Many schools assign teachers and students unique usernames and passwords as well as personal storage space to save files and images. Some schools also dedicate open-access file folders where teachers can put assignments and handouts for students to download. If you are inexperienced with your school network, ask your district or school technology specialist to give you a quick tutorial. It's easier than you think.

If your school doesn't yet have a network, then each machine must be able to hook up to the Internet on its own. This may mean starting up a modem or activating a cable connection that requires a password. However, in many cases, the Internet connection is already running and all you need to do is launch Internet browser software (described below) and you're ready to surf the Web. The main disadvantage of using non-networked machines is that a student must sit at the same computer every time, since that student's work will be stored on that computer. This is a hazardous file storage method, because computers can crash or be unavailable at the time students are trying to retrieve their work. Alternately, they can keep their work on a floppy disk, CD-ROM, or memory disk (sometimes called a "flash card") and transport it from machine to machine. Note that floppy disks can't hold very much data and CD-ROMs can be used for file storage only if you have a CD-ROM burner on each machine. Memory disks, which can hold a lot of data and come in a wide variety of shapes and sizes, usually plug into a USB (Universal Serial Bus) port located in the front (in newer machines) or back of the computer. Memory disks are very useful for enabling students to work on computer projects at home and at school.

Hardware

At minimum, you will need enough computers for each student to use at least 30 minutes each day while working on inquiry projects. Periods of 45-60 minutes are better for grades 3–5, and 60–90 minutes is preferred for grades 6–8. These suggested times are ideal, so if this amount of time is not possible in your situation, don't let that stop you from initiating inquiry projects. Teachers are highly skilled at squeezing every minute out of the instructional day, so for a short time you may have to "borrow" time from other subjects in order to ensure adequate time for Internet inquiry.

The computers should be less than 3 years old, with the latest operating systems for fastest performance on the Internet. Each computer should have a file storage option (described above). There must also be a functional monitor, keyboard, and mouse for each computer. If you have students with special needs in your classroom, be sure to inquire about any assistive technologies they may need, such as height-adjustable computer tables, touch screens, or augmentative communication devices.

If your school is using laptop carts, make sure the laptops are always fully charged and that you have any power boosters turned on. As with desktop computers, laptops should have file storage options, network access, and be less than 3 years old. Again, if this ideal situation does not match yours, don't despair. You can still teach transferable strategies for learning on the Internet by having your students do paper-based practice activities and then do the computer-based activities at home or at the public library.

In addition to the hardware described thus far, you may also want to have speakers and/or headsets for some or all of the computers so kids can listen to audio files and/or text-to-speech software (described below). You will need at least one reliable printer, but make sure your students don't abuse printing privileges or you will find yourself replacing ink cartridges and paper at an alarming rate. We don't allow students to print out webpages—only their own work may be printed for review or submission.

Finally, we recommend that you have fairly easy access to an LCD (liquid crystal display) projector and screen to use for modeling, instruction, and presentation of student work. You most likely will need to share with some colleagues. If you don't have an LCD projector, you can use a TV to display a computer screen if you have the right type of connection cables. Ask your technology specialist to help you get set up for projection.

Scanners and digital cameras are nice extras to have around if you have a sufficient budget. A scanner enables students to digitize original artwork or photo prints, and a digital camera allows them to take pictures of anything relevant to their inquiry project and instantly upload the images to a computer. Note that digital cameras often capture pictures at a very high resolution such as 300, 600, or 1200 dpi (dots per inch), so they'll look sharp in print. When the images are transferred to the computer, your students will need to reduce the file sizes of these pictures using image editing software (discussed below) so they don't appear too large on-screen or take up too much disk space; 150 dpi is usually sufficient for printing, and 72 dpi is generally recommended for Web publishing.

Software

One type of software that is absolutely essential for surfing or searching the Web is a Web browser such as Internet Explorer (*www.microsoft.com*) or Netscape Navigator (*www.netscape.com*). If not already installed on your computers, these can be freely downloaded. Many of your students will already know how to use them.

Another essential piece of software for young children, struggling readers, and students with visual impairments is a text-to-speech (TTS) or screen reader software tool. These tools read digital texts aloud, providing enhanced access to the content by alleviating the burden of decoding. Some offer accessibility features like highlighting words as they are read aloud, saying the names of tabs, buttons, and links, and describing images, while others only perform the function of reading. Some use synthetic speech, and others use natural voices. Newer computer systems come with TTS already installed, but if you need to obtain your own or if any of your students require more sophisticated accessibility features, we recommend the *CAST AspireREADER* (*www.cast.org*) for PC or Mac because it has numerous features that aren't available in freeware products. If you have no software budget, try searching the Web for freeware TTS tools such as *Speakonia* for PC and *HearIt* for Mac using the keywords <TTS + free>.

For full-scale inquiry, you may want some additional software programs that allow students to create multimedia projects. Chances are you already have the Microsoft suite of tools, including Microsoft Word and PowerPoint for desktop publishing. These are great for creating written documents, fliers, brochures, scrapbooks, and multimedia slide shows. Microsoft Publisher, which can be purchased separately (*www.microsoft.com*), is a handy layout tool for creating cards, banners, and newspaper articles using images and text.

If you would like to teach your students to make webpages so they can publish their work to a broad audience, you can obtain a free webpage editor called Netscape Composer (*www.netscape.com*). However, if you have a software budget, you may be able to provide a more sophisticated tool such as Macromedia Dreamweaver (*www.macromedia.com*) or Microsoft FrontPage (*www.microsoft.com*), which most students prefer. All of these web authoring tools have become as easy to use as word processors, and all have great online tutorials. All you really need to know is how to publish the kids' pages on the Web. Ask your technology specialist for details—in general, you'll need to know the ftp (file transfer protocol) address or domain name, the directory (a master file folder), a username, and a password.

Finally, you may wish to purchase some image editing software such as Photoshop Elements (*www.adobe.com*) so that your students can create and make alterations to images. If you've got no budget, you can use basic image editing software such as Microsoft Photo Editor, which comes free with Microsoft Office (*www.microsoft.com*).

Am I Conceptually Prepared?

In addition to being technically prepared, make sure you and your students are conceptually prepared for online inquiry. Some of the fundamental teaching points that you will want to reinforce are listed below and are reiterated in Chapter 5.

The Internet

The Internet is a huge computer network that includes e-mail, chat rooms, and the World Wide Web. Computers are connected to the Internet through phone lines, cables, or wireless connections that transmit digital information around the world. The Web, which is a subset of the Internet, is all the websites published by companies, universities, nonprofit organizations, and individuals. Anyone can publish on the Web; therefore, you shouldn't trust every website to contain reliable information. We will return to this topic in Chapter 6.

URLs and Domain Names

Every website needs a unique identifier so that your computer will know where to find it on the network. It's like an e-mail address or a postal address that enables people to send mail to you and only you. A URL (Uniform Resource Locator) is the "address" or location of a website or other Internet service, for example, *www.pbs.org*.

Each website has a domain name extension that indicates the type of organization that published the information. When you visit a website, it is important to notice the domain name of the website so you have an idea where the information originated. The domain name extension is the three-letter extension at the end or just before the first single slash in a web address, or URL. For example:

- .edu = educational (*www.arizona.edu/sports*)
- .gov = government (*www.whitehouse.gov*)
- .org = non-profit organization (*www.cast.org*)
- .mil = military (*www.army.mil*)
- .com = commercial and individual (*www.bonus.com*)
- .net = commercial—alternate to .com (*www.ReadingTheWeb.net*)
- .az = state (*edweb.tusd.k12.az.us*)
- .uk = country (*www.britishcouncil.org.uk*)

Search Engines

Search engines such as Google, Yahoo, MSN search, and AOL search are software tools that search the Internet using keywords that you type or select. Search engines use different methods of finding websites, but all of them categorize topics to manage all the information. Search engines don't actually go out and search the Web right when you type in your terms; rather, they have already located and categorized the information before you search—that's why your search results come back so fast.

A popular search engine that functions differently from the others is Ask.com, which uses Natural Language Processing (NLP) to identify keywords when you type in a long phrase or full question. It is likely that more search engines will move in this direction, since people are more comfortable using natural language than artificial "computerspeak."

Keywords

One of the biggest secrets to searching the Internet is knowing which words to use in your search. These are called "keywords," "key terms," or "key phrases." Search engines that don't use NLP (described above) use these words to find categories of information on the Internet. For example, if you want to find out about the history of skateboarding, the best words to use in your search might be <skateboard> and <history>.

It's usually a good idea to search for a combination of two to three keywords rather than just one keyword by itself. In the skateboarding example, it would *not* be a good idea to simply search for <history> because that term is too broad and will give you every website in that search engine's database about history, including the history of the world. Similarly, if you just search for <skateboarding>, you will get websites trying to sell you skateboards in addition to informational sites about the sport.

Sometimes your keywords consist of phrases rather than single words; for example, you may need to search for <"tree frogs"> instead of just <frogs>. Or you might search for <"jazz musicians"> instead of just <musicians>. It is always a good habit to put quotation marks around phrases, because without them, some search engines will separate the phrase into individual words, which can drastically alter the results of your query. It is not a good idea to string too many words together because it is unlikely that all of those words will be found right next to each other on any one webpage. For example, searching for <"appearance of African killer bee nests"> may result in no matches because no Web designers have elected to use that exact phrase in their websites.

Some smart search engines such as Google will drop common words such as "of" and "the" automatically, so if you *do* want them included, use quotation marks. For example, if you're searching for information about the <"Straits of Gibraltar">, be sure to put it in quotation marks so the "of" isn't unintentionally dropped. Keyword strategies are discussed further in Chapter 5.

Boolean Operators

Boolean operators are mathematical punctuation marks that are used by many search engines to narrow a search. The most common operator is the plus sign (+), which means "and." In the killer bee example above, a good keyword combination might be <"African killer bee" + nest + appearance>. This tells the search engine that you want it to show you all the websites in its database that contain the phrase "African killer bee" and the words "nest" and "appearance." Most search engines will accept the word <AND> in all capitals in lieu of the plus sign.

Sometimes it is helpful to use the minus sign <–> or the word <NOT> instead of the plus sign. This tells the search engine to omit webpages that contain an undesirable word. For example, a fifth-grade student was doing research on Hawaii's climate, but kept getting advertisements for resorts. She used the keyword combination <Hawaii + climate –resort> to eliminate all the resort sites from the search results list. *Note that the minus sign must be adjacent to the undesirable word, whereas the plus sign can either be adjacent or have a space.*

Less commonly used Boolean operators include <OR> <OR NOT>, <AND NOT>, and parentheses; however, since neither of us have ever needed to use these, most likely you will not need this knowledge either. If you would like to know more about Boolean operators, try searching the Web for <"Boolean operator" + tutorial>.

Are My Students Prepared?

Before launching a Web inquiry project, you will want to have a sense of your students' spelling skills, decoding ability, reading comprehension strategies, reading fluency, vocabulary, and writing ability (see Chapter 2). You'll want to know how well they understand the research process using traditional sources such as the library, and whether they are adept at staying on task and are well organized. If your students have weaknesses in any of these areas, they will need extra scaffolding in order to be successful with Web inquiry. It's especially advantageous to know your students' keyboarding ability because this critical skill is a gatekeeper to successful online activities. There are many inexpensive keyboarding software games that students can use at school and/or at home to improve their keyboarding speed and accuracy.

We strongly recommend that you conduct some pre-assessments to determine what your students already know about the research process and the Web. Many students have gaps in their understanding about what the process of inquiry entails, and most have misconceptions about search engines, keywords, and/or the Web. Below, we offer several types of assessment tools from which to choose, depending on your class size and access to computers. Some of these assessments can then be used for group discussion and reflection, thus serving as highly effective teaching tools. Note that we would not expect a teacher to use *all* of the assessments we provide with all students. Think of them as a menu of possibilities, from which you can select the assessments that best meet the needs of your students and best match your instruction.

The first two assessments are individually administered, so they require more time than the subsequent whole-class measures. If possible, it is optimal to use one or the other of the individual assessments in conjunction with some of the whole-class instruments. With any of the whole-group assessments, allow young learners and older students with writing difficulties to dictate their responses so that you can get a more accurate measure of their Web experience and knowledge. Similarly, you may want to make a transparency of the assessment so you can read aloud the questions, ensuring that your weaker readers are not stymied by decoding.

Web Search Strategies

The most accurate assessment tool is the 10-minute *Web Strategies Assessment—Computer/Individual* (Handout P-2), in which you sit right next to each individual student on the computer and ask her to *show* you how she typically goes about finding information on the Web. You can video- or tape-record the session for later analysis and/or take notes using the *Web Strategies Scoring Guide—Computer/Individual* (Handout P-3) while you watch each student carry out the task. In addition to noting each student's keyboarding skills, you will want to observe and record students' strategies for (1) turning the computer on; (2) logging on to the school network; (3) launching browser software (such as Internet Explorer or Netscape Navigator); (4) going to a search engine (such as Google or Yahoo); (5) entering keywords (such as lory + care); (6) choosing a website; (7) scanning for information (such as dietary or housing needs for a lory); and (8) finding relevant information. If no relevant information is found on the first site, observe and record students' recovery strategies for (1) choosing a new website; (2) choosing a new search engine; or (3) choosing new keywords.

Once each student feels that she has found relevant information, ask how she knows if it's "good" information, what she would do with this information, and what she would do next if this were a real research project. Stop after 10 minutes, regardless of whether the student has been successful. This tool can be used as a posttest as well.

If you have too many students or lack easy access to a computer, you can glean some of the same information by doing the 5-minute *Web Strategies Assessment—Oral/Individual* (Handout P-4). With this tool, you ask a student to *tell* you how he would go about finding specific information on the Web, while you record his responses on a notepad and/or tape recorder.

If you cannot afford the time it takes to administer individual assessments, the most time-saving tool to measure your students' Web strategies is the group-administered *Web Strategies Assessment—Written/Group* (Handout P-5). You can score responses to the both the oral and written tools using the *Web Strategies Scoring Guide—Oral or Written* (Handout P-6). For the written assessment, we recommend that you have students trade papers for scoring. This serves as an excellent teaching and group discussion tool. Figures 3.1 and 3.2 show two contrasting Web Strategies Assessments written by eighth-graders.

Computer Survey

Another quick assessment is the *Computer Survey* (Handout P-7), which helps you gauge which students are likely to be proficient and which are likely to struggle, based on their computer experience and answers to survey questions. It is also a

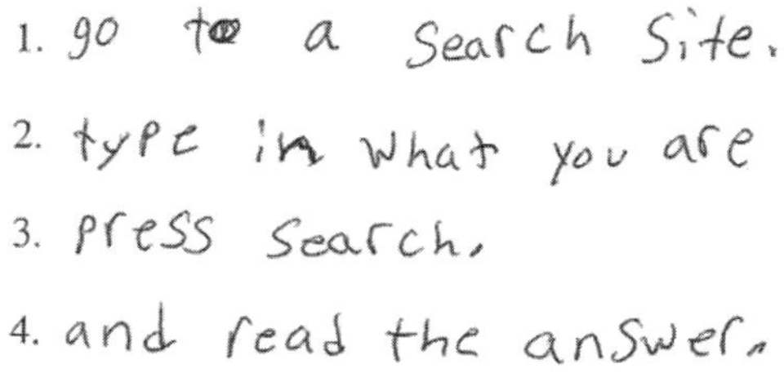

FIGURE 3.1. Web Strategies Assessment—weak.

1. go to a search site.
2. type in what you are looking for,
3. press search,
4. and read the answer.

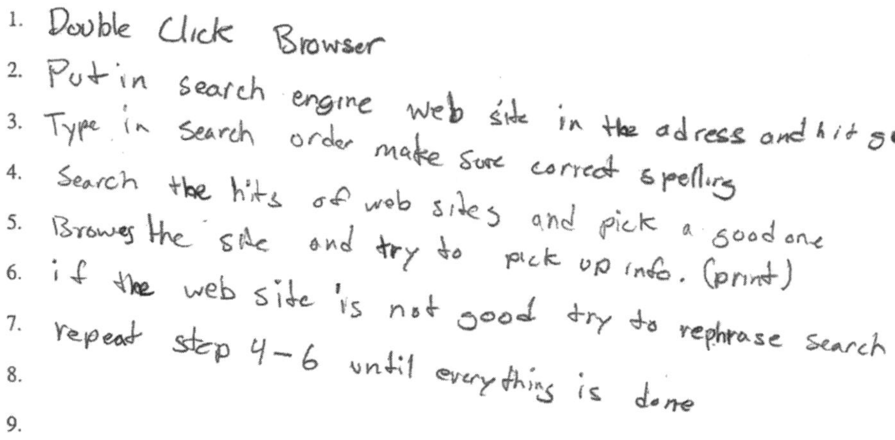

1. Double Click Browser
2. Put in search engine web site in the adress and hit go
3. Type in search order make sure correct spelling
4. Search the hits of web sites and pick a good one
5. Browse the site and try to pick up info. (print)
6. if the web site is not good try to rephrase search
7. repeat step 4-6 until everything is done
8.
9.

FIGURE 3.2. Web Strategies Assessment—strong.

great way to find out who your "tech-savvy" students are so that they can be recruited to serve as in-house technical support for you and the rest of your class(es).

Internet Drawing

A very interesting assessment tool we like to use is the *Internet Drawing* (Handout P-8), which simply asks students to draw a picture of the Internet and use captions if desired. This is a quick method for evaluating the degree of sophistication of students' mental models of the Internet as a place to find information (Guinee & Eagleton, unpublished manuscript). For example, do they accurately depict it as a global network of computers (Figure 3.3), or do they just draw a picture of a computer monitor with a webpage on it (Figure 3.4)? Do they have only a vague mental image of the Internet (Figure 3.5), or do they have serious misconceptions about the Internet, such as thinking that there are robots behind the walls finding webpages for you (Figure 3.6)? Since the Web is most likely going to be the most frequently used resource for student research, let's make sure our kids really understand what it is—and isn't. We usually describe the Internet as a huge network of computers (computers that are all hooked together so they can share data) and the Web as a bunch of interconnected websites containing information (some of it valuable and some of it not), rather like a large, disorganized virtual library. Search engines are tools for finding the information you want in this immense, disorganized collection of websites.

Internet Vocabulary

Finally, we offer a tool for assessing students' *Internet Vocabulary* (Handout P-9), which you can measure with the *Internet Vocabulary Scoring Guide* (Handout P-10). This quick assessment will not only inform you of your students' fluency with "computerspeak" and help identify your tech-savvy students, but will serve as a

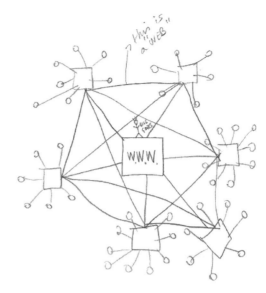

FIGURE 3.3. Internet as a global network.

guide for you as you're teaching with the Internet. The terms that are on the test are the terms with which your students should be conversant in order to be considered Web literate.

Once you have administered some of the assessments above, show students the *QUEST Inquiry Model* (Handout P-11) and have a discussion about what each phase of Internet inquiry involves. It's always advisable to begin with short "mini-inquiries" before diving into major inquiry projects.

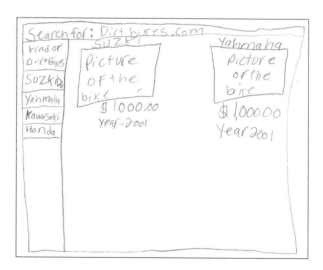

FIGURE 3.4. Internet as Web browser software.

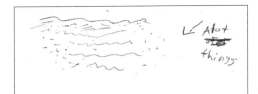

FIGURE 3.5. Vague image of Internet.

Summary

Just as you must gather equipment and knowledge for a hike in the woods, you need to be technically and conceptually prepared for Internet inquiry. Technical preparation includes making sure you have appropriate networking and file storage, hardware, and software. Conceptual preparation includes knowing some basics about the Internet, URLs and domain names, search engines, keywords, and Boolean operators. You also need to determine your students' level of readiness for a QUEST so that you know what needs to be taught and scaffolded; therefore, we provide several assessment tools from which to choose. Many of these assessments can be used before, during, and after a QUEST so that you and your students are aware of the progress that is being made.

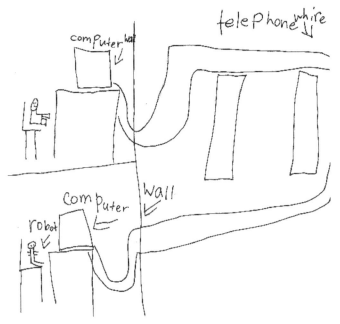

FIGURE 3.6. Serious misconceptions of Internet.

In the next chapter, on Questioning, we offer research-based suggestions for helping young inquirers figure out what they want to know and develop a plan for finding the information they seek. This first step in the QUEST Internet inquiry cycle often includes research themes, topics, focus areas, and questions, while considering the audience, purpose, and methods for demonstrating what's been learned.

Handouts

The following chart lists the handouts discussed in this chapter on Preparing for the QUEST. Each handout is printed on a separate reproducible page for easy copying. If you have the time, we strongly suggest that you administer one of the individual tests, since they are analogous to conducting an informal reading inventory with each student rather than a standardized reading test for the whole class. Clearly, the former will give you much more information about each student's strategies.

Number	Name of handout	Purpose
P-1	Technical Preparation Checklist	Ensure you are prepared
P-2	Web Strategies Assessment—Computer/Individual	Assess Web strategies
P-3	Web Strategies Scoring Guide—Computer/Individual	Score Web strategies
P-4	Web Strategies Assessment—Oral/Individual	Assess Web strategies
P-5	Web Strategies Assessment—Written/Group	Assess Web strategies
P-6	Web Strategies Scoring Guide—Oral or Written	Score Web strategies
P-7	Computer Survey	Assess computer experience
P-8	Internet Drawing	Assess Internet knowledge
P-9	Internet Vocabulary	Assess technical vocabulary
P-10	Internet Vocabulary Scoring Guide	Score technical vocabulary
P-11	QUEST Inquiry Model	Model of the process

HANDOUT P-1. Technical Preparation Checklist

NETWORKING and FILE STORAGE

☐ Usernames and passwords for school network

☐ Reliable Internet connection and signed AUPs

☐ File storage method: floppies   CD-ROMs   memory disks   network

HARDWARE

☐ Multimedia computers: How many? Mac ___ PC ___ age of machines _____

☐ Operating system: Mac—OS X or newer   PC—Win XP or newer

☐ Sufficient time on computers: 30 min   45 min   60 min   90 min

☐ Speakers and/or headsets: How many? _____   _____

☐ Printer(s):   How many? _____

☐ LCD projector and screen, or TV with correct cables

☐ Scanner or digital camera (optional)

SOFTWARE

☐ Web browser: Internet Explorer Netscape Safari Firefox Other _____

☐ Text-to-speech: AspireREADER Speakonia   Hearlt   Other _____

☐ Desktop publishing: Word   PowerPoint   Publisher   Other _____

☐ Webpage authoring: Netscape Composer Dreamweaver FrontPage Other _____

☐ Image editor: Photoshop Elements Microsoft Photo Editor Other _____

Name and phone number of tech support _____

Names of tech-savvy students _____

_____

_____

_____

_____

_____

_____

_____

HANDOUT P-2. Web Strategies Assessment—Computer/Individual

1. Explain to student that you want to see how people find information on the Web. Say that this activity will take **10 minutes**.

2. Ask student's permission to tape-record. Turn on recorder and have student state his or her name and the date. Check for proper recording.

3. Say to student: **"Let's say you were doing Web research on the lory, which is a type of parrot people keep as pets. Show me how you would find information about how to feed and take care of a lory. Please talk through every step as you go so I can understand what you're thinking."** [Spell "lory" for student.]

4. Write down everything the student does on the computer. If student forgets to talk out loud, prompt him or her frequently; for example, "What are you doing now?" "Why did you click on that link?" "What is going through your head right now?"

5. If student is not consistently thinking aloud, narrate for the tape recorder; for example, "So, you typed "lory" into Google and now you're clicking "search." Now you're skimming the list of websites . . ."

6. End the test at 10 minutes. Ask what the student would do next if there were more time.

Search Engine Prompt:

If necessary, prompt, "What else could you try?" If that doesn't work, say, "Have you ever used Yahoo or Google?" If the student doesn't know how to get to a search engine, provide the URL (*google.com*; *yahoo.com*). Stop the test if the student has no other ideas about search engines.

Keywords Prompt:

If student has tried only the "main topic" approach (typing "lory" by itself into a search engine), prompt, "What else could you try?" If that doesn't work: "Are there any other words you could use that would help you find the information you need?" Stop the test if the student has no other keyword ideas.

POSTTEST PROMPT: Instead of the lory, use the anole (UH-NO-LEE), which is a type of lizard people keep as pets.

HANDOUT P-3. Web Strategies Scoring Guide—Computer/Individual

Name _____ Class _____ Date _____

☐ Pretest   ☐ Posttest

	1	2	3	Score	Comments
Keyboarding	Hunt and peck	Slow, looking at keys	Fast, not looking at keys		
Mouse Skills	Slow, jerky	Medium, smooth	Fast, facile		
Logging On	Novice	Inter-mediate	Expert		
Managing Operating System	Novice	Inter-mediate	Expert		
Launching Web Browser	Novice	Inter-mediate	Expert		
Using Search Engine	Novice	Inter-mediate	Expert		
Selecting Keywords	No idea what to do	Too big or too small	Just right		
Spelling Ability	Weak	Average	Strong		
Reading—Decoding	Weak	Average	Strong		
Reading—Comprehension	Weak	Average	Strong		
Choosing a Website from Search Results	No idea what to do	Random, numerical choices	Judicious choices		
Identifying Relevant Info	Novice	Inter-mediate	Expert		
Evaluating Info	Novice	Inter-mediate	Expert		
Navigating Websites	Novice	Inter-mediate	Expert		
Overall Speed	Slow	Medium	Fast		
Overall Effectiveness	Novice	Inter-mediate	Expert		
			TOTAL SCORE		

HANDOUT P-4. Web Strategies Assessment—Oral/Individual

1. Explain to student that you want to know how he or she usually finds information on the Web. Say that this activity will take **5 minutes**.

2. Ask student's permission to tape-record. Turn on recorder and have student state his or her name and the date. Check for proper recording.

3. Say to student: **"Let's say you were doing a research project on the history of soccer. Tell me exactly how you would gather information on the Web for your project, explaining every step so I can picture what you would actually do. Start by imagining yourself sitting down at the computer."**

4. Write down everything the student says. Prompt if needed: "What would you do next?"

5. End the test at 5 minutes. Ask what the student would do next if there were more time.

Search Engine Prompt:

If the student doesn't mention using a search engine, prompt, "Have you ever used a search engine such as Google or Yahoo?" (If so) "Explain how you would use it for this history of soccer project."

Keywords Prompt:

If student has mentioned only the "soccer.com" or "main topic" approach (putting "soccer" by itself into a search engine), prompt, "What other keywords would you try?" If that doesn't work, "Are there any other words you could use that would help you find the information you need?"

Notemaking Prompt:

If student doesn't mention making notes, prompt, "What would you do with the info once you find it?"

POSTTEST PROMPT: Instead of the history of soccer, prompt for the history of baseball or any other popular sport in your region.

HANDOUT P-5. Web Strategies Assessment—Written/Group

Name _____ Class _____ Date _____

List every step a person needs to do when searching for information on the Web.

1. _____
   _____

2. _____
   _____

3. _____
   _____

4. _____
   _____

5. _____
   _____

6. _____
   _____

7. _____
   _____

8. _____
   _____

9. _____
   _____

10. _____
    _____

11. _____
    _____

12. _____
    _____

13. _____
    _____

14. _____
    _____

15. _____
    _____

HANDOUT P-6. Web Strategies Scoring Guide—Oral or Written

Name _____ Class _____ Date _____

☐ Pretest   ☐ Posttest

	If student says/writes:	Points	Wording/Comments
Get Ready	Find a computer / turn on computer	0	
	Get online / open browser software	1	
	Sign on / log on / username / password	1	
Have a Plan	Think about your topic / have a focus	3	
	Have a research question	4	
Find a Site	Type in URL field / go to a website	1	
	Click on search button	2	
	Go to a search engine	4	
Search	Look for / click on / type in search box	1	
	Check your spelling	2	
	Click enter / go / search	1	
Use Keywords	Type in main topic	1	
	Ask the computer a question	1	
	Search for specific keywords	4	
	Narrow search / reduce keywords	3	
	Use advanced search features	4	
Assess Search Results	Look at the search results	1	
	Pick any site	1	
	Look at / read site descriptions	2	
	Pick a promising site	2	
Plan "B"	Get help	1	
	Try a new website / do the cycle over	2	
	Try a new search engine	3	
	Rephrase keywords	4	
Peruse Info	Get info / find info on page	1	
	Find the information you need	3	
	Read through / skim site	2	
	Evaluate site for relevancy	4	
Gather Info	Print/save	1	
	Copy/paste	1	
	Bookmark for future use	2	
	Take notes	4	
All Done	Sign off / log off / close window	1	
	Review information	2	
	TOTAL POINTS OUT OF 75		

HANDOUT P-7. Computer Survey

Name _____ Class _____ Date _____

☐ Pretest   ☐ Posttest

		1	2	3	4	Number
1.	Do you like computers?	I hate them	They're OK	I like them	I love them	
2.	Do you have a computer at home?	No	Yes, but I don't use it very much	Yes, and I use it a lot	I have one in my room	
3.	Do you use the Internet at home?	No	Yes, but I rarely use it	Yes, I get on it a lot	I get on in my room	
4.	Are you good at using computers?	No	I'm OK	I'm pretty good	I'm really good	
5.	Are you good at using the Internet?	No	I'm OK	I'm pretty good	I'm really good	
6.	Do you use the Web to find information?	No	Sometimes	Pretty often	Really often	
7.	Are you good at finding info on the Web?	No	I'm OK	I'm pretty good	I'm really good	
8.	Are you good at downloading info from the Web?	No	I'm OK	I'm pretty good	I'm really good	
9.	Are you good at playing computer games?	No	I'm OK	I'm pretty good	I'm really good	
10.	Are you good at using computers to write papers?	No	I'm OK	I'm pretty good	I'm really good	
11.	Are you good at e-mail, chat, or instant messaging?	No	I'm OK	I'm pretty good	I'm really good	
12.	Are you good at making webpages?	No	I'm OK	I'm pretty good	I'm really good	
13.	Are you good at installing software?	No	I'm OK	I'm pretty good	I'm really good	
14.	Are you good at fixing software problems?	No	I'm OK	I'm pretty good	I'm really good	
15.	Are you good at fixing hardware problems?	No	I'm OK	I'm pretty good	I'm really good	
					TOTAL OUT OF 60	

HANDOUT P-8. Internet Drawing

Name _____ Class _____ Date _____

Directions: Draw a picture of the Internet.

HANDOUT P-9. Internet Vocabulary

Name _____ Class _____ Date _____

☐ Pretest   ☐ Posttest

Directions: Put a letter in front of each vocabulary word to match its definition.

	VOCABULARY	DEFINITION
	Bookmark/Favorites	a. A worldwide network of computers
	Boolean operator	b. Move information to your computer from another computer
	Browser	c. Save a webpage for later viewing
	CPU	d. A method for finding information when using a search engine
	Domain name	e. Words that connect to other pages on the Internet
	Download	f. A group of connected webpages
	Homepage	g. The address of a website
	html	h. Move information from your computer to another computer
	Internet	i. Software used to surf the Web
	Keyword	j. The brain of your computer
	Link	k. The starting page of a website
	Search engine	l. A language used to write pages for the Internet
	Upload	m. A mark such as the plus sign (+) to connect keywords
	URL	n. The organization that hosts a website
	Website	o. Software that helps you find information on the Internet

Give 1 point for each answer for a total of 15 possible points.

	VOCABULARY	DEFINITION
c	Bookmark/Favorites	a. A worldwide network of computers
m	Boolean operator	b. Move information to your computer from another computer
i	Browser	c. Save a webpage for later viewing
j	CPU	d. A method for finding information when using a search engine
n	Domain name	e. Words that connect to other pages on the Internet
b	Download	f. A group of connected webpages
k	Homepage	g. The address of a website
l	html	h. Move information from your computer to another computer
a	Internet	i. Software used to surf the Web
d	Keyword	j. The brain of your computer
e	Link	k. The starting page of a website
o	Search engine	l. A language used to write pages for the Internet
h	Upload	m. A mark such as the plus sign (+) to connect keywords
g	URL	n. The organization that hosts a website
f	Website	o. Software that helps you find information on the Internet

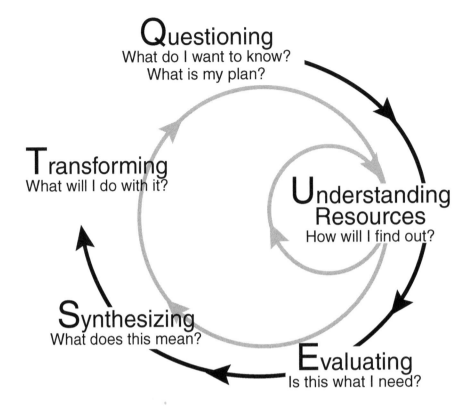

4 QUESTIONING

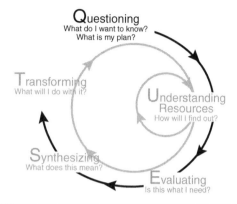

KEY IDEAS

▶ Children and young adolescents often initiate research without explicit research questions or a plan of action.

▶ Key questions that guide the Q phase of the inquiry process are, "What do I want to know?" and "What is my plan for finding out?"

▶ We ask questions before, during, and after reading and inquiry.

▶ Student choice is crucial for successful inquiry.

▶ Research questions must be of an appropriate scope and must be researchable.

▶ The Q phase includes theme selection, topic selection, focus areas, research questions, audience, purpose, final format, and project planning.

> **Questions are the door to human wonder.**
> **—Harvey (1998, p. 23)**

This chapter covers the first phase of Internet inquiry, the Questioning phase. Using an easy-to-follow Why, When, What, and How format, we present background information, teaching ideas, and numerous tools for teaching an instructional unit focused on Questioning. Questioning strategies are useful in many content areas and in life, so the time you spend guiding your students through this process will be time well spent.

Language Arts Standard: Generate questions to set the purpose for reading.

Why Is Questioning Important?

Humans are natural questioners. Anyone who's been around a 4-year-old for more than 5 minutes can attest to the innate human need to know (Figure 4.1). Unfortunately, this passion for asking questions seems to diminish as students reach the upper grades, most likely because schools have traditionally prioritized answers over questions (Harvey, 1998). In Chapter 2 we discussed the cognitive strategy of asking questions when reading so as to activate prior knowledge, check comprehension, clarify unclear ideas, and focus attention on the task. In this chapter we expand our definition of questioning to include its role as the first step in the inquiry process, in addition to its ongoing role as a method of activating prior knowledge, monitoring, and decision making during online reading. Note that the Questioning phase of inquiry is similar for library and Web-based research, with the exception that with the latter we try to help students for-

> **"Everything they do in school is answering questions, so they rarely get that opportunity to develop a question. It's a new skill, and new skills take a long time to master."**
> —Jenna, library media specialist

FIGURE 4.1. Young children are natural inquirers.

mulate questions that lend themselves to keyword generation, as discussed in the next chapter.

Key questions that guide the Q phase of the inquiry process are, "What do I want to know?" and "What is my plan for finding out?" Numerous researchers have found that children and young adolescents initiate research without clear goals or explicit research questions, which obscures their sense of purpose and their ability to target and recognize the information they seek (e.g., Eagleton & Guinee, 2002; Schachter, Chung, & Dorr, 1998; Wallace, et al., 2000; Watson, 1998). Keeping a strong focus on a guiding question while reading on the Web is crucial because of the incredible volume of information that can distract a reader from his original intent (McNabb et al., 2002; Kuiper et al., 2004).

> **Rather than learning how to solve well-structured problems of the kind seen in textbooks, there is a need to know how to engage with a complex situation and turn it into a problem that can be solved; thus, to find problems rather than just solve them.**
> —Bruce (2002, p. 18)

Just as we must thoughtfully plan and prepare for a hike in the woods or a trip to the beach, learners need to have a plan of action before beginning their QUEST for information on the Web, or they will waste valuable time aimlessly surfing. Just as the goal-setting process is critical for learning and reading, it is essential for effective (accurate) and efficient (fast) Web searching (Jakes et al., 2002; Kajder, 2003; Leu, Leu, & Coiro, 2004; Rose & Meyer, 2002). In addition to asking questions, planning for inquiry includes defining research topics and focus areas, identifying audience and purpose, and (when appropriate) deciding on a final format (e.g., report, poster, website) to demonstrate what's been learned (Eagleton et al., 2003; Wilhelm, 2004).

Teacher: "Can you write a 250-page book without planning?"

Student: "Yes, but it wouldn't be very good."

When Do We Ask Questions?

We ask questions all the time in our daily lives. We ask ourselves questions, such as "What do I want to do today?" and "Where did I put my shoes?" We ask questions of our family and friends, such as "What do you want for your birthday?" and "Why do you think so-and-so should be president?" We even ask questions of strangers, such as "What time is it?" or "How do I get to the library?" Questioning is so fundamental to life that we may not even notice how often we ask questions throughout the course of a typical day.

To prepare students to be good questioners, ask them to start noticing how often they ask questions and what types of questions they use. Perhaps they can keep a questioning journal for a while. It also helps to have students think about when and why we ask questions in the classroom. You might have them discuss the following (Armstrong, 2000, p. 52):

- What are the most common types of questions asked in our classroom?
- Why do we ask questions in our classroom?
- Why are questions valuable?
- When is it hard to ask good questions?
- When is it easy to ask good questions?
- Which kinds of questions lead to interesting discussions?

Science Standard: Identify questions that can be answered through scientific investigation; design appropriate investigation to answer different questions.

We ask questions before, during, and after reading and inquiry. Questions that come before inquiry are used to guide the process, but learners must also ask numerous decision-making questions during and after online reading, such as "Where do I want to go next?" "Is this the information I need?" "Do I have enough information?" and "What am I going to do with this information?" As students become more engrossed in an inquiry topic, they naturally generate more questions based on new information. This is an excellent outcome; however, students and teachers do need to find a balance between adherence to an original question or set of questions and capricious topic-hopping based on haphazard findings, reactive decision making, or fears that the original question will require too much work.

Research is not intended to eliminate questions but to generate new questions.
—Short and Burke (1991, p. 59)

What Characterizes "Good" Questions?

Although all questions are important, some make better research questions than others. The most compelling inquiry questions are student-generated. Teacher-generated questions are fine for certain teaching activities such as scavenger hunts (which are short Web searches for specific pieces of information); however, student choice is critical for sustaining interest in long-term inquiry projects. For example, when a teacher tried to persuade one of her eighth-graders to change research topics, the young adolescent's enthusiasm plummeted. Angrily flipping through a book on presidents, she randomly selected Franklin D. Roosevelt, retorting, "I'm not psyched about anything in school anyway, so who cares?" In order to address learners' affective needs, we need to let them choose their own topics, focus areas, and questions. If teachers want to select a central theme for the whole class, Short et al. (1996) recommend broad concepts such as cycles, change, conflict, adaptation, culture, community, mysteries, perspectives, systems, sense of place, interdependence, and discovery, since they provide "many possible points of connection that naturally

Inquiry projects born of learners' passion and curiosity encourage students to understand what they learn, rather than merely retell it.   —Harvey (1998, p. 2)

weave across the day and year and do not limit the topics and questions that students can pursue" (pp. 19–20).

Sometimes young children and older students with learning difficulties need support in choosing topics within broad themes. For example, a teacher assigned the inquiry theme "Down to the Sea in Ships" in preparation for a field trip to some local offshore islands. Although some students were able to generate interesting topics and questions on this theme, others struggled greatly, producing awkward questions such as, "How are surfboards and ships similar in riding on the waves?" and "How does a huge cruise ship float and how much does it weigh?" Categorical knowledge is helpful for asking questions. For example, when researching a famous person, it helps to know that "career" and "family" are subcategories within which one might ask questions (Eagleton & Guinee, 2002). In our teaching, we always require that students seek approval on research questions before they engage in inquiry so that modifications can be made early on.

 Other people's questions do not interest us as much as our own questions. We are not born passive . . . curiosity is natural to our lives. We are born researchers.
    —Short and Burke (1991, p. 56)

Educators have identified "types" of questions to help teachers and students find an appropriate scope for inquiry projects. Reading teachers often make the distinction between explicit and implicit questions about texts, whereas research questions are often characterized as thin versus thick or skinny versus fat (McMackin & Siegel, 2001; Jakes et al., 2002). What each of these constructs has in common is the notion that a research question is inappropriate if it is either too small or too large in scope. Questions that are too small can be answered in a few words or sentences after minimal research; for example, "When was Louisa May Alcott born?" In contrast, questions that are too large cannot be answered in one inquiry project (if at all), such as, "What was the Civil War?" Many students need guidance in asking appropriately scoped research questions based on their age, ability, and the constraints of the task.

 Social Studies Standard: Formulate historical questions from multiple perspectives using multiple primary and secondary sources.

In addition to having an appropriate scope, an inquiry question must be "researchable." By this we mean that the answer to the question can be found using available resources. Examples of unresearchable questions include evaluative questions that rely on opinion, vague questions that have no real answers, and personal questions that can't be answered using public resources such as interviews, primary documents, print materials, or the Web.

Another type of question to avoid is one about which the student has either too much or too little prior knowledge.

 When students feel that they are not starting from scratch and that they already know something about a topic, they will be much more likely to be interested in learning a little more about it—especially if they feel that it relates to their lives in some way.
    —Zwiers (2004, p. 13)

We have seen students select topics about which they already know everything there is to know, particularly popular culture topics such as sports and celebrities. In this case, there are no authentic questions to be asked, because the student already knows all the answers. In contrast, when a student has such a low level of prior knowledge about a topic that she can't even generate a reasonable question (one of our personal favorites is, "Where did Harriet Tubman get her education?"), then it is advisable to allow her to explore the topic a little bit before committing to it and formulating definitive research questions.

How Do We Teach Questioning Strategies?

If you haven't administered any of the pre-assessments presented in Chapter 3, we recommend that you do so first. Then, start with the *Research Questions Assessment*, described below, before moving into an instructional unit focused on questioning strategies. Before engaging in large-scale inquiry projects, we recommend assigning "mini-inquiries," which are short investigations focused on a single strategy that can be concluded within one or two class periods. We also strongly recommend that you conduct your own inquiry project alongside your students so that you can frequently model the process. Using teacher think-alouds is a fabulous method for helping make explicit the in-the-head processes that expert inquirers use.

 When projecting a website on an LCD projector, the text is sometimes too small for the whole class to see clearly. Go to View>Text Size (Internet Explorer) or View>Text Zoom (Netscape Navigator) to increase the size of the font.

Assessing Questioning Strategies

Before beginning an inquiry unit focused on Questioning strategies, we recommend that you assess your students' understanding of what makes a "good" research question for a typical school project, using a *Research Questions Assessment* (Handout Q-1), and have students trade papers for scoring while you guide them through the *Research Questions Scoring Guide* (Handout Q-2). We have found that this is an excellent tool to springboard a lively conversation about questioning.

After being assessed, students are ready to move forward with selecting themes, topics, focus areas, and research questions. If this is more than just a mini-inquiry, students should also consider audience, purpose, and final format(s). Remind the students frequently that the focus of the unit is on the Q part of the QUEST.

 Library Media Standard: Define information needs and identify effective courses of action to conduct research, solve complex problems, and pursue personal interests.

Although some students are impatient with this planning stage and eager to get going on the computers, making a plan is an essential part of the initial phase of inquiry and should not be skipped. Emphasize that initiating an inquiry QUEST is analogous to preparing for a long trip or a hike in the woods, so good planning is crucial.

The next eight sections can be completed in any order that makes sense to you and your students: theme selection, topic selection, focus areas, research questions, audience, purpose, final format, and project planning. Allow as much student choice as possible, but it is prudent to make some of the choices yourself simply to save time. For example, you may elect to choose a central theme, you may decide that everyone will present at Parent Night, or you may state that all students are going to create acrostic poems, persuasive essays, or posters to show what they've learned.

Do not assign every handout that we've provided in one project, or you and your students will bury yourselves in far too much paperwork and smother the spirit of inquiry. Choose judiciously and save the unused handouts for another time.

Theme Selection

If you teach in the content areas, such as science or social studies, you may not be able to offer much student choice regarding inquiry themes. However, if you are a language arts teacher, library media specialist, or elementary teacher and have some flexibility, you can either have the class vote on a group theme or allow individual students to select their own. Examples of broad themes that our students have selected are animals, sports, and famous people. Some teacher-generated inquiry themes that we've seen are minerals, U.S. states, and historical figures. If you need to have a whole-class theme, make sure that all your students understand what the theme encompasses and that they "buy in" to the value of conducting research in this area.

Topic Selection

Once a theme has been established, students should be free to select topics of personal interest. Topics are often chosen before questions are generated; however, some students find it easier to start with questions. Allow each student to proceed in whatever order feels natural to him. Some teachers have students keep an ongoing list of inquiry topics in their journals or writing folders so that there is always a bank of ideas from which to select. Teacher modeling is always beneficial. For example, when reading a piece of literature or a portion of a textbook, the teacher might wonder aloud, "That's really interesting. I don't know much about that topic; I might want to research it at some point."

Although some students have an endless list of inquiry topics, others don't seem to be interested in anything. These unenthusiastic inquirers should be prompted until they come up with a topic about which they are passionate. Here are some useful prompts, adapted from Tricia Armstrong (2000):

Although teacher selection of topics and negotiated choice are important, they aren't adequate by themselves. . . . If we never allow learners to make choices independently, then we have no way to assess whether they've internalized the skills and strategies they learn about topic selection.

—Chandler-Olcott and Mahar (2001, p. 44)

1. What are your favorite sports or hobbies?
2. What kinds of things do you like to collect?
3. Who are your favorite musicians, or what types of music?
4. What are your favorite foods?
5. What are your favorite movies, or who are your favorite celebrities?
6. What are your favorite TV shows?
7. What are your favorite books (or comic books)?
8. What are your favorite school subjects?
9. What animals do you find interesting?
10. Who are some people you admire?
11. Where would you like to go on vacation?
12. What issues do you care about?
13. What would you like to be an expert on?
14. What are some of your best memories?
15. What kinds of things inspire you?
16. What are you curious to know more about?

Previous student topics and projects can also serve as inspiration. We have found that avoiding the term "research" sometimes helps, since it is equivalent to a four-letter word for some reluctant learners. You can use the term "inquiry" instead—just be sure that everyone knows what it means. If a student is still struggling to find a topic, consult Table 4.1, which provides a list of inquiry topics for all ages.

At times, young students and struggling learners come up with topics that are too big, too small, too vague, or unresearchable, as discussed previously in relation to research questions. In this case, the teacher or a more capable peer can help the student adjust the topic to an appropriate scope for whatever length of time has been allotted for the project (Guinee, 2005b). Once a topic has been chosen, we ask students to use the *Topic Knowledge Assessment* (Handout Q-3) as a pretest so that we have a sense of their prior knowledge on the topic. This tool flags students who know either too little or too much about a topic, so that the teacher can intervene.

TABLE 4.1. Interesting Inquiry Topics

Superordinate category	THEMES	Topics
Animals	ENDANGERED SPECIES	Unicorns, minotaurs, dragons
	WEIRD/RARE/EXTINCT	Bigfoot, Loch Ness monster
	MYTHICAL CREATURES	Brown recluse spider, tarantula
	POISONOUS, BLIND, TINY	Pterodactyl, brontosaurus
Places	OUTER SPACE	Jupiter, Northern Lights
	CRATERS, OCEAN	Petrified forest, painted desert
	JUNGLE, DESERT	Yosemite/Old Faithful
	CAVES/CAVERNS	Mt. Rushmore, Grand Canyon
	NATIONAL MONUMENTS	Carlsbad Caverns

(*continued*)

TABLE 4.1. *(continued)*

Superordinate category	THEMES	Topics
People	HEROES, POLITICIANS	Madeleine Albright, Gandhi
	CELEBRITIES	Arnold Schwarzenegger, Oprah
	RARE/ANCIENT CULTURES	The Mayan Civilization
	ROYALTY, WRITERS	Princess Diana, Prince Charles
	NOBEL PRIZE WINNERS	Toni Morrison, Maya Angelou
	EXPLORERS, INVENTORS	Einstein, Newton, Edison
	SCIENTISTS, HUMANITARIANS	Picasso, Michelangelo
	ARTISTS, BUSINESS LEADERS	Donald Trump, Bill Gates
Popular Culture	MUSIC	Origins of jazz fusion
	MOVIES	Drum manufacturing
	EXTREME SPORTS	The making of *Jurassic Park*
	FASHION	Bungee jumping
Events	DISASTERS	Avalanches, tornadoes, tsunamis
	ASSASSINATIONS	Hurricanes, floods, wildfires
	POLITICAL COUPS	JFK, Martin Luther King Jr.
	PRESIDENTIAL ELECTIONS	Fall of Berlin Wall
	CURRENT EVENTS	9/11, Oklahoma City bombing
	REBELLIONS	Boston Tea Party
Science	INVENTIONS	Robots, walkie-talkies
	ENERGY AND CONSERVATION	Solar energy, hybrid cars
	MINERALS AND GEOLOGY	Diamonds, volcanoes
	FOOD ORIGINS	North Pole expeditions
	EXPLORATION	Shackleton's expedition
Transportation	PLANES	Boats, trains, jets, cars
	RECREATION	Space shuttles, rockets, gliders
	SHIPS	Helicopters, scooters, parasailing
	VEHICLES	Skateboarding, surfing, cycling
Phenomena	WEIRD PHENOMENA	Crop circles, UFOs
	MYSTERIOUS PHENOMENA	Spontaneous human combustion
	RELIGIOUS PHENOMENA	Stigmata, ESP
Issues	CONTROVERSIAL ISSUES	Euthanasia, abortion
	CURRENT ISSUES	Pollution, ozone layer
Wonders of the World	NATURAL WONDERS	Niagara Falls, Victoria Falls
	ANCIENT WONDERS	Hanging Gardens of Babylon
	MODERN WONDERS	Krakatoa Island
	MYSTERIOUS WONDERS	Stonehenge, Easter Island

Knowing too little about a topic may not be a problem for experienced computer users and older learners, but can present too much of a challenge to young children, computer novices, and students with learning difficulties because they lack sufficient topic knowledge to brainstorm appropriate focus areas, questions, and keywords.

 Nonfiction reading, research, and reporting is hard work. **For students to maximize their inquiry experience, they should choose a topic they care about, know something about, and wonder about. Topics that surface from passion and wonder have the best chance of engaging students over the long haul.   —Harvey (1998, p. 32)**

Conversely, choosing a topic about which the student knows too much is ill-advised because the student will have difficulty generating any new questions about that particular subject.

This pretest also alerts the teacher to students who do not know how to depict categories and subcategories of topics; for example, a student who chooses to research Walt Disney might create a concept map with his name in the center bubble, then place details about his life into subcategories such as "creations," "appearance," and "family life" (Figure 4.2). In contrast, students who produce what we term "spoke-shaped," or nonhierarchical concept maps list all their knowledge of a topic at the same level of importance, as shown in Figure 4.3. Spoke-shaped concept maps are often an early indicator that these students will have trouble searching the Internet because they don't understand that information is arranged hierarchically on the Web.

Focus Areas

Once a theme and topic have been selected, many students think they are ready to begin researching. However, we strongly suggest that students develop one or two focus areas within their topic that are of particular interest rather than trying to cover the entire topic in one inquiry project. For example, in a famous person project, a student might zero in on the person's childhood. Similarly, in a sports project, the history of the sport might serve as an interesting focus area. This not only helps

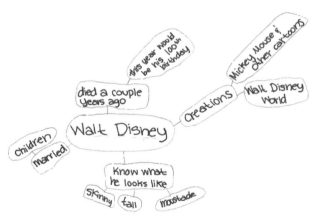

FIGURE 4.2. Topic knowledge—hierarchical.

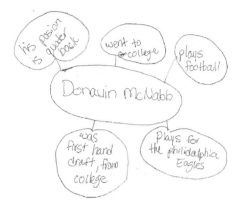

FIGURE 4.3. Topic knowledge—nonhierarchical.

direct student inquiry and results in more interesting projects, but leads to the development of specific keywords, as discussed in the next chapter.

If students are having difficulty with choosing focus areas, it might be a good idea to generate research questions first, then come back to focus areas. Focus areas can be derived by having students brainstorm as many questions as they can about their topics, then grouping similar types of questions together by using 3×5 index cards. Most students find that obvious categories of questions emerge. At this point, it is useful to come up with a label for each category and then choose one or two categories that are most interesting, saving the rest of the questions for another project. Handout Q-4, *Choosing Focus Areas*, guides students through this process.

Research Questions

As mentioned above, sometimes the generation of research questions precedes topic and focus area selection. It depends on the student. The most important consideration is the scope of a topic or research question, as discussed earlier. Is the subject something that can be researched in a few weeks, or would it take a year? Is it something that can be answered with a simple yes–no, or is it something that requires synthesis and transformation? Depending on how your students perform on the *Research Questions Assessment* (Handout Q-1), you may need to do some targeted instruction in this area.

One of the most effective inquiry planning tools that we've used is the *Category Flowchart* (Figure 4.4; Handouts Q-5, Q-6, and Q-7). The flowcharts shown in these handouts can serve as guided and/or independent practice in identifying themes, topics, focus areas, and questions. The goal is to teach students that the most effective Web research questions contain a topic and a focus area. For example, the question "What is the history of hockey?" has "hockey" as its topic and "history" as the focus area, and "Where do polar bears live?" contains the topic "polar bear" and the focus area "habitat." Handout Q-5 helps students generate topics and focus areas from words that are directly stated in the question. Handout Q-6 requires students to fill in the topic and focus area by substituting words or phrases from the questions. Finally, Handout Q-7 is left blank for teachers and students to generate their own

FIGURE 4.4. Category flowchart.

flowcharts. In the next chapter, we will see that topic and focus area words can conveniently be used as keywords for searching the Web.

A classic questioning tool developed by Ogle (1986) is the K-W-L Chart (Figure 4.5). The K stands for "What I already Know," the W stands for "What I Want to know," and the L is used to record "What I Learned" during and after reading and/or inquiry. Zwiers (2004) offers a variety of adaptations of the K-W-L, including K-W-H-L-S, which stands for "What we think we Know," "What we Want to learn," "How we will learn it," "What we Learned," and "How we will Show what we learned" (p. 71).

Another classic method of helping students generate questions is the 5WH technique, which helps students brainstorm questions using "Who," "What," "Where," "When," "Why," and "How" as sentence starters. You can also get creative by turning a lesson on questioning into a whole-class or small-group game in which one team asks questions and another team has to categorize the questions as too big, too small, or just right for a typical inquiry project. Have fun with it, and keep at it until you feel confident that your students really understand what constitutes a reasonable research question.

K	W	L
What I already KNOW	What I WANT to know	What I LEARNED

FIGURE 4.5. K-W-L chart.

If students are having difficulty generating questions about their chosen topic, an activity that we always find helpful is to have students ask each other genuine questions about the topics. This often stimulates new ideas that students had not even considered and helps to remind them that there is a real audience for their inquiries. Be sure to have someone record all the questions that are asked so nothing is forgotten.

Table 4.2 shows some themes, topics, focus areas, and questions that our students have successfully researched on the Web. While some of the questions are a bit clunky, the topics and focus areas are interesting and easily converted into keywords for searching.

Audience

Part of the initial phase of inquiry includes knowing one's audience. Whenever possible, we like to provide the broadest, most authentic audience for student inquiry. An audience of one (namely, the teacher) is not really a true audience. At the very minimum, students should present the results of their inquiries to each other, but you will find that the students' level of effort and the quality of the inquiry will rise dramatically if they are asked to present to another class or set of classes, to their grade-level peers, to the whole school, to parents, to teachers, to the community, or even to a global audience via the Web. If students are asking important questions that have real answers, they will take pride in demonstrating their findings to an authentic audience. Handout Q-8, *Knowing Your Audience*, helps students determine their audience before launching an inquiry project.

TABLE 4.2. Themes, Topics, Focus Areas, and Questions

THEMES	Topics	Focus areas	Questions
ANIMALS	Siberian tigers	Extinction	Why are Siberian tigers becoming extinct?
	Platypuses	Classification	What makes the platypus a mammal instead of a bird?
	Grizzly bears	Size	How big are grizzly bears compared to other bears?
SPORTS	Snowboarding	Equipment	How do they change snowboarding equipment for sandboarding?
	Stanley Cup (hockey)	History	What is the history of the Stanley Cup?
	Williams sisters (tennis)	Biography	What was the Williams sisters' childhood like?
HEROES	Martin Luther King, Jr.	Personality	What was Martin Luther King, Jr. like?
	Nelson Mandela	Peace Prize	Why did Nelson Mandela win the Nobel Peace Prize?
	Shirley Temple Black	Career	What did Shirley Temple Black do in her career?

Purpose

Often, students don't have a sense of purpose during the inquiry process. This is similar to not knowing the purpose of a writing assignment. Is it to inform? To entertain? To persuade? To express oneself? The purpose, whether assigned by the teacher or chosen by students, will have a significant impact on the types of questions that are pursued and the types of formats that are used to represent what's been learned (discussed below). Therefore, it is important that students identify the purpose of their inquiries in advance. Handout Q-9, *Understanding Purposes*, helps to highlight how the entire focus of a writing or inquiry project can change depending on the purpose that is selected.

Final Format

A simple search for a small fact or piece of information does not require a final product, but full-scale inquiry projects usually result in some sort of final product to demonstrate what's been learned. Whenever possible, we like to give students choices as to how they will represent their findings (e.g., poems, posters, slide shows, websites). Unfortunately, students often choose final formats according to (1) teacher requirements; (2) familiarity and comfort; (3) convenience; or (4) a perception of what seems "fun," such as colorful posters or elaborate PowerPoint slide shows that lack substantive content (Eagleton et al., 2003). Therefore, we always require that students gain approval of their intended final format very early in the inquiry process. Having a strong vision of a final format in advance really helps students stay on target while searching for information. Table 4.3 shows some common formats (adapted from Armstrong, 2000).

Final formats must be appropriately matched to research questions, purposes, and audiences; should be of a reasonable size and scope; and must demonstrate the learning that's taken place. This last point is harder to achieve than it sounds. Many students do not know how to represent knowledge; therefore, we must teach this skill through modeling and scaffolding and by providing plenty of practice and feedback (see Chapter 1). One of our favorite examples of a final format that did not demonstrate learning was an eighth-grade student's ceramic bust of Jerry Garcia (Figure 4.6). While this project showed wonderful creativity, it did not reflect 4 weeks of inquiry on the life and music of Jerry Garcia. In fact, it did not communicate any information at all other than his facial appearance. In contrast, another student's digital time line of Walt Disney's career represented a lot of information about her topic and focus area (Figure 4.7).

At the beginning of an inquiry project, we always ask students to brainstorm a list of the various ways that information can be presented and show them examples of past student projects as models. We return to the topic of final formats in Chapter 8 when we discuss the Transforming phase of inquiry.

TABLE 4.3. Final Formats

Written formats

Autobiography	Biography	Booklet
Book report	Diary	Essay
Glossary	Journal	Letter
List	Magazine article	Newspaper article
Poem	Questionnaire	Report
Review	Script	Survey

Visual formats

Advertisement	Brochure	Cartoon
Comic strip	Commercial	Diorama
Drawing	Flier	Game
Mural	Photo essay	Poster
Sign	Storyboard	Time line

Presentation formats

Dance	Drama	Interview
Mock debate	Music	Oral report
Puppet show	Role play	Speech

Multimedia formats

Audiotape	Database	Slide show
Spreadsheet	Video	Webpage

Note. Adapted with permission from Armstrong (2000). Copyright 2000 by Pembroke Publishers.

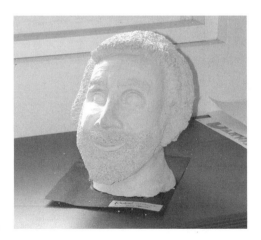

FIGURE 4.6. Final format—insufficient content.

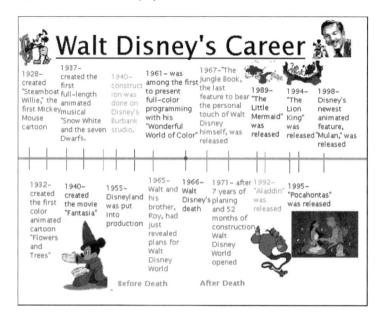

FIGURE 4.7. Final format—sufficient content.

Project Planning

Before embarking on a major inquiry project, we ask students to collaborate in designing project criteria, due dates for major milestones (Figure 4.8), and grading rubrics for how their efforts will be assessed. These are printed out as metacognitive reminders and stored in students' Reflection Log journals (discussed in Chapter 9), in which they write during the last 5 minutes of every class period (Figure 4.9). Handout Q-10, *Sample Project Criteria*, helps students monitor their progress on their projects, while the *Sample Grading Rubric* (Handout Q-11) provides a more formal way of assessing student productivity. For inquiry projects lasting more than 2 weeks, we have students complete several grading rubrics so they can receive frequent feedback on how they are progressing and can make adjustments if needed.

Because many students initiate research without a clear plan (Eagleton et al., 2003; Rankin, 1999), we also ask that some students fill out a *Project Planning Flowchart* (Handout Q-12) and that all develop a *Project Planning Template* (Handout Q-13) to cement the intended theme, topic, focus area(s), question(s), audience, purpose, and final format(s). This document serves as a road map for the QUEST, helping students and teachers stay on course toward the targeted objective of the activity. The project plan must be previewed by one or more peers, then approved by the teacher in a student–teacher conference (Figure 4.10). Handouts Q-14 and Q-15, the *Project Planning Lessons* for *Elementary* and *Middle Levels*, provide guidelines for walking your students through the planning process.

	Note: All assignments are due at the BEGINNING of the period!			
ITEM	ASSIGNMENT	DUE DATE	Student initials and date	Teacher initials and date
1	Project Plan			
2	Website Evaluation Chart			
3	Notes—first draft			
4	Notes—second draft			
5	Focus Area #1— 3 paragraphs			
6	Focus Area #2— 3 paragraphs			
7	Project—first draft			
8	Project—final			
9	Works Cited			
10	Project Presentations			

FIGURE 4.8. Due dates checklist.

Summary

The Q phase of the QUEST includes theme selection, topic selection, focus areas, research questions, audience, purpose, final format, and project planning. Children and young adolescents frequently initiate research without explicit research questions or a plan of action; therefore, we need to help them develop strategies for this important first step in the inquiry process. As teachers, we can reinforce these strategies by conducting our own inquiry projects process alongside our students while providing appropriate modeling, scaffolding, practice, and feedback. Whenever possible, we try to allow student choice so that young inquirers will sustain interest in their QUEST over the long haul.

FIGURE 4.9. Writing in Reflection Log.

FIGURE 4.10. Teacher–student planning conference.

In the next chapter on Understanding Resources, we share research and practical suggestions for helping students develop strategies for identifying resources, managing computers, utilizing the Internet, choosing search tools, and selecting keywords. While we always like to see students using as many resources as possible to answer their research questions—people, books, mass media, and computers—there is no doubt that today's students need strategies for using the Internet as a resource for inquiry and learning.

Handouts

The following chart lists the assessment tools, activities, and handouts discussed in this chapter on Questioning. Remember that it is not advisable to have students use everything we've provided in one project—choose several that appeal to you and save the rest for another time. Feel free to modify any of these tools to suit your specific needs. Color versions of the *Category Flowcharts* (Handouts Q-5 to Q-7) can be downloaded from our website, *www.ReadingTheWeb.net*.

Number	Name of handout	Purpose
Q-1	Research Questions Assessment	Assess research question knowledge
Q-2	Research Questions Scoring Guide	Score research question assessment
Q-3	Topic Knowledge Assessment	Assess topic knowledge
Q-4	Choosing Focus Areas	Help choose focus areas
Q-5	Category Flowchart—Literal	Find focus areas in question
Q-6	Category Flowchart—Substitution	Substitute words in question
Q-7	Category Flowchart—Blank	Create your own flowchart
Q-8	Knowing Your Audience	Help identify your audience

Q-9	Understanding Purposes	Transform purposes
Q-10	Sample Project Criteria	Set guidelines for projects
Q-11	Sample Grading Rubric	Method of grading work
Q-12	Project Planning Flowchart	Guide inquiry project
Q-13	Project Planning Template	Scaffold inquiry project
Q-14	Project Planning Lesson—Elementary Level	Teach project planning strategies
Q-15	Project Planning Lesson—Middle Level	Teach project planning strategies

HANDOUT Q-1. Research Questions Assessment

Name _____ Class _____ Date _____

Would these questions be effective for a Web research project?
Circle your answer, then explain your thinking.

1. What is the history of soccer?	good bad	
2. What was Mia Hamm's childhood like?	good bad	
3. Who is Mia Hamm?	good bad	
4. How are soccer balls made?	good bad	
5. Mia Hamm and her soccer career	good bad	
6. How old is Mia Hamm?	good bad	
7. What is the story of Mia Hamm's soccer career?	good bad	
8. Why is soccer the best sport?	good bad	
9. Who are all the people who have ever played soccer?	good bad	
10. What does a soccer ball look like?	good bad	

HANDOUT Q-2. Research Questions Scoring Guide

Directions: Give 1 point for each correct circled answer, then 0, 1, or 2 points for reasoning.
Total possible points = 30

1. What is the history of soccer?	(good) bad	has a topic and focus
2. What was Mia Hamm's childhood like?	(good) bad	has a topic and focus
3. Who is Mia Hamm?	good (bad) too big
4. How are soccer balls made?	(good) bad	has a topic and focus
5. Mia Hamm and her soccer career	good (bad) not a question
6. How old is Mia Hamm?	good (bad) too small
7. What is the story of Mia Hamm's soccer career?	(good) bad	has a topic and focus
8. Why is soccer the best sport?	good (bad) opinion
9. Who are all the people who have ever played soccer?	good (bad) too big
10. What does a soccer ball look like?	good (bad) too small

From *Reading the Web* by Maya B. Eagleton and Elizabeth Dobler. Copyright 2007 by The Guilford Press. Permission to photocopy this handout is granted to purchasers of this book for personal use only (see copyright page for details).

HANDOUT Q-3. Topic Knowledge Assessment

Name _____ Class _____ Date _____

□ Pretest   □ Posttest

Draw a bubble map that shows what you know about your topic.

HANDOUT Q-4. Choosing Focus Areas

Use the example below to help you choose some focus areas for your topic.

Step 1: Brainstorm 10 or more questions about your topic on 3×5 note cards—one question per card.

Step 2: Sort the note cards into categories.

Step 3: Create a name that describes each category that would make a good focus area (not too big or too small). Put the names in these boxes.

Step 4: Choose your two favorite categories and turn them into research questions.

EXAMPLE:

Step 1: Brainstorm questions.

WHO made the Hanging Gardens of Babylon (HGB)?
WHAT were the HGB?
WHEN were the HGB built?
WHERE were the HGB?

WHY were the HGB built?
HOW were the HGB built?
What did the HGB look like?
Has anyone found the ruins of the HGB?
How long did it take to build the HGB?

Step 2: Sort questions into categories.

Category 1	Category 2	Category 3	Category 4	Category 5
WHO made the HGB?	WHAT were the HGB?	WHEN were the HGB built?	WHERE were the HGB located?	WHY were the HGB built?
HOW were the HGB built?	What did the HGB look like?	How long did it take to build the HGB?	Has anyone found the ruins of the HGB?	

Step 3: Create a title for each category.

History	Appearance	Time	Location	Purpose

Step 4: Turn the two most interesting categories into research questions.

Question 1: What is the <u>history</u> of the Hanging Gardens of Babylon?
Question 2: What is the <u>appearance</u> of the Hanging Gardens of Babylon?

HANDOUT Q-5. Category Flowchart—Literal (page 1 of 2)

Name _____ Class _____ Date _____

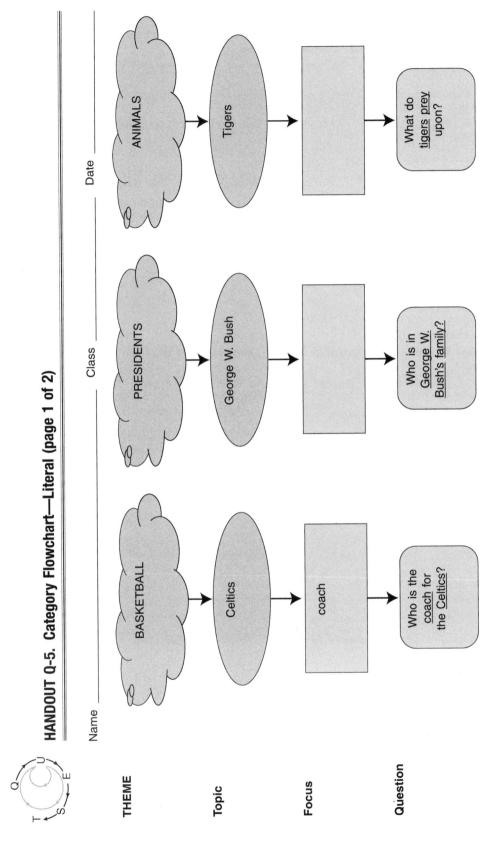

THEME

Topic

Focus

Question

HANDOUT Q-5. Category Flowchart—Literal (page 2 of 2)

THEME
Topic
Focus
Question
CARS
VW
How does the engine work in a VW?
INVENTORS
Thomas Edison
What are some of Thomas Edison's inventions?
Make up your own flowchart:

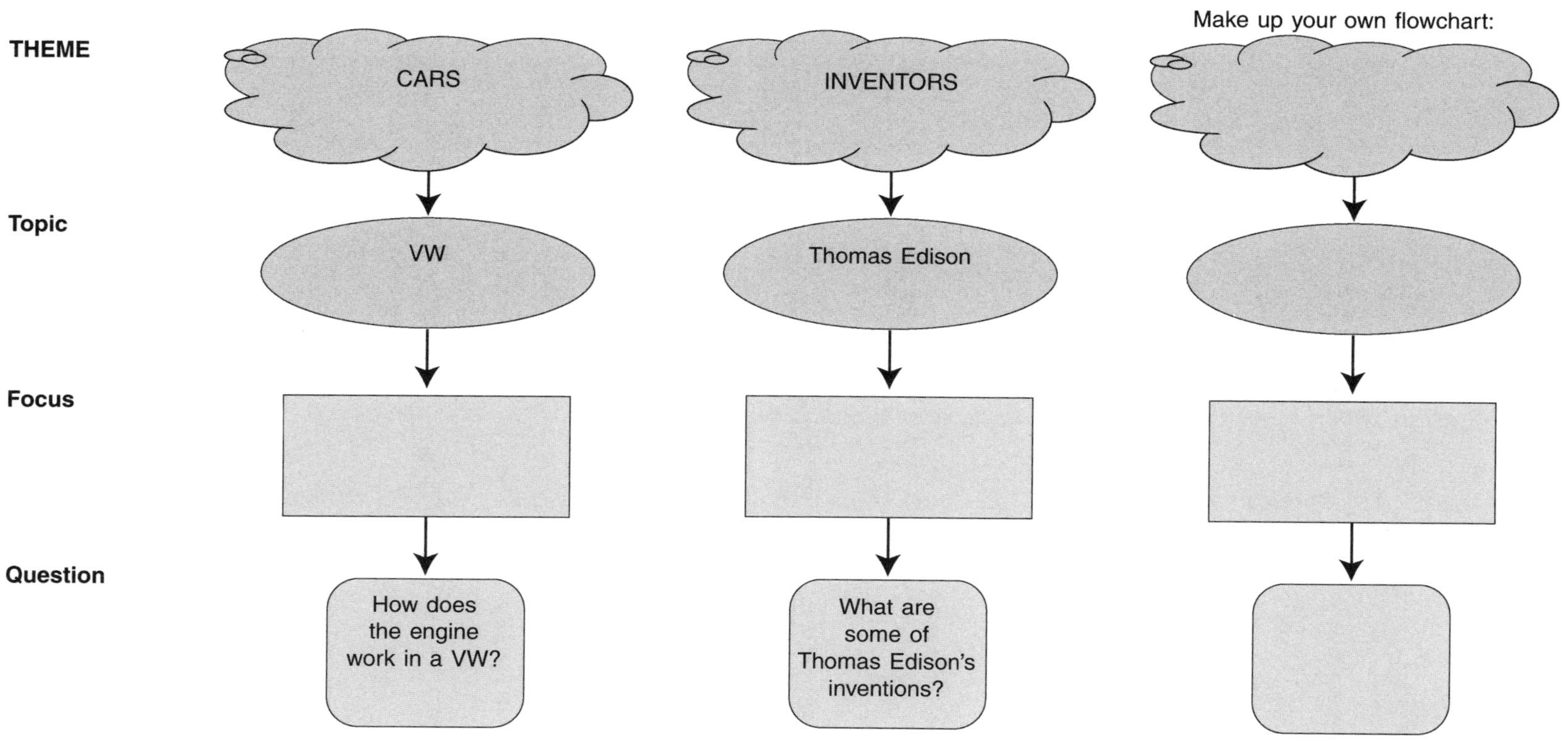

HANDOUT Q-6. Category Flowchart—Substitution (page 1 of 2)

Name _____   Class _____   Date _____

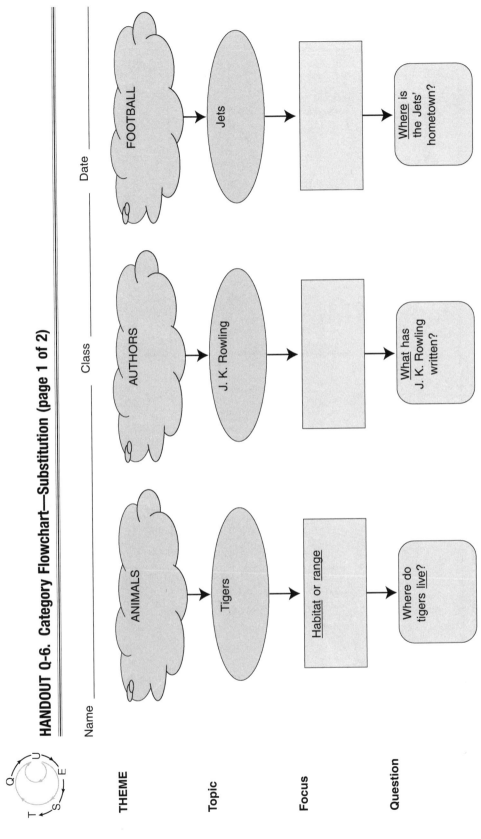

THEME

ANIMALS   AUTHORS   FOOTBALL

Topic

Tigers   J. K. Rowling   Jets

Focus

Habitat or <u>range</u>

Question

Where do tigers <u>live</u>?   What has J. K. Rowling written?   Where <u>is</u> the Jets' hometown?

From *Reading the Web* by Maya B. Eagleton and Elizabeth Dobler. Copyright 2007 by The Guilford Press. Permission to photocopy this handout is granted to purchasers of this book for personal use only (see copyright page for details).

HANDOUT Q-6. Category Flowchart—Substitution (page 2 of 2)

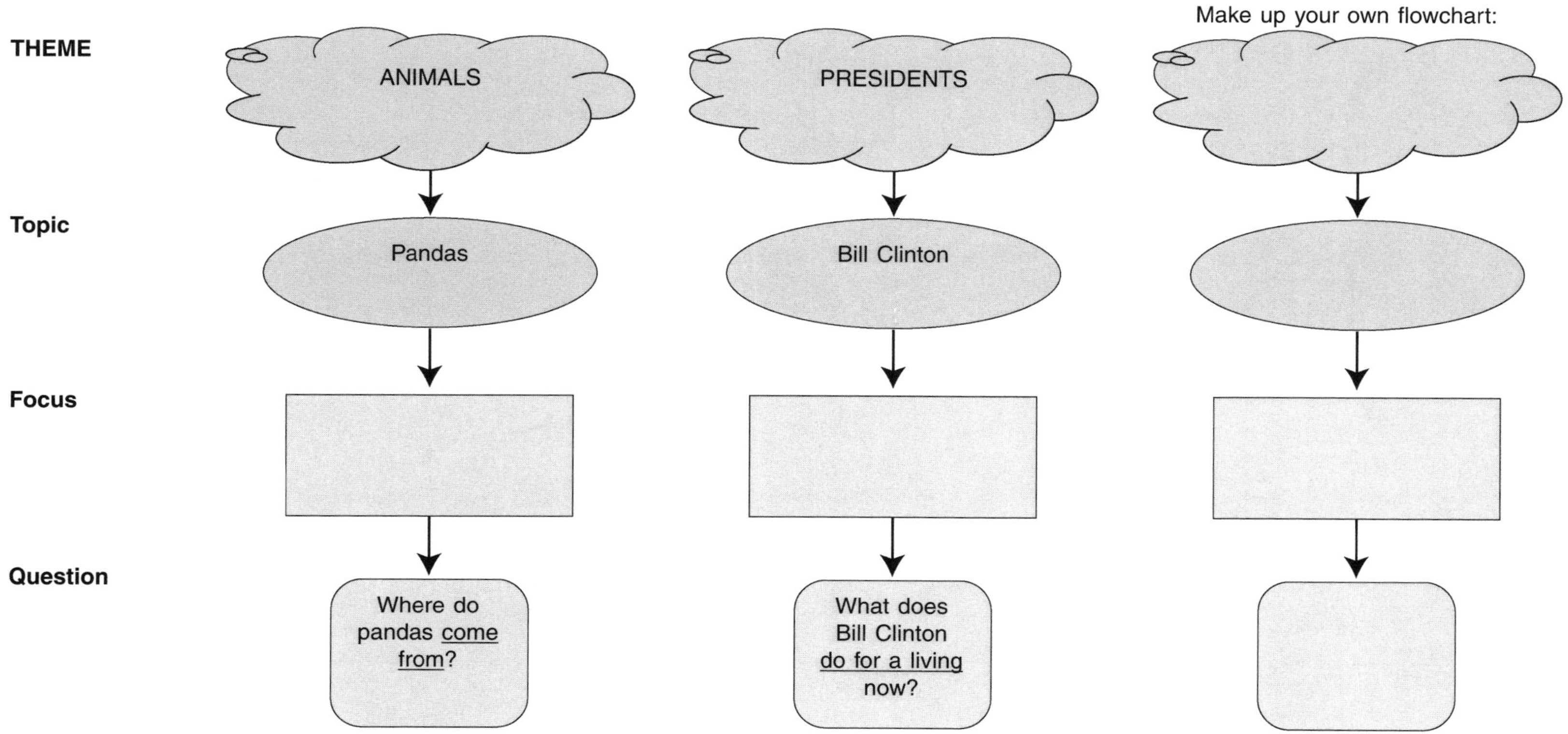

Make up your own flowchart:

THEME

ANIMALS

PRESIDENTS

Topic

Pandas

Bill Clinton

Focus

Question

Where do pandas come from?

What does Bill Clinton do for a living now?

HANDOUT Q-7. Category Flowchart—Blank

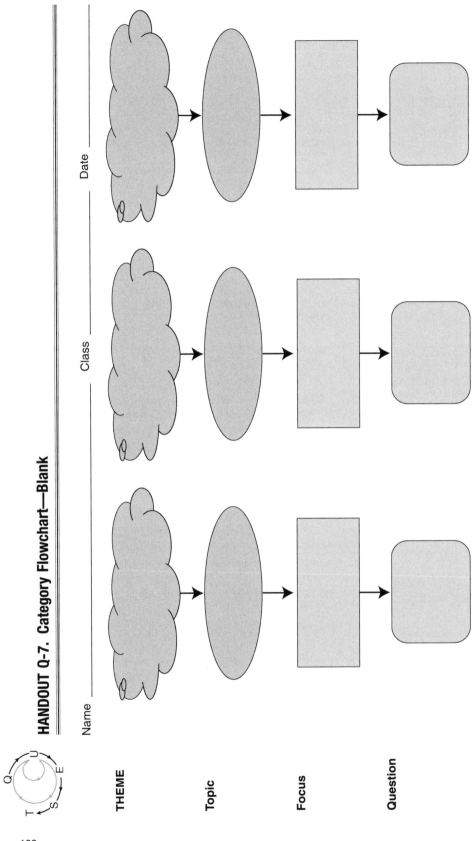

Name _____ Class _____ Date _____

THEME

Topic

Focus

Question

HANDOUT Q-8. Knowing Your Audience

Name _____ Class _____ Date _____

Understanding who your audience is will help you to decide which information to include in your project and how to present it.

	Enter your answers in this column:
1. The audience for my project includes these kinds of people:	
2. My audience is similar to me in these ways:	
3. My audience is different from me in these ways:	
4. My audience probably knows the following about my topic:	
5. My audience probably feels this way about my topic:	
6. These are questions my audience might ask me about my topic:	

HANDOUT Q-9. Understanding Purposes

Name _____ Class _____ Date _____

Almost any topic can be used for a variety of purposes. There are four basic purposes for any writing or inquiry project: to inform, to entertain, to persuade, and to express.

Read the chart and fill in the missing blanks. Create your own topics and add purposes in the blank rows.

	PURPOSES			
TOPICS	to inform	to entertain	to persuade	to express yourself
kangaroos	kangaroo babies	the crazy story of the dueling kangaroos	advertisement for saving the Australian outback	my kangaroo poem
skiing	history of skiing	skiing comics	letter soliciting funds for a ski resort	how skiing changed my life
Einstein	Einstein's childhood	weird creatures that live in Einstein's hair	why Einstein should win the Nobel prize	
whales	different types of whales	all the things you can do with blubber		collection of haunting whale sounds
rap music	famous rap musicians		why kids should be able to play rap in school	my rap song
Hawaii		surfing bloopers	poster to convince tourists to visit Hawaii	video clip of my hula dancing

HANDOUT Q-10. Sample Project Criteria

Questioning
☐ Choose two focus areas for your topic.
☐ Develop a Project Plan.

Using Resources
☐ Use a search engine.
☐ Use TOPIC + FOCUS keywords for searching.
☐ Use Edit>Find on webpages.

Evaluating
☐ Complete a Website Evaluation Chart for one of your sources.

Synthesizing
☐ Gather info on your topic from *at least* three different websites.
☐ Use CHoMP notemaking strategies.
☐ Copy and paste URLs next to your notes.

Transforming
☐ Write at least three paragraphs in your own words for each focus area.
☐ Include at least two images with captions.
☐ Create a Works Cited list.

HANDOUT Q-11. Sample Grading Rubric

PROCESS	4	3	2	1	0	STUDENT SCORE	TEACHER SCORE
Effort	I put forth a *ton* of effort	I put forth *a lot* of effort	I put forth *some* effort	I put forth a *little* effort	I didn't put out any effort		
Citizenship	I *always* respected my peers	I *usually* respected my peers	I *sometimes* respected my peers	I *rarely* respected my peers	I never respected my peers		
					TOTAL PROCESS		

PROGRESS	4	3	2	1	0	STUDENT SCORE	TEACHER SCORE
Making Notes	I *totally* had enough notes for my project	I *mostly* had enough notes for my project	I *somewhat* had enough notes for my project	I *sort of* had enough notes for my project	I didn't have any notes		
Finding Information	I found my info *super fast*	I found my info *pretty fast*	I found my info *but it took a little while*	I found my info *but it took a long time*	I couldn't find any information		
					TOTAL PROGRESS		

PRODUCT	4	3	2	1	0	STUDENT SCORE	TEACHER SCORE
Citing Sources	I gathered info from *four or more* sources	I gathered info from *three* sources	I gathered info from *two* sources	I gathered info from *one* source	I didn't gather any info		
Research Topic	I learned a *ton* about my topic	I learned *a lot* about my topic	I learned *some* stuff about my topic	I learned a *little* about my topic	I didn't learn anything new		
Final Project	My project *totally* showed what I learned	My project *mostly* showed what I learned	My project *somewhat* showed what I learned	My project *sort of* showed what I learned	My project didn't show what I learned		
					TOTAL PRODUCT		

		TOTALS	
TOTAL POSSIBLE FOR THIS CATEGORY: 8	PROCESS		
TOTAL POSSIBLE FOR THIS CATEGORY: 8	PROGRESS		
TOTAL POSSIBLE FOR THIS CATEGORY: 12	PRODUCT		
	TOTAL out of 28 points		
	PERCENT		

HANDOUT Q-12. Project Planning Flowchart

Name _____ Class _____ Date _____

Enter your theme, topic, two focus areas, and two questions into the flowchart.

THEME

Topic

Focus

Questions

HANDOUT Q-13. Project Planning Template

Name _____ Class _____ Date _____

Clear goals will help you organize your project and stay on track.

	Enter your answers in this column:
1. My theme is:	
2. My topic is:	
3. I chose this topic because:	
4. My first research question is:	
5. My second research question is:	
6. The audience for my project is:	
7. The purpose of my research is (to inform, persuade, entertain, or express):	
8. I will show what I've learned by making a (report, poster, brochure, webpage):	

Objective

Students will demonstrate the ability to plan an inquiry project by brainstorming and categorizing research questions.

Time

One or two class periods

Materials

1. *QUEST Inquiry Model* (Handout P-11)
2. *Choosing Focus Areas* (Handout Q-4)
3. *Project Planning Flowchart* (Handout Q-12)
4. 3×5 notecards (10 or more per student)
5. Rubber bands (5 or more per student)
6. Pencils

Assessment Options

1. *Web Strategies Assessment* (Handout P-2, P-4, or P-5)
2. *Web Strategies Scoring Guide* (Handout P-3 or P-6)

Introduction

1. Make sure you have covered themes, topics, audience, purpose, and formats before doing this Project Planning Lesson.
2. Tell students you will be teaching them a strategy for planning an inquiry project that many other students have found useful. Contextualize the lesson using the *QUEST Inquiry Model* (Handout P-11) by pointing out that they are in the <u>Q</u> phase of the QUEST, which includes creating a plan.
3. Have students brainstorm why planning is useful in this class, in other classes, and outside of school. This can be done in pairs, in small groups, or as a whole class.
4. Generate excitement and get student buy-in on the purpose of the lesson before proceeding. Tell students that strong project plans and appropriately scoped focus areas and research questions will improve their ability to find information on the Internet.

Modeling

1. Use the "Hanging Gardens of Babylon" example in Handout Q-4 or generate your own example to model brainstorming questions, sorting them into categories and creating a name that describes each category.
2. Pass out materials.

Practice

1. Students brainstorm what they want to know about their topics by putting one question on each index card.
2. Students sort the cards into categories and place a rubber band around each stack.
3. Students create a name for each category and enter the names in the boxes on Handout Q-4.
4. Students choose two focus areas and corresponding questions that are the most interesting and put them in the flowchart in Handout Q-12.
5. Toward the end of the class period, have each student place a rubber band around all the index cards and put his or her name in a prominent location on the top card.
6. Collect all materials.

Scaffolding

1. An excellent activity for helping students generate questions is to have them ask each other questions about their topics. This works well in small groups so long as someone who writes quickly can accurately record the questions.
2. If anyone is struggling to generate questions, you may want to have that student use the K-W-L procedure (Figure 4.5) or the 5WH technique (Who, What, Where, When, Why, How).
3. If students are struggling to categorize their questions, name their categories, or convert categories into research questions, pair them up or help them individually.
4. If anyone is struggling with writing, have a more capable student serve as a scribe.
5. For students who are overwhelmed with two focus areas, have them just do one.
6. If anyone is having serious difficulty with the whole procedure, have him or her go through the process again from the start with you or a more capable peer. Have the student talk aloud as you go through each step together. Choose another topic if necessary.

Feedback

Have individual conferences to ensure that students have appropriately scoped focus areas, "good" research questions, and well-matched purposes and formats before proceeding to the next QUEST phase: Understanding Resources.

Ticket Out the Door

Have each student tell you his or her topic and focus area(s) before leaving class.

HANDOUT Q-15. Project Planning Lesson—Middle Level (page 1 of 2)

Objective

Students will demonstrate the ability to plan an inquiry project by brainstorming and categorizing research questions.

Time

One or two class periods

Materials

1. *QUEST Inquiry Model* (Handout P-11)
2. *Choosing Focus Areas* (Handout Q-4)
3. *Project Planning Flowchart* (Handout Q-12)
4. 3×5 note cards (10 or more per student)
5. Rubber bands (5 or more per student)
6. Pencils

Assessment Options

1. *Web Strategies Assessment* (Handout P-2, P-4, or P-5)
2. *Web Strategies Scoring Guide* (Handout P-3 or P-6)

Introduction

1. Make sure you have covered themes, topics, audience, purpose, and formats before doing this Project Planning Lesson.
2. Tell students you will be teaching them a transferable strategy for planning an inquiry project that many other students have found useful. Contextualize the lesson using the *QUEST Inquiry Model* (Handout P-11) by pointing out that they are in the Q phase of the QUEST, which includes creating a plan.
3. Have students brainstorm why planning is useful in this class, in other classes, and outside of school. This can be done in pairs, in small groups, or as a whole class.
4. Generate excitement and get student buy-in on the purpose of the lesson before proceeding. Tell students that strong project plans and appropriately scoped focus areas and research questions will improve their keywords and search strategies on the Internet.

Modeling

1. Use the "Hanging Gardens of Babylon" example in Handout Q-4 or generate your own example to model brainstorming questions, sorting them into categories and creating a name that describes each category.
2. Pass out materials.

Practice

1. Students brainstorm what they want to know about their topics by putting one question on each index card.
2. Students sort the cards into categories and place a rubber band around each stack.
3. Students create a name for each category and enter the names in the boxes on Handout Q-4.
4. Students choose two focus areas and corresponding questions that are the most interesting and put them in the flowchart in Handout Q-12.
5. Toward the end of the class period, have each student place a rubber band around all the index cards and put his or her name in a prominent location on the top card.
6. Collect all materials.

Scaffolding

1. An excellent activity for helping students generate questions is to have them ask each other questions about their topics. This works well in small groups so long as someone who writes quickly can accurately record the questions.
2. If anyone is struggling to generate questions, you may want to have that student use the K-W-L procedure (Figure 4.5) or the 5WH technique (Who, What, Where, When, Why, How).
3. If any students are struggling to categorize their questions, name their categories, or convert categories into research questions, pair them up or help them individually.
4. If anyone is struggling with writing, have a more capable student serve as a scribe.
5. If anyone is having serious difficulty with the whole procedure, have the student go through the process again from the start with you or a more capable peer. Have him or her talk aloud as you go through each step together. Choose another topic if necessary.

Feedback

1. Have students share their Project Plans with each other. Have peers provide feedback.
2. Have individual conferences to ensure that students have appropriately scoped focus areas, "good" research questions, and well-matched purposes and formats before proceeding to the next QUEST phase: Understanding Resources.

Ticket Out the Door

Have each student tell you his or her topic and two focus areas before leaving class.

5 UNDERSTANDING RESOURCES

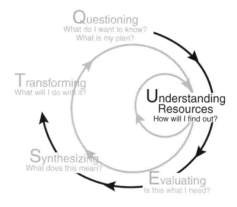

KEY IDEAS

▶ Many people, especially children and struggling learners, have a limited understanding of how to best utilize digital resources for inquiry, and lack strategies for efficiently and effectively locating information on the Web.

▶ The key question that guides the <u>U</u> phase of the inquiry process is, "How will I find the answers to my questions?"

▶ Identifying appropriate resources for inquiry requires the ability to match resources with research questions, whether these resources are people, books, mass media, computers, or the Internet.

▶ Computer-mediated learning involves being able to manage the "apparatus" of the computer effectively, including keyboarding, navigating the operating system, and minor troubleshooting.

▶ Among other things, effective utilization of the Internet includes knowing how to get on the Internet, navigate through websites, interpret URLs and domain names, use features of web browsers, and work with images, multimedia, and text.

▶ Choosing search tools means knowing the difference between typing a web address straight into the URL field, clicking the search button on a web browser, and using a search engine.

▶ Because search engines differ in their search algorithms and features, it is important to understand how several popular ones work and know when to use them. Some search engines use natural language processing, some offer categories, and others rely on keywords.

▶ The linchpin to selecting keywords for searching is to avoid being too broad or too wordy. A very reliable method is the <topic + focus> keyword strategy.

> The continuously changing technologies of literacy mean that we must help children learn how to learn new technologies of literacy. In fact, the ability to learn continuously changing technologies for literacy may be a more critical target than learning any particular technology of literacy itself.
>
> —Leu, Kinzer, Coiro, and Cammack (2004, p. 1605)

In this chapter on Understanding Resources, we share research-based practical suggestions for helping students develop strategies for identifying resources, managing computers, utilizing the Internet, choosing search tools, and selecting keywords. While many of the strategies presented in the preceding chapter on Questioning are similar for print-based and Web-based learning, the Understanding Resources phase requires unique strategies that have no print corollary. For example, since search engines are currently the primary mediators of information on the Internet, understanding how to use them effectively is critical. Moreover, since many search engines require the use of highly specific keywords, it is essential that students have strategies for selecting keywords. We conclude this chapter with numerous reproducibles to help your students become more strategic with technological resources.

Language Arts Standard: Exhibit self-direction by independently finding answers to questions.

Why Is It Important to Understand Resources?

There is so much information available to us today that it is important to have knowledge of available resources and to have flexible strategies for finding answers to compelling questions. Although traditional forms of information media are still very useful resources, there is no doubt that the Internet has far exceeded every previous information technology in breadth, depth, and recency. The Internet has become an integral part of gaining information in schools, at home, and in the workplace; however, as mentioned in the introduction to Part I, researchers have found that people of all ages are surprisingly inefficient at finding information using this uniquely flexible resource. If we want to prepare today's students to be successful in school and to compete in tomorrow's workplace, we had better start teaching them to be Web literate.

Library Media Standard: Locate and effectively use print, nonprint and/or electronic resources to solve problems and conduct research.

When Do We Need to Use Resources?

We regularly use all kinds of resources in our daily lives, everything from telephone directories to cookbooks to the Internet. It is a high compliment to describe someone as "resourceful." A resourceful person may not know all the answers, but she is strategic and tenacious at finding them; for example, she may know the right person to call, know the right reference book to peruse, or know how to find the information online. When stumped, a resourceful person does not give up but rather tries to think of another resource to consult. These are exactly the kinds of transferable strategies that we need to be teaching our students, and providing instruction in the types of resources that are available via the Internet is especially crucial in this day and age. When was the last time you ordered a complete set of printed and bound encyclopedias for your home or classroom? Probably not recently, since we are now able to purchase encyclopedias that can fit on one or two CD-ROMs that contain not only text and images, but illustrative multimedia features as well.

Strategies for Understanding Resources come into play throughout the inquiry process, but are especially helpful after the Questioning phase, when topics and research questions have been solidified and it's time to figure out the most expedient means for gathering the target information. Certain types of research questions lend themselves to primary data collection methods, such as interviewing people or conducting surveys. Others require a trip to the library or the local museum. Still others may require a combination of many different kinds of resources, including the Web. The trick is knowing which types of resources to consult at which times.

Social Studies Standard: Gather information from multiple sources, including primary and secondary sources.

What Characterizes Effective Use of Resources?

There are five fundamental aspects of Understanding Resources with which students must be strategic in order to be successful with Web-based inquiry projects, as follows: (1) identifying resources; (2) managing computers; (3) utilizing the Internet; (4) choosing search tools; and (5) selecting keywords. If you have used some of the assessment tools provided in Chapter 3, you will know which of your students need assistance in each area.

Identifying Resources

The first step in <u>U</u>nderstanding Resources is identifying the most promising (and easily accessible) resources for answering research questions. Although the chief focus of this book is on Web-based resources, we like to give students experience with all the different types of sources that "real" researchers use: primary source materials, people (adults, peers, experts), print (books, magazines, encyclopedias), media (TV, film, and video), computers (CD-ROMs, clipart collections, tutorials), and the Internet (e-mail, websites, bulletin boards). Notice how these forms of representation map directly onto the semiotic sign systems that we discussed in Chapter 1. Humans use a wide variety of representational forms to communicate information, and being literate involves interpreting and making use of culturally valued forms.

**Science Standard:
Use appropriate tools
and techniques to make
observations and gather data.**

Managing Computers

If a student decides that a technological resource is indeed a good match for his research questions, then we need to ensure that he knows how to manage various aspects of technology, such as keyboarding, navigating, and troubleshooting. The "apparatus" of a computer is much more difficult to manage than the apparatus of a book. Therefore, keyboarding and mouse skills are essential. Just as a young learner needs to know how to hold a pencil and form letters in order to write, he needs to be able to use a keyboard and a mouse (or alternate assistive technology) to work with computers. Using the laborious keyboard technique known as "hunting and pecking" is a serious barrier to learning on the Web (Figure 5.1).

As discussed throughout this book, navigation is also a fundamental computer skill (Coiro & Dobler, in press; Henry, 2006). Unlike books, which typically proceed in a linear fashion, computer operating systems and software programs require non-linear navigational strategies, or the linking of ideas in various sequences, in order to move through the system with ease. As discussed in Chapter 2, computer navigation requires an understanding of the system and the ability to make speedy, informed decisions about where to go next . . . and next . . . and next.

Finally, learners need some basic troubleshooting strategies in order to manage technology effectively (Figure 5.2). While we certainly don't advocate having youngsters pry open computer casings at school, it is helpful if your students know a few tricks to escape from frozen programs and error messages (see Chapter 3). A good rule of thumb to preserve your sanity as a teacher is to train students to solicit help from three knowledgeable classmates before coming to you with a computer problem (Wilhelm & Friedemann, 1998).

If you are starting to feel you're doing the job of a library media specialist or computer teacher, please don't despair—

**Use <Ctrl+Alt+Delete> to
unfreeze a PC program and
<Command+Option+Escape>
to unfreeze a Mac program.**

FIGURE 5.1. Hunting and pecking on the keyboard.

these skills are fairly quick to teach and are essential literacies for today's students in almost every content area in and out of school.

Utilizing the Internet

After assessing your students using some of the tools discussed in Chapter 3, you will have a sense of their level of Internet knowledge, abilities, and attitudes. The following are some additional questions you will want to ask yourself about your students:

FIGURE 5.2. Troubleshooting computers.

- Do they know how to get on the Internet?
- Do they know how to navigate websites efficiently?
- Do they know about the "refresh" and "history" tools on web browsers?
- Do they know how to interpret URLs and domain names (Chapter 3)?
- Do they know what to do when a commercial pop-up suddenly appears?
- Do they know how and where to save images, multimedia, and text they find?
- Do they get frustrated easily and "threaten" to run to the library for a book on their topic (an interesting conundrum for the 21st-century teacher)?

 Instead of allowing your students to inefficiently click the "back" button a zillion times to return to a familiar webpage, teach them to use the small triangular button next to the back button or the URL field to jump directly back to a desired page.

Choosing Search Tools

At this time in history, in order for anyone to find anything in the massive, disorganized database that is the Internet, a person must be able to understand and use search engines. Although it is possible to search by simply clicking the "search" button in a web browser or by using a search tool within a website, 71% of Web users access search engines to reach other websites, making the use of a search engine the second most popular Internet task next to e-mail (Jansen & Pooch, 2001). Interestingly, the search engine Google at *www.google.com* has so pervaded the Web that "Google" was selected by the American Dialect Society as the most useful new word of 2002 (Roush, 2004). "Google" has actually become a verb used in conversation to be synonymous with "search," as in "Did you try googling it?" and "I googled my high school sweetheart and found him still living in Des Moines!"

Although some students know of the existence of several search engines, they tend to use one search engine regularly. The search engine of choice for just over 66% of the students in a study by Gunn and Hepburn (2003) was, in fact, Google. However, these same students were often unaware of the advanced features offered by Google, and those students who were aware of them used them infrequently. One problem is that most students do not understand how search engines work. In our research with students in grades 3–8, we have found it very enlightening to pose the question, "When you ask a computer to do an Internet search, what does the computer do with your request?" Table 5.1 shows typical responses to this query, sorted into degrees of sophistication.

To choose the best search engine, we begin with asking ourselves the questions, "What does each search engine offer?" and "What are the differences between search engines developed for children and those developed for adults?" Some Internet readers, including adults, figure out how to use a search engine with little or no instruction. Maybe you are like us and began Internet searching by muddling your way through the use of a search engine. Though you may eventually find some information, are you being efficient and effectively finding the most useful information? A system relying on luck and guessing may work very well, especially if you are

TABLE 5.1. Children's Beliefs about Search Engines

How does a search engine work?

Novice

- I don't know. It gets it really fast.
- It goes to this other computer with a person on it and it types in where you want to go and it somehow connects you.
- Takes it to a computer that someone's on and they actually search and find information and send it back to your computer.
- It goes in a small cycle through a telephone wire, back through the wall, into your computer. I think it's a robot that does it.
- It has the information I type onto it and it brings it to the computer's main frame. It brings the energy pulses, the signals.

Intermediate

- It will scan a bunch of websites and it will show all the websites related to what you typed in.
- It sends what you type to this site. It analyzes all that information and sends you the links that match your description.
- Goes through every site that has the word on it, or talks about it.
- It goes through miles and miles of documents.

Advanced

- Sends it to the server and it processes it in a script and looks through the database and returns what results you have.
- It browses the registered webpages for the information that you search for and finds the closest matches.
- I think it searches the information it has on its sites for words that you've used.

---

not pressed for time when searching for information. Students, on the other hand, are often pressed for time. When searching at school or the public library, students may have a limited amount of time for using the computer. When working at home, time may also be a consideration for students who are busy with other assignments, after-school activities, and pressures from other family members who desire their own computer time.

In school settings, we have observed students using three approaches for locating information on the Web: (1) dot-com formula; (2) shopping mall; and (3) search engine (described in detail in Guinee et al., 2003). We briefly discuss the first two strategies before moving into an in-depth discussion of search engines.

Dot-com Formula

Many students attempt to find information by substituting their research topic into what Guinee et al. (2003) have dubbed the "dot-com formula" (e.g., *www. mytopic.com*), which is based on the heavily advertised convention for naming corporate Web sites. With this method, the reader creates a web address using her topic or keyword rather than beginning a search using a search engine. Fidel and colleagues (1999) also found that young adolescents often initiate searches without selecting a search engine. A novice Web user explains this phenomenon: "First of all, you go onto the Internet, and then you write alaska.com or alaskatrip.com or whatever and get onto that, and then you can go through the webpages and finally find what you need."

Commercialization of the Web has led to an abundance of corporate dot-com URLs, making the dot-com approach fairly effective when trying to find companies. For example, the Nike website at *www.nike.com* provides information and opportunities for purchase of Nike products. The proliferation of dot-com URLs gives many students the impression that the dot-com approach is a good preliminary catch-all search method. This feeling was articulated by one student, who said, "I think also . . . if you want something broad, you can just do like www and like whatever-dot-com nowadays, because there's so many different dot-coms." However, using this approach to find a relevant website for a research project can present problems because companies and their websites generally are not designed to be student refer-

 To improve success, students need to understand that companies and individuals create Web sites to share information, and that as a result, sites represent organizations, not research topics.
—Guinee, Eagleton, and Hall (2003, p. 372)

ence sources. For instance, a sixth grade student began his search by typing "www.piranna.com." Spelling error aside, this company's site wasn't related to piranhas or any other fish. Another common problem when using the dot-com approach is the retrieval of URLs that do not reference an active website, yielding a "site not found" error.

Shopping Mall

Rather than relying on the dot-com formula, some Internet users treat the Web like a shopping mall, a place with categories of information compartmentalized like stores in a mall—electronics in one store, clothes in another (Guinee et al., 2003). These students go straight to sites they think might contain their desired information. For example, one experienced Internet user said, "I'd go to *expedia.com* and go to the tour guide info and type in "Alaska" and find out what's there." Another said, "First I'd look to see if there was a brochure of the cruise ship, I'd go to that website . . . and then go to the Coast Guard to see if they rated the safety." Recently, Maya was trying to find out what time a certain children's television program airs so she could record it for commercial-free viewing. Her first approach was the shopping mall strategy, one that she had used successfully for this purpose in the past. She went straight to *www.tvguide.com*; however, since this site now requires users to register before viewing the listings, it was faster to search Google for <"TV listings" + Tucson>.

As students gain Internet experience, they become more familiar with various websites, which increases their chances that applying the shopping mall approach will be effective. However, the approach fails when the student is unsure of where to look or the selected website does not contain the target information. This situation is well demonstrated by the following navigation sequence by an older student with identified learning disabilities, who searched for information on the lory bird during the individual Web Strategies Assessment (see Chapter 3). This is where he went: National Geographic.com → Discovery.com → Petco.com → asked researcher, "Is this an extinct bird?" → finally went to Ask.com. Unfortunately, some students, like this one, tend to rely on search engines as a last resort rather than as an appropriate place to start.

Search Engines

Table 5.2 shows examples of four search engine categories: (1) those appropriate for younger students; (2) those appropriate for older students; (3) meta-search engines; and (4) portals and directories. Meta-search engines are huge engines that collect results from many different search engines, thus increasing the number of hits. Portals and directories are smaller databases of preselected websites, usually presented in categories. Because the list may be outdated by the time you read this book, check our companion website to explore some of the most current search engines.

TABLE 5.2 Types of Search Engines

Search engine	URL
For younger students	
Ask for Kids	www.askforkids.com
Yahooligans	www.yahooligans.com
Kids Click	www.kidsclick.org
Ask an Expert	askanexpert.org
Kid's Tools for Searching	rcls.org/search.htm
For older students and adults	
Google	www.google.com
AOL	search.aol.com
Ask.com	www.ask.com
MSN	www.msn.com
Meta-search engines	
WebCrawler	www.webcrawler.com
Dogpile	www.dogpile.com
Vivisimo	www.vivisimo.com
Kart00	www.kartoo.com
Portals and directories	
Yahoo	www.yahoo.com
Librarians' Index to the Internet	lii.org
Virtual Library	vlib.org
Galaxy Directory	www.galaxy.com
Web Brain	www.webbrain.com

There are many search engines on the Web competing for your students' inquiries. As in any competitive product market, different engines work in slightly different ways to try to provide a better product than the competition. Some offer standard-looking textual lists of results while others, such as Kart00 and Web Brain, present a visual display of results. Although they are becoming more and more similar, each engine still tries to distinguish itself with features not found elsewhere. Teachers and students can take advantage of these differences by becoming familiar with a few search engines, learning each one's strengths, and knowing when to use each one (Eagleton & Guinee, 2002). The following discussion of five well-established search engines provides background information for the selection of an appropriate search engine. We discuss three that are appropriate for younger students (Ask.com for Kids, Yahooligans, and KidsClick) and two that are popular with older students (Google and Yahoo). Most meta-search engines, such as WebCrawler and Dogpile, return results from Google, Yahoo, and Ask.com in addition to several others.

ASK FOR KIDS

Ask for Kids (*www.askforkids.com*), like its adult counterpart, Ask.com (*www.ask.com*), uses *natural language processing*, so is useful when you are having difficulty articulating your research question in the specific, concise manner required by other search engines (Eagleton & Guinee, 2002). Ask for Kids results are screened for appropriateness for children. When using this search engine, the learner begins by typing a question, phrase, or keywords into the search bar. After clicking on the "ask" button, the student receives various choices. The user's initial question encourages the search engine to provide MORE questions. This may be a surprise to students who are not familiar with Ask for Kids and expect to be instantly taken to a website with information about their questions. Such a variety of choices may either help the student to focus in on specific details or to become off task by being overwhelmed with too many choices. Students who are less skilled readers or who struggle with vocabulary may have some difficulty understanding the choices presented by Ask for Kids, let alone knowing which choice to make for finding information. Ask for Kids also returns choices based on websites visited by other people who asked similar questions, as well as the length of time visitors stayed on the sites. Finally, Ask for Kids supplies meta-search results, which link to answers it found using other search engines.

When faced with the topic of the solar system, Ask for Kids replies with several different choices from its search engine and also gives learners the option to see results found by other search engines (Figure 5.3). The choices presented by Ask for Kids include linking directly to a preferred website, viewing a photo, searching for related terms, selecting more specific information about the solar system, and taking a virtual tour sponsored by National Geographic. The student can also select one of two reading levels. Level 1 contains shorter text, less complex vocabulary words, and larger print. Ask for Kids also includes the feature of allowing the learner to check the spelling of her search question, a handy feature for readers who are unsure of how to spell technical terms.

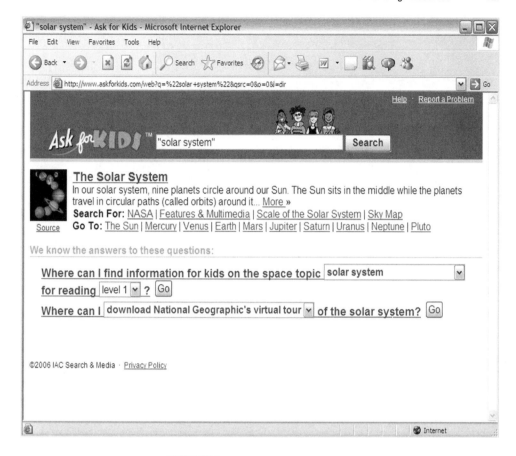

FIGURE 5.3. Ask for Kids search engine.

YAHOOLIGANS

Yahooligans (*www.yahooligans.com*) uses *categories*, so it is a useful starting place for students with limited background knowledge on a topic. Yahooligans provides readers ages 7–12 with a wide variety of places to begin their search. Readers may choose to type a term in the search box or may want to first browse through the categories in the Yahooligans directory, much like a shopper might do during a leisurely trip to the mall. Yahooligans also provides the option of reading for various purposes by selecting one of the categories on the left toolbar, such as games, jokes, or cool sites. Yahooligans selects websites that are appropriate for children but does not allow the reader to select the reading level of materials.

When searching for the term "solar system," Yahooligans provides the learner with three different choices for accessing more information (Figure 5.4). First, the student can choose from links that take him to various departments within the Yahooligans search engine. These choices include visiting the science department, watching a movie about the solar system, reading in the reference department, and using the Ask Earl feature. Second, the searcher can choose from category matches within astronomy and space or solar system. Third, the reader can select a link from

FIGURE 5.4. Yahooligans search engine. Reproduced with permission of Yahoo! Inc. © 2006 by Yahoo! Inc. YAHOO! and the YAHOO! logo are trademarks of Yahoo! Inc.

within the 65 website matches that were returned. Here he is faced with many choices of various websites along with the web address and a brief description of each website.

KIDSCLICK

KidsClick (*www.kidsclick.org*) uses a *librarian-selected database*, so it is useful when a teacher wants to protect children from visiting inappropriate sites, low-quality sites, or webpages with difficult text. The categories on the homepage follow the Dewey decimal system so as to make a connection between sites and library materials.

When viewing search results for "solar system," the learner sees the link and an annotated description along with an approximate reading level and an indication of the use of illustrations on the website (Figure 5.5). The number of search results (29) is somewhat smaller than the hit list produced by the Yahooligans search engine. Because these websites are handpicked, the quality and the reading level may be a closer match to the needs of the Internet reader even though there are fewer choices. The list of websites in the search results are listed alphabetically in KidsClick.

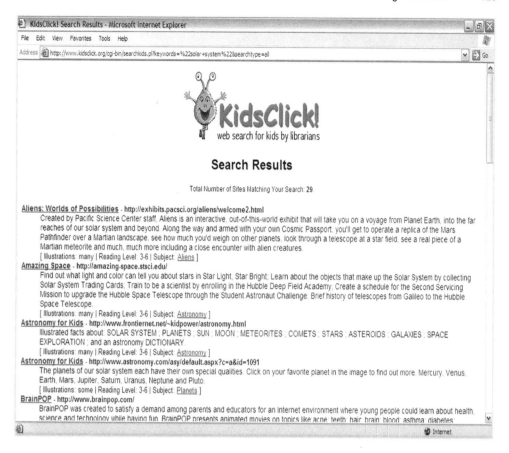

FIGURE 5.5. KidsClick search engine.

GOOGLE

Google (*www.google.com*) uses *text matching*, so it is useful when you already have a good idea of the information you hope to find (Eagleton & Guinee, 2002). At the time of this writing, Google searches 8 billion websites to determine the most relevant and popular ones related to the reader's search terms. Popularity ranking prioritizes sites that other people have chosen to visit, so the top results are likely to be the ones you seek. Google also uses a stemming technique to search not only for your indicated search terms but also for other terms that are closely related. Google is not case sensitive, so it doesn't matter whether you use capitals or lowercase. If Google thinks you may have misspelled a search term, it displays the phrase "Did you mean?" at the top of the results list. If you did make a spelling error, you can click on the Google-supplied correct spelling to see the correct search results.

In addition to its sophisticated Web search engine, Google offers numerous additional features, some of which are still in the early phases of development. A very popular tool for students is the "image search" feature, which exclusively searches the Web for images. Note that these images are not free, so appropriate citations should be collected in order to respect copyright laws. Instead of combining all Internet resources into its Web search tool, Google performs separate searches for interest groups, news, shopping, and even satellite images. Other unique features include the ability to limit search results to local resources or scholarly works. Finally, to prevent explicit sexual content from appearing in your search results list, you can activate the "SafeSearch" feature which can be found by clicking on the link for preferences.

A search for information on the solar system in Google yields almost 36 million websites (Figure 5.6), with sponsored links (paid for by advertisers) listed to the side. Such a large number of search results may have one of two effects on learners. Some will feel totally overwhelmed and incapable of making the navigational decisions needed to narrow this huge amount of information. Other students look to that number as a sign that they are good at searching on the Internet, because they can find so many websites. Either way, searchers need keyword strategies for narrowing their search to make information retrieval more manageable (discussed below).

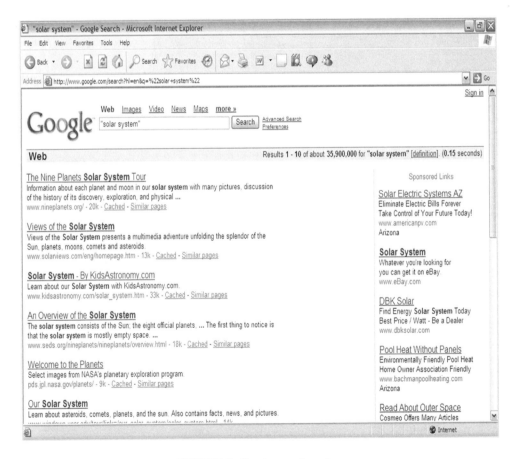

FIGURE 5.6. Google search engine.

YAHOO

Like Yahooligans, Yahoo (*www.yahoo.com*) uses *categories*, so it is useful when you have a general idea of the information you desire, but not a clear idea about where to start searching. Yahoo is a directory of webpages that have been organized into categories by Yahoo staff members. For instance, for a "famous person" project, a student might drill through the categories of Society & Culture > People > Scientists > Women to locate websites that can help her identify a famous female scientist to research (Eagleton & Guinee, 2002). In addition to category browsing, Yahoo also accepts search terms. If the specified search terms do not match one of the human-compiled categories in the Yahoo directory, Yahoo sends the search to Google to complete. Recently, Yahoo has begun providing many of the same special features as does Google, such as the ability to do separate searches for webpages, images, video, local information, news, and products instead of lumping them all together in one big hit list.

A search for the term "solar system" in Yahoo returns nearly 16 million websites, including sponsored sites listed on the right hand side (Figure 5.7). One of

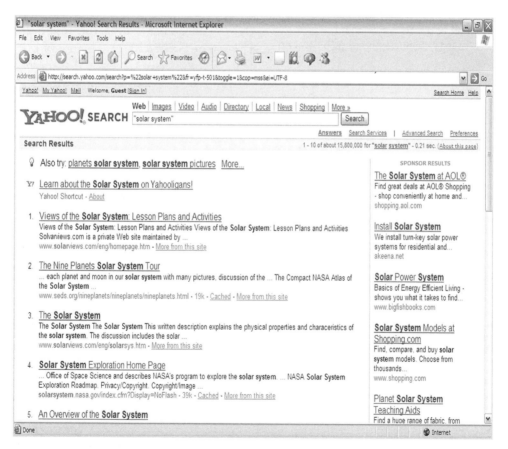

FIGURE 5.7. Yahoo search engine. Reproduced with permission of Yahoo! Inc. © 2006 by Yahoo! Inc. YAHOO! and the YAHOO! logo are trademarks of Yahoo! Inc.

the many critical literacy skills we must teach our students is to question the credibility of sponsored links, since these are likely to be commercially oriented and may not be the best source for their information need. We explore the topic of critical literacy in more depth in Chapter 6.

Selecting Keywords

As noted previously, research has repeatedly shown that people of all ages are often inefficient (slow) and ineffective (inaccurate) at searching the Web. For example, almost 25% of searchers don't find what they're looking for in the first set of results returned by a search engine (Roush, 2004). This, in addition to slow loading webpages, may explain why more than half of all Internet users admit to losing their temper when online, a phenomenon known as "Web rage" (BBC News, 2002). The challenge of searching the Web centers on keyword selection, a unique task that eludes many people.

 [When searching the Web], users do not apply the normal rules of English syntax in any coherent or consistent manner.
—Jansen, Spink, and Pfaff (2000, p. 172)

The vast majority of Web searchers use only two keyword combinations per session, do not use complex keyword strategies, and typically view no more than 10 documents from the results list (Jansen & Pooch, 2001). The use of Boolean operators (see Chapter 3) to narrow a search is practically nonexistent, ranging from 2 to 8% (Jansen & Pooch, 2001); in fact, even when adults try to use Boolean operators, they usually do so incorrectly (Moukdad & Large, 2001). In one large study, 191 high school students from six different schools made the following errors when constructing keywords during a unit on Boolean operators (Nahl & Harada, 1996):

- 44% of students made Boolean inversions
- 28% of the time, students failed to use operators
- 36% of the search statements contained a natural language phrase or sentence
- 22% of students misspelled words
- 22% added unnecessary concepts
- 100% neglected word form variations (truncation)

 [The students'] search behavior was incomprehensibly random.
—Wallace, Kupperman, Krajcik, and Soloway (2000, p. 96)

Similarly, in a series of studies that analyzed *millions* of keyword combinations entered into the Excite search engine, Jansen and colleagues concluded that most people who search the Web do not employ sophisticated strategies to construct keywords (Jansen, Spink, & Pfaff, 2000; Jansen, Spink, & Saracevic, 2000). For example, 67% of users don't go beyond their first and only search query, and even if they do attempt new searches, the modifications they make to their keywords are negligible (Jansen, Spink, & Saracevic, 2000), such as reversing the word order, substituting capitals and lowercase letters, or adding unnecessary words.

> Some strategies seem to reflect that the user thinks of the search engine as one would a small child who only understands single words. . . . Other strategies seem to reflect that the user thinks of the computer as an "all-knowing" entity that can easily comprehend complex expressions.
> —Jansen, Spink, and Pfaff (2000, p. 176)

According to extensive research conducted by Eagleton and Guinee (e.g., Eagleton & Guinee, 2002; Eagleton et al., 2003; Guinee, 2005a; Guinee et al., 2003), children and young adolescents employ at least five basic strategies for constructing keywords: (1) single words; (2) topic + focus; (3) multiple words; (4) phrases; and (5) questions. For simplicity, we present them in three overarching categories: too broad, just right, and too wordy (Figure 5.8), similar to gauging the appropriate scope for a topic or a research question (Chapter 4).

Too Broad

The most prevalent keyword strategy we've observed in classrooms is the submission of a single word, usually a research topic, to a search engine. When asked about searching procedures, numerous students report that all you have to do is "type in the topic word that you're searching for."

Typical examples of the main topic approach are <volcano>, <penguins>, and <Arnold Schwarzenegger>. Worse, some children approach keywords from the theme level, using highly inefficient keywords such as <animals> and <states>. Still worse, some students use such broad search terms that there is no possibility of success—for example, <stuff>, <free>,

 When searching the Web, brainstorm synonyms for keywords that are likely to match an existing category in a search engine. Use Boolean operators, particularly the plus sign, as in <topic + focus>. Put quotation marks around phrases and proper names.

Too Broad	basketball	SEARCH
Just Right	basketball + inventor	SEARCH
Too Wordy	Who is the inventor of basketball?	SEARCH

FIGURE 5.8. Scoping out keywords.

and <info>. It is easy to imagine a child asking himself, "What do I want to find?", answering himself quite literally, "Info," and naively plunking this term into a search engine. Although typing in a single keyword can be an effective approach when a student has weak prior knowledge about his topic and needs to learn more before continuing, it is not efficient when searching for something specific.

Just Right

There is research evidence to support what Eagleton and Guinee have coined the "topic + focus" strategy (Figure 5.9) for choosing keywords (Guinee et al., 2003). Students who use this approach are able to locate target information more quickly because they've identified a specific focus area within a research topic. Examples of keywords for this method are <wrestling + techniques> and <"Mia Hamm" + childhood>. Note that while using the Boolean operator <+> is not necessary in every search engine, it is a good habit for children to internalize. We strongly recommend that you use some of the *Category Flowcharts* from Chapter 4 to teach this keyword method (Handouts Q-5 to Q-7).

An extension of the topic + focus method is to use more than two discrete terms when searching, which we call "multiple keywords" (Guinee et al., 2003). There are times when two keywords are insufficient to narrow the number of search results from a search engine. When searching for something very specific, such as "Who were the first African Americans to win the Nobel Prize for literature?" students must enter three keywords <"African American" + "Nobel Prize" + literature> to find the answers. Students who neglect to include the keyword <literature> will incorrectly identify Ralph Bunche (who won the Nobel Peace Prize in 1950) rather than poet Derek Wolcott (1992) or writer Toni Morrison (1993). One of our favorite examples of a multiple keyword search is <president + stuck + bathtub>, which takes the user straight to amusing websites that recount how a portly U.S. president got stuck in his bathtub on his inauguration day. We share instructional materials for teaching the topic + focus and multiple keyword strategies later in this chapter.

During online searching, remind students to spell things correctly, and to use capitals and lowercase letters as appropriate. Many search engines are case sensitive.

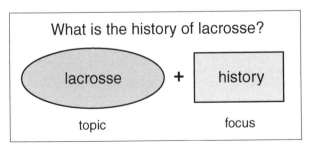

FIGURE 5.9. Topic + focus keyword strategy.

Too Wordy

Many children and adults tend to use natural language phrases and sentences for keyword searching. Search engine designers, such as the developers of Ask.com and Ask for Kids, are aware that natural language processing (NLP) is an effective search feature because people are more comfortable using natural language than computerspeak. However, in other search engines, this strategy is ineffective because potentially useful websites about the desired topic will not show up because

 Some search engines, such as Google, automatically drop high-frequency words, thus converting some phrase searches into topic + focus searches—for example, history of lacrosse will be turned into history + lacrosse. If you intentionally want to find a page that contains a common word, such as "where," you can use +where (space before the plus, but no space between the plus and the common word) to force Google to include that word in its search.

those exact words in that exact order did not appear on any websites. Examples of phrases we've seen students use are <President stuck in his bathtub> and <types of wrestling moves>.

Like using phrases, another popular but highly ineffective keyword strategy is to submit an entire research question to a search engine—for example, <What was Jim Carrey's childhood like?>. The only search engines that can effectively parse out essential keywords from whole sentences are those that use NLP technology, such as Ask.com. Students who habitually use the question keyword strategy probably do not understand how standard search engines work and are in need of instruction and guidance. It is best to help students get in the habit of using the <topic + focus> strategy instead of natural language, because Boolean equations will work in any search engine.

"Keywords are critical for kids' doing research regardless of how they're searching, whether it be from the index of a book or using our online catalog here in the library, or searching on the Internet. And search strategies are such an incredible weakness, they're just not taught enough." —Jenna, library media specialist

Clearly, many of our students are desperately in need of instruction in robust Web search strategies. The activities at the end of this chapter will help your students gain a better understanding of how to make effective use of electronic resources.

How Do We Teach Strategies for Understanding Resources?

If you haven't administered any of the assessments presented in Chapter 3, we recommend that you do so first. Then start with one of the pre-assessments discussed below (Technical Knowledge, Search Engines, or Keywords) before moving into an instructional unit focused on one of these three areas. Do not attempt to teach strategies for all three areas at once; rather, choose one and scaffold the rest. Frequently remind the students that the emphasis of instruction is the U part of the QUEST and that the strategies they learn during these inquiries are highly transferable to other school subjects and to life in general. Our aim is to teach students to be as resourceful as possible, and these days that necessitates a strong working knowledge of the Internet.

Technical Knowledge

A quick way to assess your students' knowledge of computer and Internet resources is to administer the *Technical Knowledge Assessment* (Handout U-1) both before and after an Internet inquiry unit. Have your students trade papers to score and then discuss their answers using the *Technical Knowledge Scoring Guide* (Handout U-2). The best way to turn this assessment into a teaching tool is to have a computer with an LCD projector set up so everyone can see the features that are on the assessment.

An effective way to launch a unit on Understanding Resources is to draw a large Venn diagram on a transparency, chalkboard, or chart paper and have the students brainstorm the similarities and differences between conducting research using books versus using the Internet. Figure 5.10 shows a Venn diagram created by a group of students led by the school library media specialist.

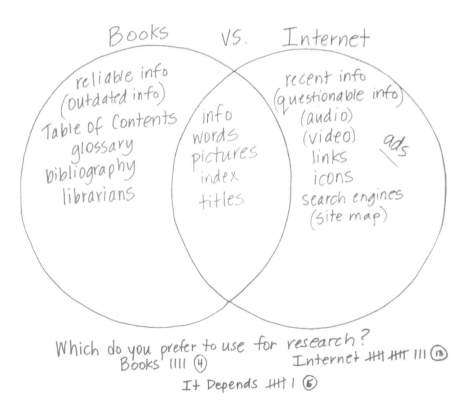

FIGURE 5.10. Venn diagram of books versus Internet.

We've also found it informative to have students brainstorm the literacy skills they think they'll be learning at the start of an inquiry unit and share them, and then have them revisit the list at the end. Many students (and teachers) are pleased to discover how many essential literacy skills are engaged during Internet inquiry—everything from spelling, vocabulary, reading, and writing to strategies for handling Web browsers, search engines, and keywords.

Search Engines

Many students seem to prefer "browsing" the Internet over "searching" it (Large, Beheshti, & Moukdad, 1999; Leu, Leu, & Coiro, 2004; Schachter et al., 1998); however, for most school activities, searching is a necessary skill. If the focus of your instruction is on search engines, you may wish to start with the *Search Engines Assessment* (Handout U-3) and have students trade papers to score and discuss their answers using the *Search Engine Scoring Guide* (Handout U-4). As with the other assessment tools, this can serve as an excellent teaching tool as well.

To better understand the differences between major search engines, your students can try out the *Search Engine Comparison—Elementary Level* (Handout U-5) or the *Search Engine Comparison—Middle Level* (Handout U-6) individually, in pairs, in small groups, or as a class, depending on the level of scaffolding they need. Afterward, they should be ready to conduct some mini-inquiries or full-scale inquiries on topics of their choosing. You will probably wish to use some of the materials discussed in the section "Project Planning" in Chapter 4 to scaffold their inquiries. Have them keep track of the search engines they use so that they become more metacognitive about their own searching habits. Throughout the inquiry project, have the students keep Reflection Logs and regularly share their search engine strategies with each other.

Keywords

As you can imagine, keyword selection is a linchpin to successful reading and learning on the Web. If you can't *find* any relevant information, you certainly can't *read* it! After having carried out numerous keyword units with upper elementary, middle school, and even high school students, we feel strongly that this is an area that deserves attention every year in school. We have done 6-week units focused just on keywords alone. During keyword units, we heavily scaffold all the other aspects of the QUEST process so that students can concentrate on keywords. As an added bonus, focusing on keywords will also stimulate and reinforce students' spelling and vocabulary skills.

 A good rule of thumb is to use the root form of a keyword; for example, use <ski> instead of <skis>, <skiing>, <skier>, or <skiers>. You can also place an asterisk after the root word if you want the search engine to find all the variations of the word; for example, <ski*> will find all the variations shown above. The asterisk is called a "wildcard" in computerspeak.

One way to quickly assess your students' keyword knowledge is to use the *Keywords Assessment* (Handout U-7) and the accompanying *Keywords Scoring Guide* (Handout U-8). Have students trade papers for scoring so that you can use the pretest as a teaching and discussion tool. For additional practice, you can use the *Keywords Practice 1* (Handout U-9) and the *Keywords Practice 2* (Handout U-10) activities. These are not only excellent diagnostic assessment instruments for you, but fabulous teaching tools when used for class discussion and reflection afterward.

 An easy way to keep track of the keywords students have used is to use the drop-down menu in the search box. Modern Web browsers list all the keywords that have been tried during a search session in case the user wishes to go back to an earlier search.

A more direct method for assessing students' keyword strategies is to use the *Scavenger Hunt Assessment* (Handout U-11). It's fun for the kids and very revealing for you. If you have the luxury of time, administer the test in small groups so you are better able to observe each student's approach to the task. In addition to trying to find the answers quickly, students must record the keyword combinations they try and the URL where they finally found the answer. This is analogous to "showing your work" on a math question because we're more interested in the process than in the answer. Beware of students who are tempted to sneak a peek at a neighbor's screen or yell out the answer. However, even if they do, everyone must still use effective keywords to arrive at a website that contains the answer. As always, save time for a group strategy discussion and/or Reflection Log entry at the end of the activity.

If you find that some of your students need guidance in focused keyword selection, you can assign additional scavenger hunts, such as the *Literal Scavenger Hunt* (Handout U-12), the *Substitution Scavenger Hunt* (Handout U-13), and the *Double Focus Areas Scavenger Hunt* (Handout U-14). Answers to all the Scavenger Hunts are found in Handout U-15, *Scavenger Hunt Answers*. Note that these activities may seem decontextualized if you haven't yet introduced the *Category Flowcharts* (Handouts Q-5 to Q-7) from Chapter 4.

Please note that we are not suggesting that topic + focus is the only effective keyword strategy. It's just that we want to ensure that every student has at least *one* reliable keyword method in her inquiry strategy toolbox. With struggling learners, we have even resorted to having three students stand in front of the class and bob up and down in sequence, repeating, "TOPIC—AND—FOCUS!" This is so hilarious and embarrassing that every student is quick to remember the mantra.

After instruction and practice in keyword selection, most students will notice a dramatic change in their speed and accuracy and will be very pleased with themselves. We have fond memories of students of all ages and abilities who have rushed home to share the topic + focus strategy with their family members, thus assuming the "mantle of the expert" that is so desirable in constructivist education. In fact, all the teachers with whom we've worked have bemoaned that it's taken this long for someone to help *them* learn how to search effectively.

After a week or two of keyword assessment and instruction, students are usually eager to try their own inquiry projects. Be sure to make the IMPORTANT POINT that a scavenger hunt is qualitatively different from an inquiry project. The former is a quick search for a tiny piece of information, whereas the latter is much more complex, requiring the synthesis of ideas and information from a variety of resources. We recommend that you use some of the project planning materials in

 Use the information you find on a hit list or website to think of new keywords; for example, when searching for the history of skiing, you might find the word "origin" on a website. Try using "origin" in your next search.

Chapter 4 to scaffold students' inquiries, especially Handout Q-13, the *Project Planning Template*. Have them keep track of the keywords they use so that they become metacognitive about their keyword habits. Throughout the inquiry project, have the students keep daily Reflection Logs and take time to share everyone's keyword strategies regularly.

At the end of each of the QUEST chapters in this book, we supply a lesson plan that you can adapt for use in your classroom. In this chapter, we offer the *Search Engine Lesson Plan—Elementary Level* (Handout U-16) and the *Search Engine Lesson Plan—Middle Level* (Handout U-17).

"I wish I'd known these things in my master's program! I was getting hits of 15,000 and I was just scanning through them for hours and not getting what I needed."
—Deborah, seventh-grade special educator

Summary

This chapter on Understanding Resources focused on strategies for identifying resources, managing computers, utilizing the Internet, choosing search tools, and selecting keywords. Researchers have repeatedly found that many people, even adults, have difficulty searching for information on the Web; therefore, these skills must be taught, practiced, and reinforced. Because computer teachers and media specialists do not have sustained time with students, classroom teachers need to help students develop strategies for Understanding Resources.

In the next chapter, on Evaluating, we present strategies for determining the "usefulness" and "truthfulness" of information found on the Web. Not only do students need to be able to determine whether a website is worth visiting when viewing the search engine results, but once there, must decide whether the website actually contains the desired information. Further, they must determine whether the information is reliable.

Handouts

The following chart lists the assessment tools, activities, and handouts that were discussed in this chapter on Understanding Resources. Feel free to modify any of these tools, especially if some have become outdated. If you download them from our companion website, you can print the handouts in color and/or make changes to suit your students' needs. As with the handouts in all other chapters, do not attempt to use all of them in one lesson or unit. Decide which seem most useful for your students, and save the rest for another time.

Number	Name of handout	Purpose
U-1	Technical Knowledge Assessment	Assess technical knowledge
U-2	Technical Knowledge Scoring Guide	Score technical knowledge
U-3	Search Engines Assessment	Assess search engine knowledge
U-4	Search Engines Scoring Guide	Score search engine knowledge
U-5	Search Engine Comparison—Elementary Level	Practice search strategies
U-6	Search Engine Comparison—Middle Level	Practice search strategies
U-7	Keywords Assessment	Assess keyword knowledge
U-8	Keywords Scoring Guide	Score keyword knowledge
U-9	Keywords Practice 1	Assess keyword knowledge
U-10	Keywords Practice 2	Assess keyword knowledge
U-11	Scavenger Hunt Assessment	Assess keyword strategies
U-12	Literal Scavenger Hunt	Practice keyword strategies
U-13	Substitution Scavenger Hunt	Practice keyword strategies
U-14	Double Focus Area Scavenger Hunt	Practice keyword strategies
U-15	Scavenger Hunt Answers	Score keyword strategies
U-16	Search Engine Lesson Plan—Elementary Level	Model search strategies
U-17	Search Engine Lesson Plan—Middle Level	Model search strategies

HANDOUT U-1. Technical Knowledge Assessment

Name _____ Class _____ Date _____

☐ Pretest   ☐ Posttest

Choose the best answer by circling the letter.

---

1. How do you turn on a PC?

   a. Put in a CD   b. Power button   c. Enter button   d. Put in a disk

---

2. How do you turn off a PC?

   a. Log off   b. Unplug it   c. Start>Turn off   d. Off button

---

3. How do you unfreeze a PC computer?

   a. Ctrl+Alt+Delete   b. Power button   c. Unplug it   d. Ctrl+Tab+Shift

---

4. How do you open a software program?

   a. Program button   b. Taskbar   c. Open button   d. Start Menu

---

5. What is the Internet?

   a. A network   b. A chat room   c. A web   d. A highway

---

6. What is the name of a popular Web browser?

   a. PowerPoint   b. Web Surfer   c. Browse It   d. Internet Explorer

---

7. How do you save a website address?

   a. Edit>Save   b. Favorites   c. Edit>Save As   d. Save button

---

8. What is the name of a popular search engine?

   a. Topic + Focus   b. Engine Works   c. Google   d. Searcher

---

9. How do you reload a website?

   a. Refresh   b. Stop   c. Home   d. Back

---

10. How can you see which websites you've visited on a certain day?

   a. Back   b. Favorites   c. Edit>Find   d. History

HANDOUT U-2. Technical Knowledge Scoring Guide

Give 1 point for each correct answer.

1. How do you turn on a PC?   b. Power button
2. How do you turn off a PC?   c. Start>Turn off
3. How do you unfreeze a PC computer?   a. Ctrl+Alt+Delete
4. How do you open a software program?   d. Start Menu
5. What is the Internet?   a. A network
6. What is the name of a popular Web browser?   d. Internet Explorer
7. How do you save a website address?   b. Favorites
8. What is the name of a popular search engine?   c. Google
9. How do you reload a website?   a. Refresh
10. How can you see which websites you've visited on a certain day?   d. History

HANDOUT U-3. Search Engines Assessment

Name _____ Class _____ Date _____

Choose the best answer by circling the letter.

1. Which search engine is designed for entering whole research questions?

   a. Google   b. WebCrawler   c. Yahoo   d. Ask.com

2. Which search engine is designed for entering keywords?

   a. Google   b. WebCrawler   c. Yahoo   d. Ask.com

3. Which search engine is designed for browsing categories?

   a. Google   b. WebCrawler   c. Yahoo   d. Ask.com

4. Which search engine is designed for searching other search engines?

   a. Google   b. WebCrawler   c. Yahoo   d. Ask.com

5. How does a search engine work?

   a. searches the   b. searches   c. searches its   d. searches its
      Internet   the Web   database   server

Circle ALL the answers that fit.

6. Which search engines let you search just for images?

   a. Google   b. WebCrawler   c. Yahoo   d. Ask.com

7. Which search engines have a spellchecker?

   a. Google   b. WebCrawler   c. Yahoo   d. Ask.com

8. Which search engines show the number of search results?

   a. Google   b. WebCrawler   c. Yahoo   d. Ask.com

9. Which search engines include sponsored links?

   a. Google   b. WebCrawler   c. Yahoo   d. Ask.com

10. Which search engines let you search just for video?

    a. Google   b. WebCrawler   c. Yahoo   d. Ask.com

HANDOUT U-4. Search Engines Scoring Guide

Give 1 point for each correct answer (5 possible).

1. Which search engine is best for entering whole research questions?   d. Ask.com
2. Which search engine is designed for entering keywords?   a. Google
3. Which search engine is designed for browsing categories?   c. Yahoo
4. Which search engine is designed for searching other search engines?   b. WebCrawler

5. How does a search engine work?
 	
                        c. searches its
                            database

Give as many points as indicated after each question (15 possible).

6. Which search engines let you search just for images? (4)   a. Google   b. WebCrawler   c. Yahoo   d. Ask.com
7. Which search engines have a spellchecker? (2)   a. Google   d. Ask.com
8. Which search engines show the number of search results? (4)   a. Google   b. WebCrawler   c. Yahoo   d. Ask.com
9. Which search engines include sponsored links? (3)   a. Google   c. Yahoo   d. Ask.com
10. Which search engines let you search just for video? (2)   b. WebCrawler   c. Yahoo

Note: Since search engine features change regularly, check our website for updates.

HANDOUT U-5. Search Engine Comparison—Elementary Level

Name _____ Class _____ Date _____

You are trying to find out the five most popular cat breeds. See what happens in each of these search engines before you search a website for the answer.

Go to Yahooligans @ *www.yahooligans.com*

Try a broad search: **cat** How many hits did you get? _____

Try a misspelled phrase: **poplar cat breed** Did a spellchecker come up? _____

Try keywords: **popular + cat + breed** How many hits did you get? _____

Try a question: **What are the most popular cat breeds?** Which words does Yahooligans search for? _____

Go to Ask for Kids @ *www.askforkids.com*

Try a broad search: **cat** How many hits did you get? _____

Try a misspelled phrase: **poplar cat breed** Did a spellchecker come up? _____

Try keywords: **popular + cat + breed** How many hits did you get? _____

Try a question: **What are the most popular cat breeds?** Which words does askforkids.com search for? _____

AND NOW FOR THE ANSWER!

What are the five most popular cat breeds? _____

_____

What search engine did you use to find this info? _____

_____

What keywords did you use to find this info? _____

_____

Which website had the info? http:// _____

_____

HANDOUT U-6. Search Engine Comparison—Middle Level

Name _____ Class _____ Date _____

You are trying to find out the five most popular cat breeds. See what happens in each of these search engines before you search a website for the answer.

Go to Google @ *www.google.com*

Try a broad search: **cat** How many hits did you get? _____

Try a misspelled phrase: **poplar cat breed** Did a spellchecker come up? _____

Try keywords: **popular + cat + breed** How many hits did you get? _____

Try a question: **What are the most popular cat breeds?** Which words does Google search for?

_____

Go to Yahoo or Yahooligans @ *www.yahoo.com* or *www.yahooligans.com*

Try a broad search: **cat** How many hits did you get? _____

Try a misspelled phrase: **poplar cat breed** Did a spellchecker come up? _____

Try keywords: **popular + cat + breed** How many hits did you get? _____

Try a question: **What are the most popular cat breeds?** Which words does Yahoo search for?

_____

Go to Ask.com or Ask for Kids @ *www.ask.com* or *www.askforkids.com*

Try a broad search: **cat** How many hits did you get? _____

Try a misspelled phrase: **poplar cat breed** Did a spellchecker come up? _____

Try keywords: **popular + cat + breed** How many hits did you get? _____

Try a question: **What are the most popular cat breeds?** Which words does Ask.com search for?

_____

Go to WebCrawler @ *www.webcrawler.com*

Try a broad search: **cat** How many hits did you get? _____

Try a misspelled phrase: **poplar cat breed** Did a spellchecker come up? _____

Try keywords: **popular + cat + breed** How many hits did you get? _____

Try a question: **What are the most popular cat breeds?** Which words does WebCrawler search for? _____

AND NOW FOR THE ANSWER!

What are the five most popular cat breeds? _____

What search engine did you use to find this info? _____

What keywords did you use to find this info? _____

Which website had the info? _____

HANDOUT U-7. Keywords Assessment

Name _____ Class _____ Date _____

☐ Pretest ☐ Posttest

Decide if these keywords would be effective in a search engine like Google.
Circle your answer and explain why, **using the reasons below**.

1. soccer + history	good bad	
2. sports	good bad	
3. What is the history of soccer?	good bad	
4. soccer + equipment	good bad	
5. world history of soccer	good bad	
6. "soccer teams"	good bad	
7. soccer	good bad	
8. soccer history	good bad	
9. soccer + sports	good bad	
10. soccer balls and nets	good bad	

Good keywords have: topic + focus, topic focus, or "topic focus"
Bad keywords have: no topic, no focus, or extra words

From *Reading the Web* by Maya B. Eagleton and Elizabeth Dobler. Copyright 2007 by The Guilford Press. Permission to photocopy this handout is granted to purchasers of this book for personal use only (see copyright page for details).

147

HANDOUT U-8. Keywords Scoring Guide

☐ Pretest   ☐ Posttest

Give 1 point for the correct answer and 2 points for the reason. Total possible is 30.

1. soccer + history	(good) bad	topic + focus
2. sports	good (bad)	no topic
3. What is the history of soccer?	good (bad)	extra words
4. soccer + equipment	(good) bad	topic + focus
5. world history of soccer	good (bad)	extra words
6. "soccer teams"	(good) bad	"topic focus"
7. soccer	good (bad)	no focus
8. soccer history	(good) bad	topic focus
9. soccer + sports	good (bad)	no focus (TRICK QUESTION)
10. soccer balls and nets	good (bad)	extra words

HANDOUT U-9. Keywords Practice 1

Name _____ Class _____ Date _____

Decide if these keywords would be effective in a search engine like Google.
Circle your answer and explain why, **using the reasons below**.

1. tigers	good bad	
2. tiger + habitat	good bad	
3. What is the tiger's habitat?	good bad	
4. tiger + animal	good bad	
5. tigers around the world	good bad	
6. "tiger habitat"	good bad	
7. animals	good bad	
8. tiger prey and diet	good bad	
9. tiger + prey	good bad	
10. tiger diet	good bad	

Good keywords have: topic + focus, topic focus, or "topic focus"
Bad keywords have: no topic, no focus, or extra words

Name _____ Class _____ Date _____

Decide if these keywords would be effective in a search engine like Google.
Circle your answer and explain why, **using the reasons below**.

1. "Ben Franklin"   good   bad

2. "Ben Franklin" + invention   good   bad

3. inventors   good   bad

4. "Ben Franklin" invent   good   bad

5. Famous inventions of Ben Franklin's   good   bad

6. "Ben Franklin" + career   good   bad

7. Ben Franklin's career and inventions   good   bad

8. inventions + career   good   bad

9. What did "Ben Franklin" invent?   good   bad

10. "Ben Franklin" + "famous invention"   good   bad

Good keywords have: topic + focus, topic focus, or "topic focus"
Bad keywords have: no topic, no focus, or extra words

HANDOUT U-11. Scavenger Hunt Assessment

Name _____ Class _____ Date _____

☐ Pretest   ☐ Posttest

DIRECTIONS

- Open an Internet browser (such as Internet Explorer or Netscape Navigator)
- Go to a search engine (such as *www.google.com* or *www.yahoo.com*, NOT Ask.com)
- Find answers to the following three questions, noting how and where you found the information.
- You have 10 minutes to complete each search. Your teacher will tell you when to move on to the next question.

PRE: How many actors have played James Bond? POST: What is the capital of Denmark?

Answer _____

Search Engine(s): _____

Keyword(s): _____

URL: http:// _____

PRE: Where is Mount Rushmore? POST: Where do anteaters come from?

Answer _____

Search Engine(s): _____

Keyword(s): _____

URL: http:// _____

PRE: Which American president got stuck in a bathtub? POST: Who is the head coach for the Sun Devils hockey team?

Answer _____

Search Engine(s): _____

Keyword(s): _____

URL: http:// _____

HANDOUT U-12. Literal Scavenger Hunt

Name _____ Class _____ Date _____

Determine your topic and focus, then use them as keywords for searching.

Question 1: Who was the inventor of basketball?

topic ⬭ **+** ▭ focus

Answer _____

Search Engine(s): _____

URL: _____

EXTRA: What year?

Question 2: How many directors did *Shrek I* have?

topic ⬭ **+** ▭ focus

Answer _____

Search Engine(s): _____

URL: _____

EXTRA: Name them.

Question 3: In which country is Mount Everest?

topic ⬭ **+** ▭ focus

Answer _____

Search Engine(s): _____

URL: _____

EXTRA: How tall?

HANDOUT U-13. Substitution Scavenger Hunt

Name _____ Class _____ Date _____

Determine your topic and focus, then use them as keywords for searching.

Question 1: Where is the Country Music Hall of Fame?

topic + focus

Answer _____
Search Engine(s): _____
URL: _____

EXTRA: What other tourist spots are here? _____

Question 2: Who played Chewbacca in the original *Star Wars* movies?

topic + focus

Answer _____
Search Engine(s): _____
URL: _____

EXTRA: How tall is he? _____

Question 3: When was King Tut's tomb found?

topic + focus

Answer _____
Search Engine(s): _____
URL: _____

EXTRA: Who found it? _____

HANDOUT U-14. Double Focus Area Scavenger Hunt

Name _____ Class _____ Date _____

Write your topic with two focus areas, then use them as keywords for searching.

Question 1: What is the most popular girl's name in the United States?

topic ○ + focus ▢ + focus ▢

Answer _____

Search Engine(s): _____

URL: _____

EXTRA: Boy's name? _____

Question 2: In what year did women gain the right to vote in America?

topic ○ + focus ▢ + focus ▢

Answer _____

Search Engine(s): _____

URL: _____

EXTRA: What were these female activists called? _____

Question 3: Who was the first African American to win the Nobel Prize for Literature?

topic ○ + focus ▢ + focus ▢

Answer _____

Search Engine(s): _____

URL: _____

EXTRA: What has she written? _____

HANDOUT U-15. Scavenger Hunt Answers

Scavenger Hunt Pretest (Handout U-11)

QUESTION	KEYWORDS	ANSWER	TYPE OF QUERY
How many actors have played James Bond?	"James Bond" + actors	6	keywords in question
Where is Mount Rushmore?	"Mount Rushmore" + location	South Dakota	one substitution needed
Which American president got stuck in a bathtub?	president + stuck + bathtub	William Taft	three keywords

Literal Scavenger Hunt (Handout U-12)

QUESTION	KEYWORDS	ANSWER	EXTRA
Who was the inventor of basketball?	basketball + inventor	James Naismith	1891
How many directors did *Shrek I* have?	"Shrek I" + directors	2	Andrew Adamson & Vicky Jenson
In which country is Mount Everest?	"Mount Everest" + country	Nepal	29,035 ft. (8,850 m)

Substitution Scavenger Hunt (Handout U-13)

QUESTION	KEYWORDS	ANSWER	EXTRA
Where is the Country Music Hall of Fame?	"Country Music Hall of Fame" + location	Nashville, Tennessee	Opryland Hotel
Who played Chewbacca in the original *Star Wars* movies?	Chewbacca + actor	Peter Mayhew	7'3"
When was King Tut's tomb found?	"King Tut's tomb" + year	1922	Howard Carter

Double Focus Area Scavenger Hunt (Handout U-14)

QUESTION	KEYWORDS	ANSWER	EXTRA
What is the most popular girl's name in the United States?	"popular name" + girl + United States	Emily or Emma	Jacob
In what year did women gain the right to vote in America?	vote + women + year	1920	suffragists
Who was the first African American to win the Nobel Prize for Literature?	"Nobel Prize" + literature + "African American"	Toni Morrison	Beloved

Scavenger Hunt Assessment (Handout U-11)

QUESTION	KEYWORDS	ANSWER	TYPE OF QUERY
What is the capital of Denmark?	Denmark + capital	Copenhagen	keywords in question
Where do anteaters come from?	anteater + origin	South America	one substitution needed
Who is the head coach for the Sun Devils hockey team?	"Sun Devils" + hockey + coach	Mike De Angelis	three keywords

HANDOUT U-16. Search Engine Lesson Plan—Elementary Level (page 1 of 2)

Objective

Students will demonstrate the ability to distinguish between ineffective and effective search strategies and will compare the features of two popular search engines.

Time

One or two class periods

Materials

1. *QUEST Inquiry Model* (Handout P-11)
2. Teaching computer and LCD projector
3. Internet computers for students (OK for students to share)
4. Timer or clock
5. *Search Engine Comparison* (Handout U-5) on paper or on the computers

Assessment Options

1. *Computer Survey* (Handout P-7)
2. *Internet Vocabulary* (Handout P-9)

Introduction

1. Tell students you will be teaching them a strategy for searching the Web that many other students have found useful. Contextualize the lesson, using the *QUEST Inquiry Model* (Handout P-11), by pointing out that they are in the U phase of the QUEST, which includes using good search strategies.
2. Have students brainstorm why Web searching is useful in this class, in other classes, and outside of school. This can be done in pairs, in small groups, or as a whole class.
3. Generate excitement and get student buy-in on the purpose of the lesson before proceeding. Tell them that strong search strategies will help them find information faster on the Web.

Modeling

1. Tell the kids to imagine that you're doing a pretend research project on cats.
2. Show students what happens when you use the "dot-com" approach by typing *www.cat.com* straight into the URL field instead of using a search tool (the Caterpillar machinery site will appear).
3. Ask the class, "Did we find the info we wanted?" Remark that the "dot-com" strategy is not useful for searching. It is only useful for finding known websites.
4. Solicit student suggestions for websites that might have info on cats (petco, discovery, etc.). This is the "shopping mall" approach.

5. Before trying any of these sites, say that what you really want to learn is about the types of *cat breeds*.
6. Use a timer or clock to see how long it takes to find info on cat breeds by going straight to some of these commercial sites. Talk out loud as you and the class try to find the info. Stop after 10 minutes.
7. Now do a Yahooligans search for <cat breed> and have everyone note the improvement in speed, as compared to the shopping mall and dot-com strategies. You will probably find a perfect website on the first hit and find the cat breed information in less than a minute.
8. Finally, show your students the differences between:
   a. intentionally going to a search engine website (such as Yahooligans),
   b. clicking on the search button on a browser (which typically brings up a default search engine such as msn), and
   c. searching within a website that has an embedded search tool (a good example is *pbskids.org/go*, which has its own search tool).

Practice

1. Pass out the *Search Engine Comparison* (Handout U-5) or have kids bring it up on their computers.
2. Have kids work individually, in pairs, or in small groups at the computer.
3. Circulate to observe and offer support.

Scaffolding

1. For anyone with visual disabilities:
   a. Increase the font size in the Web browser (View>Text Size>Largest), or
   b. Make the print larger on the handout.
2. Provide a scribe for weak writers.
3. Provide a typist for weak keyboarders.
4. Pair up weaker readers with stronger readers for decoding.
5. Allow more time for slower workers.

Feedback

1. Have students gather as a whole class to debrief.
2. Discuss the differences between the search engines.
3. Share answers to the "popular cat breed" question.
4. Share any additional observations, opinions, or questions.

Ticket Out the Door

Have each student name two popular search engines for kids (Yahooligans and Ask for Kids).

HANDOUT U-17. Search Engine Lesson Plan—Middle Level (page 1 of 2)

Objective

Students will demonstrate the ability to distinguish between ineffective and effective search strategies and will compare the features of four popular search engines.

Time

One or two class periods

Materials

1. *QUEST Inquiry Model* (Handout P-11)
2. Teaching computer and LCD projector
3. Internet computers for students (OK for students to share)
4. Timer or clock
5. *Search Engine Comparison* (Handout U-6) on paper or on the computers

Assessment Options

1. *Computer Survey* (Handout P-7)
2. *Internet Vocabulary* (Handout P-9)

Introduction

1. Tell students you will be teaching them a transferable strategy for searching the Web that many other students have found useful. Contextualize the lesson, using the *QUEST Inquiry Model* (Handout P-11), by pointing out that they are in the U phase of the QUEST, which includes using good search strategies.
2. Have students brainstorm why Web searching is useful in this class, in other classes, and outside of school. This can be done in pairs, in small groups, or as a whole class.
3. Generate excitement and get student buy-in on the purpose of the lesson before proceeding. Tell them that strong search strategies will help them find information faster on the Web.

Modeling

1. Tell the kids you're doing a mock research project on cats.
2. Show students what happens when you use the "dot-com" approach by typing *www.cat.com* straight into the URL field instead of using a search tool (the Caterpillar machinery site will appear).
3. Ask the class, "Did we find the info we wanted?" Remark that the "dot-com" strategy is not useful for searching. It is only useful for finding known websites.
4. Solicit student suggestions for websites that might have info on cats (petco, discovery, etc.). This is the "shopping mall" approach.
5. Before trying any of these sites, say that what you really want to learn is about the types of *cat breeds*.

6. Use a timer or clock to see how long it takes to find info on cat breeds by going straight to some of these commercial sites. Talk out loud as you and the class try to find the info. Stop after 10 minutes.
7. Now do a Google search for <cat breed>, and have everyone note the improvement in speed, as compared to the shopping mall and dot-com strategies. You will probably find a perfect website on the first hit and find the cat breed information in less than a minute.
8. Finally, show your students the differences between:
   a. Intentionally going to a search engine website (such as Google),
   b. Clicking on the search button on a browser (which typically brings up a default search engine such as msn), and
   c. Searching within a website that has an embedded search tool (a good example is *www.nasa.gov*, which has a prominent "Find it @ NASA" search tool).

Practice

1. Pass out the *Search Engine Comparison* (Handout U-6), or have kids bring it up on their computers.
2. Have kids work individually, in pairs, or in small groups at the computer
3. Circulate to observe and offer support.

Scaffolding

1. If someone is overwhelmed by all the text on the handout, change the spacing to 2.0 and print it back to back.
2. For anyone with visual disabilities:
   a. Increase the font size in the Web browser (View>Text Size>Largest), or
   b. Make the print larger on the handout.
3. Provide a scribe for weak writers.
4. Provide a typist for weak keyboarders.
5. Pair up weaker readers with stronger readers for decoding.
6. Allow more time for slower workers.

Feedback

1. Have students gather as a whole class to debrief.
2. Discuss the differences between the search engines.
3. Share answers to the "popular cat breed" question.
4. Share any additional observations, opinions, or questions.

Ticket Out the Door

Have each student name three popular search engines. (Google, Yahoo or Yahooligans, Ask.com or Ask for Kids, WebCrawler, other).

6 EVALUATING

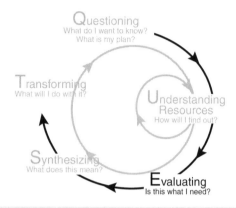

KEY IDEAS

▶ Evaluation of information is important in order for citizens to make informed choices as they participate in democracy.

▶ The guiding questions for this chapter are, "Is this information useful?" and "Is this information true?"

▶ Evaluating websites is challenging because anyone is free to publish anything on the Internet.

▶ Clues about the quality of information can be found in the web address (URL) and on the website once an Internet reader knows what to look for and what is meant only as a distraction.

▶ Comparing and contrasting information found on various websites is an effective way to validate information and develop critical literacy skills.

We build up our store of knowledge not so much for its own sake but in order to develop insight. With insight, we think more deeply and critically. We question, interpret, and evaluate what we read. In this way, reading can change thinking.

—Harvey and Goudvis (2000, p. 9)

In this chapter, we focus on the skill of Evaluating ideas and information, especially those found on the Web. This third—and ongoing—phase of the QUEST Internet inquiry process involves making decisions about whether information is needed and whether it is true. Evaluation skills also play an important role in all of the information we receive through reading, listening, and viewing.

Information Literacy Standard: Evaluate information critically and competently.

Why Is It Important to Evaluate?

Evaluation facilitates the separation of the wheat from the chaff, the important from the unimportant, and the useful from the useless. If, as learners, we gave every bit of information we encountered equal consideration, we would drown in a sea of thoughts and ideas. Evaluation helps us to prioritize our time, energy, and money as we strive to make the most informed decision possible when seeking the value or judging the worth of an object or idea. This skill is critical in a society where citizens are expected to make informed choices as they participate in decision-making processes. So, one of our goals as educators is preparing students to find, evaluate, and use quality information in an efficient manner. We must teach students to think critically about what they see and hear and to ask questions of themselves and others as they seek to validate new ideas.

Language Arts Standard: Monitor selection for viewing based on purpose and quality; make critical judgments when reading and viewing; recognize propaganda, stereotyping, and statement of bias; recognize and communicate author's purpose.

Such a lofty goal is made even more challenging when students are finding, evaluating, and using information from the Web. The novelty of technology and the captivation of multimedia graphics have created an expectation that an answer to every question can be located on the Web with only a few clicks of the mouse. Information on the Web looks authentic through what appear to be official publications of everything from rumors to facts, with the boundaries between the two blurred. Traditional indicators of credibility, such as author and publishing information, are often difficult to find or perhaps even missing from websites. Asking critical questions about information becomes challenging when the origin of the information is not accounted for, or is done so using other unreliable sources. Determining the importance of ideas can become a complex task when information is gathered from the integration of different media—text, graphics, sound, video, and animation—and the learner must determine what is useful and what is meant to distract.

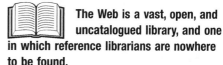

The Web is a vast, open, and uncatalogued library, and one in which reference librarians are nowhere to be found.
—Sorapure, Inglesby, and Yatchisin (1998, p. 410)

Our traditional view of critical thinking and critical reading is now more important than ever (Jonassen, 2000; Luke, 2002). For students, this means becoming critical consumers of information by comparing and contrasting facts and ideas within a website and from multiple websites. For teachers, this means an increased responsibility for teaching students how to recognize bias, how to balance information with other sources, and how information fits in a larger context—in other words, teaching students to consider everything they see, hear, and read on the Internet with a critical eye. Leu (1997) refers to the term "healthy skeptic" when describing the role that both teachers and students must play in effective Internet reading. This role of questioning information extends beyond just the text of the website and includes multimedia features as well. Learners should question what they see and be aware that visual information in the form of images and graphics can be manipulated or used to convey a certain idea in the way an author chooses.

Visual literacy, or the ability to understand and create visual images, takes on an important role for the critical reader. Written text has become slightly less prominent as other modes of conveying ideas—namely, visual representations—have helped to reshape the ways texts present ideas (Kress, 1998). Today our students frequently encounter informational text with visuals that enhance, explain, and replace ideas once typically found in written text. Teachers can prepare students to understand the visual images they encounter by teaching about the ways in which

 Authorship is no longer rare.
—Kress (2003, p. 6)

images persuade us, the connections (or lack of them) between the text and images, and the importance of locating and scanning images for details.

Critical literacy goes beyond reading the Web to focus on critically thinking about information by interpreting meaning and assessing appropriateness (Burbules, 1997), whether that information comes from media, print text, or Internet text. Critical literacy also goes beyond our classroom, to promote critical and creative thinking across content areas. "Critical literacy is but one literacy that combines with other literacies to develop a continually inquiring human mind" (Langford, 2001, p. 18). Langford, a teacher and library media specialist, describes the connection between the process of accessing and understanding information and the development of thinking skills. This connection forces us to "adopt a manner of continuous learning in order to function well in society" (Langford, 2001, p. 18). Such deep

 Library Media Standard:
Apply evaluative criteria to selection and interpretation of information; explore information and arguments from various points of view.

thinking calls upon the skills of analysis, evaluation, and synthesis. The concept of critical literacy is tightly woven among the steps of the inquiry process by empowering learners to be creative, critical, constructive users of information.

When Do We Evaluate?

Evaluating information is already a part of our lives and the lives of our students. When we encounter new information, we compare the ideas to what we already know to determine if there is a place to fit this new information into our current understanding. When seeking information about the world's tallest man, for example, a learner asks himself if this information found in a world records book matches what he already knows from past experience about the height of most people. He may also read other record books, magazines, or newspapers for further information. At various points in his search, he may pause to wonder if this information will be useful. Can he impress his friends and family with this little-known fact? He may also want to know if the information is true. "Can a man really be over 7 feet tall? Where does he buy pants? How does he fit in a car?" During these thoughts and questions, the learner is informally evaluating the information from his collection of print resources. Although his informal evaluation is important and useful, our world record sleuth has had some help with determining the quality of information he has encountered. He is not the first stop in the evaluation chain, which initially begins with authors, editors, and publishers, all of whom have provided additional layers of evaluation before the printed text reaches his hands. Facts have been checked and the authenticity of visuals has been determined.

Access to vast amounts of information is not the whole answer. The power to discover the right info quickly and easily, to separate nice to know from need to know info is essential if superhighway users do not drown in electronic junk info. . . . An info flood does not necessarily mean that people become informed.   —Kehoe (1993, p. 11)

The forms of text and multimedia that we encounter in our everyday lives come with some type of evaluation made by others who are in the business of making judgments about quality. We may make a cursory evaluation of what we see and read, knowing that others have made an in-depth evaluation before it reaches our eyes. Books, magazines, and newspaper articles are proofread by editors and must meet the standards of the publisher. Even multimedia such as television, movies, and video games are scrutinized before they are available for viewing or purchase. Television programs have a labeling system, with a symbol displayed at the beginning of a program indicating that the program has met the standards set by the network and the Federal Communications Commission, along with serving as a guide to parents who are monitoring the viewing of their children. Movies receive a rating to inform the audience of the appropriate age level and level of guidance needed for those viewing a movie. Even video games carry symbols representing the age for which a video game is appropriate. Some might say these labels are not accurate, do not screen out enough inappropriate content, or do not have sufficiently high standards. Others, especially parents, recognize the need for some assistance in evaluating the quality of multimedia children are encountering. Regardless, we are not left totally on our own to evaluate the appropriateness of print or these other multimedia sources.

Math Standard: Evaluate problems with variable expressions; make approximations and judge the reasonableness of results.

Unlike these other media, the Internet has no system of checks and balances for evaluating, labeling, or providing any indication of appropriateness. The learner is directly linked to the author or website creator, with no layers in place to filter out untrue or inappropriate information. The responsibility for evaluation falls directly on the learner, which can be a daunting task for our students. Parents and teachers share concerns about students encountering incorrect and/or inappropriate website information, which forms one of the foundational reasons for teaching students strategies for evaluation.

What Characterizes Evaluation?

When they are evaluating information, we want learners to "weigh information carefully and wisely to determine its quality" (American School Library Association, 1998, p. 2), whether that information is found in print text or on the Internet. Readers of all types of information must know how to locate and determine the quality of information, along with recognizing their own biases and how these may influence their search for answers to their questions. However, readers of the Internet must especially focus on determining the *usefulness* and the *truthfulness* of information encountered on websites because the reader is the primary evaluator of this information (Figure 6.1).

 **Internet technologies raise new issues about our relationship to information. As students scan search results and select particular websites to examine more closely, they'll need strategies for efficiently evaluating the credibility and usefulness of the information they find.**
—Leu, Leu, and Coiro (2004, p. 86)

Evaluating Usefulness

In determining the *usefulness* of information, the Internet reader asks herself, "Does this information meet my needs and interests?" This question is the learner's guiding focus as she makes decisions about what to read, when to read, how fast to read, and when to stop reading. Decisions about the usefulness of information on the Internet are often made in a matter of seconds. Frequently, a learner glances over a webpage and quickly determines if the information is going to be useful and interesting. In our work with Internet readers, we have found that elementary and middle school learners often make hasty decisions about what to read on the Web, which causes them to either waste time on irrelevant information or to bypass useful sources

FIGURE 6.1. Evaluating usefulness and truthfulness.

of information (Eagleton et al., 2003). Teaching students to determine the usefulness of information found on the Web is a matter of instructing them to take a more careful look and their having the background knowledge to understand what they see.

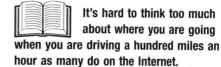 **It's hard to think too much about where you are going when you are driving a hundred miles an hour as many do on the Internet.**
—Kajder (2003, p. 61)

Evaluating Search Engine Results

An Internet reader's evaluation skills come into use from the moment an Internet search begins. So, in a sense, evaluating begins with the selection of a search engine, although many learners typically find their favorite search engine and return to it regularly. In Chapter 5, we described specific search engines and provided information for determining the search engine that meets your needs based on your purpose for reading and the type of information needed. We also shared several strategies for selecting keywords for beginning your Internet search.

After a user selects a search engine and types in a keyword, a list of websites is presented. The search results list, or hit list, is the first exposure students have to the information they're seeking and is critical for guiding their progress. Right away a learner uses evaluation skills to select the website that seems to be the most useful by asking himself the question, "Which website will match my informational needs?" Many students have a hard time identifying good sites from the hit list (Kafai & Bates, 1997) and have difficulty distinguishing between appropriate and inappropriate results (Large & Beheshti, 2000). When a search engine returns a hit list of potential websites, novices and weak readers sometimes click on all the hits in numerical order, whereas stronger searchers are more selective, using their knowledge of domain names and URLs to determine the likelihood of a good match. Figure 6.2 shows typical middle schoolers' responses to the question, "When you're looking at a hit list, how do you decide which websites to visit?"

Regardless of which strategy they employ, it is critical that learners have a research focus firmly in mind by this stage or they will lose valuable time surfing websites that may not contain answers to their questions. Selecting a useful website

TYPE OF STRATEGY	TYPICAL RESPONSE
Random Strategy	"I randomly pick one, and if that doesn't work then I pick the others."
Numerical Strategy	"I just, well, usually I click on the first one, and if that's not the one I want, I go to the second one, and I just go down the list."
Judicious Strategy	"I read the little paragraphs they have underneath and see which one I think is the best for what I want."

FIGURE 6.2. Students' website selection strategies.

Our students must become proficient in accessing and analyzing information so that a level of understanding can be reached. When this is achieved, information has been converted to knowledge and stored for future reference.
—Sutherland-Smith, (2002, p. 662)

involves a learner's prior experiences and skills in critically analyzing the quality of a website, based on the limited information provided by the search engine. A lack of prior knowledge about using search engines or experience with the skill of evaluating can cause a learner to struggle with evaluating search results and become frustrated when faced with many choices of website links. Without evaluation tools on which to rely, a frustrated learner may resort to making uncritical decisions by clicking on a site that catches his eye or one that is simply next on the list. We return to the topic of analyzing URLs below.

Evaluating Information within a Website

Once a website has been selected, a learner must quickly evaluate the usability of the website along with the quality of information. She makes a determination as to whether the website is "user friendly" by determining the ease of access to information within the site through the use of a site map, or electronic table of contents. She also looks for information that is concise, and multimedia that supports the

Researcher: "How do you know if a website has the information you want?"

Student: "I don't."

content of the site. She checks for hyperlinks that are intact and operable. Throughout this check of usability, the learner also evaluates the specific information available on the site to determine whether the facts and ideas will effectively answer her search question.

Before the learner can determine whether the information is useful, she must locate the needed information on the webpage. Sometimes this is easier said than done. The formats of webpages vary greatly, as discussed previously. With such varied forms of websites and pages, it's difficult to provide novice Internet readers with consistent information about where to find information on a website. Teachers can begin by encouraging students to notice the "reader friendliness" of a website. When reading a website, look for key ideas listed as hyperlinks across the top or down the side of the screen. Check for a way to search for a topic within the site by using an internal search engine. Watch for links across the upper part of the screen (also called a bread crumb trail) that show the path the learner has taken within the website, so it's easy to go back to previously encountered information. Notice an introductory or welcoming message describing the purpose of the site and a sponsor's name or logo to identify the site host. Determine whether the graphics help you understand the information or whether they draw your attention away through the use of bright colors, animation, or sound. All of these features can help or hinder the learner, as the creators of websites know and understand all too well.

After selecting a website with many positive characteristics, a reader begins by skimming the webpage to gain an overall perception of the type of information found at the website. If the information appears to be useful, he then returns to the page for a closer look by scanning to seek certain facts such as dates, statistics, people, or topics. When this information

 In schools, effective teachers are those who engage in continued prompts to get children to plan and monitor their own activities. Effective teachers model many forms of critical thinking. . . .
—Brown, Palincsar, and Armbruster (2004, p. 784)

appears to be present, the learner takes another pass over the website, this time pausing longer for a more careful reading because his initial evaluation has determined the information to be useful. He often makes notes, either written or typed, containing a paraphrasing of the key ideas (Chapter 8) and references to the location of these ideas.

We have just described a skilled and knowledgeable reader. Wouldn't it be nice if all of our students could read with such confidence and ease? The reality is that not all of our students are so skilled at adjusting their reading rate or making reasonable decisions about the usefulness of information. Experienced searchers and strong readers are able to skim a website and make a quick decision about relevancy, perhaps even using the Edit>Find feature to scan for their keywords on the page. However, computer novices and weaker readers often attempt to read entire webpages too thoroughly or, alternately, copy or print whole webpages without evaluating them at all. Some rely on the "snatch and grab" (Sutherland-Smith, 2002) method of collecting information rather than paraphrasing key ideas. They often look for a key word, phrase, number, or image within the body of the website. When this text "chunk" is located, it's copied and saved or the site is bookmarked for later review. More often than not, the text is not thoroughly read and might be pasted verbatim into a final project (Guinee & Eagleton, 2006).

We have also seen cases in which students with severe reading disabilities sit staring at webpages that are not even written in English, at a loss as to why they can't find any information. Conversely, we've watched strong readers zip right past "perfect" information for their inquiries, completely oblivious that they've overlooked relevant facts. For the sake of efficiency and time, students need to be taught specific skills and strategies for identifying and understanding the most useful information available on the Web.

Social Studies Standard: Interpret oral traditions; evaluate data within the historical, social, political, and economic context in which it was created; test its credibility and evaluate its bias; examine data to determine adequacy and sufficiency of evidence, bias, distortion, and propaganda; distinguish fact from opinion.

Evaluating Truthfulness

Determining the *truthfulness* of information found on the Internet is challenging for both teachers and students, since each learner must grapple with competing perspectives and conflicting facts that are apparent or underlying within Internet text. The learner must constantly be asking herself, "Is this information true?" which can be a challenge when so much information and so many different types of information are available within a website. A learner may encounter accurate information, misinformation, and useless information during just one Internet reading session.

We travel a narrow road toward our goals with a sea of seductive information to distract us on one side and a spiraling abyss of confusion and information overload on the other.
—Marchionini (1995, p. 2)

One can easily see the importance for learners to read with a critical eye, because the burden of evaluating falls on readers rather than creators of sites. We must constantly determine "what to believe, what to doubt, what to pay attention to, and what to care about" (Todd, 1998). Not only must the Internet reader make these determinations based on information encountered in the text, but she must also consider visual or nontextual features such as icons, multimedia clips, and interactive graphics. Learners must be able to distinguish between important and useful visual images versus graphics that are used to enhance the site by making it more colorful, visually appealing, or entertaining. With all of these elements to consider, we are not surprised that even high school students have difficulty explaining how they determine the quality of information on the Web (Lorenzen, 2001).

When determining the truthfulness of Internet information, whether text or visual, learners can draw from an array of clues provided by a quality website. Learners can think of themselves as detectives seeking clues in solving a mystery. Some clues are apparent and some are hidden, but all can provide the puzzle pieces for solving the mystery of the truthfulness of a website. Students can be taught to evaluate websites with respect to authority, purpose, objectivity, and timeliness.

Authority

Determining who wrote the information may be one of the most important factors in assessing truthfulness. A credible source can provide students with a good first step toward trusting the information. Typically, the host is identified on the homepage in a banner across the top of the screen or in an opening or welcoming statement. This information may be listed as a personal, company, or organizational name and may include a logo or design to symbolize the host. The author of the site may be the host or someone hired by the host to write the text for the website and should be a person who has the educational background and experience needed to be considered an "expert" on the topic. The most helpful websites provide information about the qualifications of the website author and an e-mail address so he can be contacted.

Purpose

The purpose of the website guides the types of information available and the way the information is displayed. A quality website typically includes an opening paragraph or welcoming statement that provides the reader with the purpose. For example, at the site *World Almanac for Kids* (*www.worldalmanacforkids.com*), learners find the following welcoming statement: "Welcome to The World Almanac for Kids Online! Millions of kids read The World Almanac for Kids every year. Now the bestselling book has a companion Web site—The World Almanac for Kids Online. So dive in and explore. You might even get smarter!" Purposes for websites include sharing information, persuading the reader to believe or do something, or entertaining. Determining the purpose helps a learner to recognize the view the author is taking and how this view may cause ideas to be written in a certain way.

Objectivity

Objectivity involves portraying all sides of an issue fairly, without bias or opinion. Internet readers can tell when a website is biased by identifying propaganda, untrue information, or strong opinions. Unfortunately, when a learner is new to the topic and has little prior knowledge, she may have difficulty detecting bias or opinions versus truth and facts. Website designers may even take advantage of this lack of experience by designing information to contain games, giveaways, or contests as a way to hook the learner. Watch for overgeneralizations and simplifications that have opinions not backed up with facts.

Timeliness

One of the major advantages of Internet text over printed text is timeliness, or currency. Websites are able to present information that is up-to-date because it is so easy to post updated material. This consideration is most important with information in which change occurs rapidly, such as weather reports, current events, or stock quotes. Credible websites usually contain a footer that shows the date on which the site was created or last updated. Failure to find such a date may be a clue to the learner about the lack of timeliness of the information.

Analyzing URLs

One place to begin when seeking answers to questions that arise in evaluating information on a website is with a brief study of the URLs, or Web addresses, on a hit list returned by a search engine. A tremendous amount of useful information can be gleaned from these dots, slashes, abbreviations, and words. A URL can be broken down into parts, with each part providing identification of the path leading to the website host, as follows:

http://	www.nationalgeographic.com/	solarsystem/	splash.html
type of protocol	domain name, or host	path or directory to the file	name and type of file

Teaching learners to deconstruct URLs goes a long way toward helping them to get their search off on the right foot. Then, the individual descriptions in the search results provide learners with additional clues for determining if the website will be useful and truthful. Figure 6.3 displays one choice listed in the search results for the term "solar system" using the search engine Yahooligans. The following clues help to determine the relevance of the website, the host of the website, and the potential quality of the website:

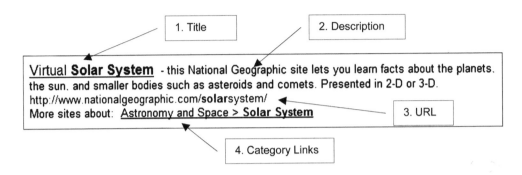

FIGURE 6.3. Clues in the search results list.

1. Title. The website title can be quite useful in determining what the website is about; however, sometimes a website has no title or the title does not clearly reflect the topic of the website. A click on this title will take the learner directly to the site.
2. Description. A brief description of the types of information found on this website is usually included. This description helps the learner to decide if the website has the needed information. Because the descriptions are brief, some important ideas may not be mentioned.
3. URL. The URL, or web address, contains bolded keywords from our search. From the URL, we can see that this website is hosted by National Geographic, a well known and respected print source of information. The domain name, such as .gov (government), .org (organization), or .edu (education), can be a clue to the reliability of the host.
4. Category Links. Search categories found within the Yahooligans directory are included as other possible links to information. A click on any of these categories will lead the learner to more links and websites related to the topic.

Understanding the various parts of a search list entry gives the reader a wealth of knowledge about the type of information likely to be encountered with a click on the link. For learners to make well-informed choices, they must take time to make a careful reading of each link. Time spent at this early search step may prevent the learner from having to sift through mountains of information—some useless—in order to answer her search question. When students know what to look for and where to look, the URL can provide a wealth of clues for determining both the usefulness and the truthfulness of information. This process does require the Internet reader to be an active participant by constantly making decisions about what to read and whether the material she has read meets her informational needs.

Plan B Strategies

What happens when students apply evaluation techniques and determine that the information they have located does not meet their needs? Some students may give up, having determined that the Internet is too confusing, takes too long, or requires too much thinking. Other students will have the drive and desire to persevere with locating information, especially when they are armed with alternative skills and strategies. When students are unsuccessful during their initial attempts to find information on the Web, they need to engage in what we refer to as "Plan B" strategies. Guinee, Eagleton, and Hall (2003) describe four strategies used by students when their initial search queries fail or when they need to verify or gather information from other sites: (1) switching topics; (2) visiting new websites; (3) trying new keywords; and (4) changing search engines.

Researcher: "What were some search strategies you used last year?"

Student: "Um, I didn't choose keywords last year. I used books."

Switching Topics

Based on our research and that of others (e.g., Fidel et al., 1999), it seems that many students take a reactive stance to searching the Internet, reframing their inquiries around what can be easily found rather than persevering in the face of difficulty. Interestingly, switching research topics midstream can be considered a dysfunctional or an adaptive technique, depending on the situation. When students select poor keywords for their searches, switching topics will not improve things. This was the case for a youngster with learning disabilities who switched topics several times, from Bahamas to Cuba, and back. However, if a search fails owing to a lack of available information, it's prudent to promptly switch topics, as one fourth-grade student realized during his research project, asking, "Can I change [my topic] 'cause I don't think I can find anything on it?" Alternatively, a student may switch focus within a topic. For example, when one eighth-grader could not find sufficient information about the Olsen twins' involvement in charitable organizations, she switched her focus to the actresses' careers (Guinee et al., 2003).

Visiting New Websites

If a website visit proves unhelpful, most students know they should go back to select new websites from the hit list (beware: if the keywords weren't good, the hit list won't be good either!). Since some students continue searching well beyond the initial 10 sites listed, we teach a general rule of thumb that if nothing useful is found in the first 10 or 20 sites, it's time to try new keywords or a new search engine.

Trying New Keywords

One of the most effective, yet least used, Plan B strategies is to try new keywords. This can be done by substituting synonyms or variations of the root words, narrowing or broadening the focus, truncating words (see below), or checking keyword spelling. As one girl explained, "If the website is not good, try to rephrase your search." This strategy was successful for a searcher who changed his keywords from <Red Sox + Nomar Garciaparra + Money he makes a year> to <Red Sox + Nomar Garciaparra + Salary>.

Researcher: "What else might you try since you're having trouble finding what you want in your Web search for the lory bird?"

Student: "How about if I just drive down to Petco?" (*exasperated laugh*)

Unfortunately, many students make inconsequential changes to their keywords, such as when one student switched from "How many actors played James Bond?" to "How many actors *have* played James Bond?" Keyword selection requires fluency with computerspeak, the ability to anticipate what words or phrases will appear on a relevant webpage, and the knowledge of how each search engine processes keywords. While computerspeak is a language that can be learned over time through trial and error, we advocate an early introduction by knowledgeable teachers.

Switching Search Engines

Another way people can modify unsuccessful search attempts is to switch search engines. As one of our students advised, "If you don't find any results that suit your purpose, try another search engine." Some students apply this technique blindly, using the same broad keywords in multiple search engines. For example, one student searched for <Nashville Tennessee> in Google, visited several sites, and then searched for <Nashville Tennessee> in Yahoo, still without specifying her focus area. More experienced students make more thoughtful and selective switches.

When students understand that search engines use different algorithms and require different types of data entry, they change search engines to maximize the fit between these characteristics and their current search needs (Guinee et al., 2003). For example, an older student explained, "If you're looking for something broader, try Yahoo, because it puts it into subcategories."

"When you use search engines, don't give up just because you tried one wording and that didn't work. Because sometimes search engines are picky on how many words you use and what order your put them in, if you use articles or not, and other picky stuff." —Marie, sixth-grader

How Do We Teach Evaluating Strategies?

Teaching evaluation strategies involves helping students to develop a discerning eye in order to become technology critics along with being technology users (Sutherland-Smith, 2002). When applying evaluating strategies to Web searching, we need a set of fundamental skills to effectively critique and use the information.

- Choose appropriate search engines.
- Select websites from the search engine hit list.
- Determine the validity of websites.
- Efficiently sort through large amounts of information.
- Recognize the usefulness and truthfulness of information.
- Collect and organize large amounts of information.

In order for students to develop these skills, we strongly suggest scaffolding students' Internet searching before placing them in an online environment on their own. As with any good instruction, a gradual release of responsibility gives students the chance to develop foundational skills while they move toward more independence. As described throughout this book, the teacher can provide fundamental support through the use of modeling and thinking aloud during whole-class activities. For example, model and describe how you select a website from a search engine hit list; also explain why you did *not* select certain websites, because these insights can be just as valuable. Of course, your ultimate goal is to have students negotiate the Web on their own, but until that time, a "follow the leader" approach can be quite effective. Teachers can help students transition into independent practice by providing a limited number of links students can access or a shortcut list of predetermined websites bookmarked for students. Support can also be given by first relying on whole-class, teacher-led activities, then moving to activities with small groups or partners and then to independent work (Figure 6.4). Throughout these transitions, a teacher should continue to think aloud about the way websites are evaluated and how information is filtered for truthfulness and usefulness.

FIGURE 6.4. Scaffolding learning by working with others.

Evaluating Search Engine Results

As mentioned above, one way to begin the evaluation process is to take a closer look at the clues found in the URL. Handout E-1, *URL Clues*, provides a format for breaking down the parts of the URL to analyze the trustworthiness of the website and provides several examples for guided practice. As a partner activity, *Questions about the URL* (Handout E-2) is designed to take an even more in-depth look at URLs. A study of search engine results, *Hit List Evaluation* (Handout E-3) provides practice in closely analyzing the links available from search engine results. This handout can be used first by students as a whole group and then, after some practice, with partners or individually. Taking a close and careful look at search engine results literally puts the Internet reading process into slow motion, forcing students to critically analyze the information provided within each link on the list. This is analogous to asking students to slow down when reading printed text so that they can be more metacognitive about their comprehension.

Evaluating Websites

A wealth of resources for evaluating websites is easy to find on the Internet. With a little exploring, teachers will find background information about evaluation, student activities for developing evaluation skills, a plethora of evaluation checklists and "bogus" websites for practice in developing evaluation skills. In this section, we share the websites and activities we have found to be the most useful, but we also invite you to conduct your own search. Begin with your favorite search engine, type in the keywords <website + evaluation>, and you will generate a list of more websites than you can fathom. Our search using Google yielded over 53 million sites! We found the top ten sites to be very useful, and below are four of our favorites that are appropriate for teachers.

1. *Yahooligan! Teachers' Guide* (*www.yahooligans.yahoo.com/tg*). This site focuses on providing teachers of 7–12-year-olds with teaching activities for locating information using the Internet, as well as clues to evaluate the quality of a website. Evaluation of a website focuses on the four A's: accessibility, accuracy, appropriateness, and appeal.
2. *Finding Information on the Internet: A Tutorial* (*www.lib.berkeley.edu/TeachingLib/Guides/Internet/FindInfo.html*). Geared for adults, this website is hosted by the University of California at Berkeley and provides useful information about various aspects of using the Internet, including links from key vocabulary to a glossary of terms such as "html," "link," and "server." A self-guided tutorial provides answers to common Internet search questions.
3. *Exercise Your Search Skills: A WebQuest* (*www.milforded.org/schools/simonlake/ebaiardi/wq/searchskills.html*). Students and teachers alike will benefit from this WebQuest activity, which guides the learner through the use of different search engines, focusing on ways to evaluate and use information displayed

by these search engines. The description of the WebQuest activity includes key vocabulary that is highlighted and linked to a glossary. In addition, a brief description is provided for each of the search engines used in the activity.

4. *Kathy Schrock's Guide for Educators—Critical Evaluation Information* (*school. discovery.com/schrockguide/eval.html*). This site focuses on tools for teaching students to evaluate webpages with consideration of the usefulness and authenticity of information, authorship, and bias. Tools available to teachers include critical evaluation surveys for elementary, middle, and high school levels and various articles about website evaluation, including "The ABC's of Website Evaluation" and "How to Tell the Good Sites from the Bad."

Evaluation Checklists

Each of the websites described above provide resources for evaluating information found on a website. Typically, some type of checklist is used for the learner to locate and consider various information presented on the website, such as our *Reader Friendliness Checklist* (Handout E-4). The handouts for *Quick Website Evaluation* (Handout E-5), *Elementary Website Evaluation* (Handout E-6), and *Middle School Website Evaluation* (Handout E-7) provide students with a list of various website elements to consider when trying to determine the quality of online information. We like these checklists because the ideas are clear, information can be easily recorded, and the wording and length are a good match to the developmental needs of students. Begin by using the age-appropriate checklist during a whole-class activity in which the website is displayed with a projector for all to see. Before the lesson, identify and bookmark examples of strong and weak websites. Display these sites and complete the checklist as a class, pausing to think aloud and discuss various website elements. A variation of this activity is to provide students with a list of five preselected websites. The students visit the sites and use an evaluation checklist to rank them in order from strongest to weakest, then discuss these rankings. Agreement is not necessary, but a rich discussion about the rankings will prove interesting and educational.

Questioning the Source

If there is one thing we should teach our students about evaluating, it should be to question the source. Being suspicious involves questioning whether information is accurate or not, either asking such questions of ourselves or asking the experts. When facts are found in more than one location, then the reliability of the information increases dramatically (Figure 6.5). Thinking critically about a webpage also requires the learner to question information, beliefs of the author, and the purpose of the website. Handout E-8, *Bias or Not?*, encourages students to consider and question the various ways a website author may try to persuade the learner to believe or do something.

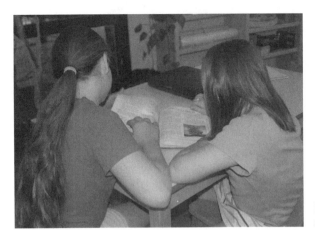

FIGURE 6.5. Fact-checking multiple sources.

Another way to encourage the querying of website information is the instructional use of bogus or hoax websites. These realistic, but untrue websites are fun ways for students to practice determining truthfulness of information. We have included a list of bogus websites (*Is It True?*, Handout E-9), but there are tons of others that you can access through your favorite search engine by typing the terms <hoax + website>. Read carefully, or you may be fooled by some of the seemingly official information.

The Teacher's Guide at Yahooligans, *www.yahooligans.com/tg*, provides activities to use with students for determining truthfulness through a comparison of two websites about the television character Barney. One website, *The Taxonomy of Barney*, at *www.improb.com/airchives/paperair/volume1/v1i1/barney.htm*, provides seemingly credible information about Barney. The information appears to be real, so learners have to rely on critical reading skills to determine the accuracy of the information. This website can be compared with the *Official Barney* page at *www.barneyonline.com/index_new.php*, containing links to various sites for purchasing toys. An additional comparison can be made with the *Barney and Friends* website at *pbskids.org/barney/*. Comparing and contrasting various forms of information causes students to think at higher levels and begin to identify what's true and useful.

Our *Is It True?* activity (Handout E-9) and the *Advertisement versus Error* activity (Handout E-10) have questions designed to encourage the development of critical literacy skills. In *Is It True?*, students peruse a bogus website to determine the accuracy of the information. Our favorite is the Dog Island website at *thedogisland.com*, because we can easily imagine what a dog "heaven" would be like, if it really existed, and students must read very carefully to discover that it does not.

Engaging Plan B Strategies

Even after becoming experts at identifying topics, focus areas, and research questions (Chapter 4); choosing search engines and selecting keywords (Chapter 5); and evaluating hit lists and websites (this chapter), students still need to engage in "Plan B" strategies when the first site they visit does not meet their information needs. During an Internet QUEST, it is expected that students will visit more than one website. Therefore, we created the *Plan B Checklist* (Handout E-11), which helps students remember five strategies for deciding what to do next. Finally, we offer *Edit>Find Lesson Plans* for elementary and middle levels (Handouts E-12 and E-13), which teach a simple method for determining if a website has the desired information.

Summary

The E phase of the QUEST focuses on evaluating search engine results and websites as learners seek to determine whether the information they find during Internet inquiry is truthful and useful. Because there are no editorial filters in Web publishing, students must become skilled at sifting out the true from the untrue, a daunting task for emergent or struggling readers who are still giving much attention to decoding and fluency. Instruction in these strategies should focus on a gradual release of responsibility from the teacher to the student through modeling and think-aloud procedures, then guided and independent practice. Teachers can help students to become super sleuths throughout the inquiry process by viewing information on the Internet as a collection of clues useful for evaluating.

In the next chapter on Synthesizing, we explore the "in the head" strategies that Web learners use to integrate ideas within and across websites. While many of these strategies are similar to those used by readers of print text (Chapter 2), the speed at which many students move through the Internet sometimes makes it difficult for them to take time to ask themselves what the information means.

Handouts

The handouts for Evaluating, listed in the following chart, are meant to give students practice in developing evaluation skills that can be applied as they move into independently seeking answers to their questions using the Internet. Note that because these activities slow down the Internet reading process, they are not meant to be used every time students seek online information.

Number	Name of handout	Purpose
E-1	URL Clues	Determine authenticity
E-2	Questions about the URL	Determine reliability
E-3	Hit List Evaluation	Evaluate search engine results
E-4	Reader Friendliness Checklist	Evaluate reader friendliness
E-5	Quick Website Evaluation	Evaluate website info
E-6	Elementary Website Evaluation	Evaluate website info
E-7	Middle School Website Evaluation	Evaluate website info

E-8	Bias or Not?	Determine bias
E-9	Is It True?	Determine truthfulness
E-10	Advertisement versus Error	Determine truthfulness
E-11	Plan B Checklist	Strategies beyond 1st site visit
E-12	Edit>Find Lesson Plan—Elementary Level	Method for finding specific information and evaluating usefulness of site
E-13	Edit>Find Lesson Plan—Middle Level	Method for finding specific information and evaluating usefulness of site

Name _____ Class _____ Date _____

A URL, or web address, can give you valuable clues for determining the credibility of the website. Here is an example of how a URL can be broken down to determine information:

SAMPLE URL: _http://www.nationalgeographic.com/solarsystem/splash.html_

Type of Protocol	Domain name (the host, or author, of the site)	Path or Directory on the server to this file	Name and type of file
http://	www.nationalgeographic.com/	solarsystem/	splash.html

DIRECTIONS: Select a term from science or social studies. Type this term into the search engine Yahooligans at _www.yahooligans.com._ Select three websites from the hit list and break down the URL for each one. Then answer the questions below each URL box to determine whether this is a site that can be trusted. If you run into trouble or are unsure, we will discuss your findings in class.

URL #1: _____

Type of Protocol	Domain name	Path or Directory	File name

Do you recognize the domain name? Is it connected to education, government, or a company with a trustworthy reputation?

Do the path/directory and file name contain words or parts of words that relate to your topic of interest?

URL #2: _____

Type of Protocol	Domain name	Path or Directory	File name

Do you recognize the domain name? Is it connected to education, government, or a company with a trustworthy reputation?

Do the path/directory and file name contain words or parts of words that relate to your topic of interest?

URL #3: _____

Type of Protocol	Domain name	Path or Directory	File name

Do you recognize the domain name? Is it connected to education, government, or a company with a trustworthy reputation?

Do the path/directory and file name contain words or parts of words that relate to your topic of interest?

HANDOUT E-2. Questions about the URL

Name _____ Class _____ Date _____

The URL is the first place to look for clues to evaluate a website. Identify two websites, then use these charts to see what types of information the websites contain.

URL #1: _____

Who published the webpage or made it public by putting it on the Web? Look for a host that has a reliable reputation.	

What type of domain does the webpage come from? Domains include:
    .edu (education, college or university)
    .gov (government agency)
    .net (network related)
    .com (commercial)
    .org (nonprofit and research organizations)
    .k12.ks.us (school district)	

Is this a personal webpage hosted by a private individual? Look for the word "users," "members," or "people." Check for a person's name, the use of a tilde (~), or a percent sign (%).	

URL #2: _____

Who published the webpage or made it public by putting it on the Web? Look for a host that has a reliable reputation.	

What type of domain does the webpage come from? Domains include:
    .edu (education, college or university)
    .gov (government agency)
    .net (network related)
    .com (commercial)
    .org (nonprofit and research organizations)
    .k12.ks.us (school district)	

Is this a personal webpage hosted by a private individual? Look for the word "users," "members," or "people." Check for a person's name, the use of a tilde (~), or a percent sign (%).	

HANDOUT E-3. Hit List Evaluation

Identify a keyword or combination of keywords for your inquiry. Type the words into the search box in Yahooligans! Then, select three links to closely analyze. All of the information you need should be collected from the link on the hit list. Don't go to the website.

URL #1: _____

Website title	Brief description	Links to categories

Does this site match your inquiry question? Why or why not?

URL #2: _____

Website title	Brief description	Links to categories

Does this site match your inquiry question? Why or why not?

URL #3: _____

Website title	Brief description	Links to categories

Does this site match your inquiry question? Why or why not?

HANDOUT E-4. Reader Friendliness Checklist

Identify a website on a search results list. Use the Reader Friendliness Checklist to determine if this website will be helpful for finding information.

URL:	Yes	No
Does a site map provide hyperlinks to key ideas and display the organization of the website?		
Are the hyperlinks easy to distinguish from the rest of the text by color, size, or shape?		
Is the path you have taken through the website listed, so you can easily see where you have come from and how to return?		
If you go to another page, is there link to get back to the first page?		
Does the title of the page tell you what it is about?		
Is there an introduction or welcoming message on the page telling you what is included?		
Is each section labeled with a heading?		
Is the structure uncluttered and easy to use, with space separating ideas?		
Is there a lack of annoying features (flashing banners, distracting animations, ugly colors)?		
Do the graphics help you to better understand the ideas of the text, and do they load easily?		

Would you use this website to help you learn more about the topic? Why or why not?

HANDOUT E-6. Quick Website Evaluation

Name _____ Class _____ Date _____

Directions: Choose a website and evaluate it using this quick method.

URL: _____

	LOW SCORE → → → → → → → HIGH SCORE				
	1	2	3	4	5
CONTENT How useful was the content?					
ACCURACY Did the info seem reliable and up-to-date?					
APPEARANCE How interesting and inviting was the site?					
SPEED Did everything load up quickly?					
NAVIGATION How easy was it to move around the site?					
TOTAL POINTS =					

Would you recommend this site?   Yes   No

Please explain your reasoning:

HANDOUT E-6. Elementary Website Evaluation
(page 1 of 2)

Name _____ Class _____ Date _____

1. How are you hooked to the Internet?
   ____ Modem and phone line
   ____ Direct connection at school/home

2. What web browser are you using? _____

3. What is the URL (address) of the webpage you are using?
   http://_____

4. What is the name of the site? _____

Part 1: How does it look? As you look at the questions below, put an X in the "yes" or "no" column for each.	YES	NO
Does the page take a long time to load?		
Are there big pictures on the page?		
Is the spelling correct on the page?		
Is the author's name and e-mail address on the page?		
Is there a picture on the page that you can use to choose links? (Image map)		
Is there information in columns on the page? (Table)		
If you go to another page, is there a way to get back to the first page?		
Is there a date that tells you when the page was made?		
If there are photographs, do they look real?		
If there are sounds, do they sound real?		

Part 2: What did you learn? As you look at the questions below, put an X in the "yes" or "no" column for each.	YES	NO
Does the title of the page tell you what it is about?		
Is there an introduction on the page telling you what is included?		
Are the facts on the page what you were looking for?		
Would you have gotten more information from an encyclopedia?		
Would the information have been better in the encyclopedia?		
Does the author of the page say some things you disagree with?		
Does the page lead you to some other good information (links)?		
Does the page include information you know is wrong?		
Do the pictures and photographs on the page help you learn?		

Part 3: Summary

Looking at all of the questions and answers above, write a paragraph telling why this website is helpful (or not helpful) for your project.

Name _____ Class _____ Date _____

1. What type of connection do you have to the Internet?
    ____ Dial-in connection: modem speed (circle one) 28.8 33.6 56k
    ____ Direct connection: (circle one) 56K DSL T1 T3 Broadband/cable Other: _____

2. What Web browser are you using? _____

3. What is the URL of the webpage you are evaluating?

http://_____

4. What is the name of the site?

_____

Part 1: Looking at and using the page As you look at the questions below, put an X in the "yes" or "no" column for each.	YES	NO
Does the page take a long time to load?		
Are the pictures on the page helpful?		
Is each section of the page labeled with a heading?		
Did the author sign his or her real name?		
Did the author give you his or her e-mail address?		
Is there a date on the page that tells you when it was last updated?		
Is there an image map (big picture with links) on the page?		
Is there a table (columns of text) on the page?		
If you go to another page on the site, can you get back to the main page?		
Are there photographs on the page? • If so, can you be sure that the photographs have not been changed by the author? • If you're not sure, should you accept the photos as true?		

HANDOUT E-7. Middle School Website Evaluation
(page 2 of 3)

Summary of Part 1
Using the data you have collected above, write a paragraph explaining why you would or wouldn't recommend this site to a friend for use with a project.

Part 2: What's on the page and who put it there?	YES	NO
Does the title of the page tell you what it is about?		
Is there a paragraph on the page explaining what it is about?		
Is the information on the page useful for your project? • If not, what can you do next? _____		
Would you have gotten more information from an encyclopedia?		
Can you tell if the information on the page is current?		
Does up-to-date information make a difference for your project?		
Does the page lead you to some other good info (links)?		
Does the author of the page present some info you disagree with?		
Does the author of the page present some info that you think is wrong?		
Does some information contradict information you found elsewhere?		
Does the author use some absolute words (like "always" or "never")?		
Does the author use superlative words (like the "best" or "worst")?		
Does the author tell you about him- or herself?		
Do you feel that the author is knowledgeable about the topic?		
Are you positive the information is true? • What can you do to prove the information is true? _____ _____ _____		

Summary of Part 2

Looking at the data you have collected in Part 2, compose a note to the author of the website explaining how you are going to use the website in your project and giving your opinion of the page's content.

HANDOUT E-8. Bias or Not?

Name _____ Class _____ Date _____

Follow the steps in the boxes to decide if a website is biased.

1. Write your research question.	2. List potential biases before reading the website.

3. Choose a website and write the URL.

4. Check off bias clues if you see them and give an example.

☐ Stereotypes _____

☐ Exaggeration _____

☐ Appeals to feelings/emotions _____

☐ Overgeneralizations _____

☐ Opinions stated as facts _____

☐ Imbalance in presentation _____
(were both sides considered?)

5. Based on clues, is this website biased? _____ yes _____ no
If yes, what is the bias?

HANDOUT E-9. Is It True?

Name _____ Class _____ Date _____

Select a website to explore from the list below. Some of the sites are real websites with truthful information. Some of the sites are not. Determine if the info at your site is true by answering the following questions.

- Velcro Crop at *home.inreach.com/kumbach/velcro.html*
- Dog Island at *thedogisland.com*
- The Venom Cure at *www.pbs.org/wnet/nature/venomcure/*
- Worm Watch at *www.naturewatch.ca/english/wormwatch/*
- The Pacific Northwest Tree Octopus at *zapatopi.net/treeoctopus.html*
- Brain Transplant at *216.247.9.207/ny-best.htm*
- Aluminum Foil Detector Beanie at *zapatopi.net/afdb.html*

1. Does the homepage look and work like a typical website? Give specific examples.

2. Does the information seem as though it makes sense? Explain why/why not.

3. Where else can you look to confirm this information? Look somewhere else on the Internet and share what you find.

4. Who created the website? List the author or webmaster's name and qualifications for being an expert.

5. Can you contact the author or webmaster? List the contact information, such as phone number, address, e-mail address.

6. Is the information on this site true? Why was it created?

HANDOUT E-10. Advertisement versus Error

Name _____ Class _____ Date _____

Pop-up messages often appear when you are reading on the Internet. How do you know whether the message is an advertisement, or whether an actual problem or error has occurred with the computer? Sly advertisers have developed sneaky ways to trick you into reading their messages. Don't get tricked! Look for these signs to decide if the message is an ad or an error.

Pop-up ad:

   ✓Blinking graphics (pictures, symbols, words)

   ✓No apparent way to close or minimize the message

   ✓Music or sounds

   ✓Message reappears, even after closing it

Error message:

   ✓Plain background, little color

   ✓No blinking graphics

   ✓No music or sound

   ✓Message does not reappear

   ✓Message can be closed by clicking on the X in the upper right corner

   ✓Message can be minimized

Draw an example of a pop-up advertisement versus a computer message below.

POP-UP AD	ERROR MESSAGE

HANDOUT E-11. Plan B Checklist

Name _____ Class _____ Date _____

Can't find what you want on the Web? Try these strategies.

Step 1: Check your keywords

_____ Are your keywords spelled correctly?

_____ Did you use topic + focus?

_____ Did you put quotation marks around phrases?

_____ Other:

Step 2: Check the website

_____ Did you use Edit>Find to scan for your keywords?

_____ Did you look for a site map?

_____ Did you check to see if there's a search tool on this site?

_____ Did you look for links that might lead somewhere useful?

_____ Did you find a link that lets you send an e-mail to the author?

_____ Did you notice related keywords that you could try next?

_____ Other:

Step 3: Try a new approach

_____ Did you try a new website?

_____ Did you try different keywords (in a keyword driven search engine like Google)?

_____ Did you try different categories (in a directory-based search engine like Yahoo)?

_____ Did you try a different question (in an natural language search engine like Ask.com)?

_____ Other:

Step 4: Try a new search engine

_____ Have you tried Yahooligans, KidsClick, and Ask.com?

_____ Have you tried Google, Yahoo, and WebCrawler?

_____ Other:

Step 5: Try a new topic or focus

_____ Did you try a new focus area?

_____ Did you try a new topic that's similar?

_____ Other:

HANDOUT E-12. Edit>Find Lesson Plan—Elementary Level
(page 1 of 2)

Objective

Students will learn a simple method for locating target words and phrases on a website to determine if it's likely to have the information they seek.

Time

One class period

Materials

1. Internet computer with LCD projector
2. At least two free web browsers, such as Internet Explorer (*www.microsoft.com*) and Netscape Navigator (*www.netscape.com*)
3. *QUEST Inquiry Model* (Handout P-11)

Assessment Options

1. *Web Strategies Assessment* (Handout P-2, P-4, or P-5)
2. *Web Strategies Scoring Guide* (Handout P-3 or P-6)

Introduction

1. Tell students you will be teaching them an easy way to tell if a website has the information they need to answer their questions. Display the *QUEST Inquiry Model* (Handout P-11) and remind students of the QUEST phases, specifically the phase of Evaluating, in which we determine if the website is useful and truthful. Say that today's focus is on deciding if the information is useful.
2. Discuss the difference between useful information and useless information. Give an example, such as: If we want to learn about cheetahs, and the website mostly has information about tigers, we would want to choose another website. Even though tigers are interesting, we would not want to keep reading that website because we need to move on and look for information about cheetahs.

Modeling

1. Pose the question, "What do cheetahs eat?" Brainstorm possible foods for cheetahs, then provide the synonym "diet."
2. Pull up Internet Explorer, go to *www.yahooligans.com* and search for <cheetah + diet>.
3. Choose a site that looks promising (explain why you think it looks promising).
4. Go to the Edit>Find feature located on the toolbar across the top of the screen in the Edit drop-down menu. Click on Find and search for the word "diet." If it's there, read the surrounding info to learn more about the diet of the cheetah. Click "Find Next" to see if diet comes up again (on a Mac, go to Edit>Find Again multiple times). If not, quickly leave the site and try other sites until you find something about the diet of cheetahs. Remark that this is a FASTER way to see if a website has the specific info you want than reading or skimming. Mention that Edit>Find works in all software programs, as well as on hit lists.

5. Now say that you want to verify the info about the cheetah's diet by fact-checking with another website.
6. Pull up Netscape Navigator and go to *www.yahoo.com* to demonstrate that this feature works in any web browser and with any search engine. Search again for <cheetah + diet>.
7. Discuss the way this little trick can help you find information quickly on a website.

Practice

1. Identify a unit of study within the curriculum (e.g., Civil War, inventions). Have students brainstorm possible words related to the topic. Direct students to a predetermined website with information relating to the topic. Have students practice using the Edit>Find feature and keep a running total for the number of times they find the target words.
2. If students are already involved in an inquiry project, have them try the Edit>Find feature on any hit list and website related to their topic.

Scaffolding

Pair weaker students with stronger students. However, always be sure that the weaker student has control of the mouse and that the mentor student understands how to support a peer without taking over.

Feedback

1. Circulate around the classroom or computer lab and ask students what they are doing and how it is helpful. If anyone seems unclear about the purpose of this lesson or how to implement it, remediate on the spot.
2. Praise students who are successfully using the Edit>Find feature.

Ticket Out the Door

Have each student tell you a fast method for finding specific words on a hit list or website (Edit>Find).

Objective

Students will learn a simple method for locating target words and phrases on a website to determine if it's likely to have the information they seek.

Time

One class period

Materials

1. Internet computer with LCD projector
2. At least two free web browsers, such as Internet Explorer (*www.microsoft.com*) and Netscape Navigator (*www.netscape.com*)
3. *QUEST Inquiry Model* (Handout P-11)

Assessment Options

1. *Web Strategies Assessment* (Handout P-2, P-4, or P-5)
2. *Web Strategies Scoring Guide* (Handout P-3 or P-6)

Introduction

1. Tell students you will be teaching them a transferable strategy for evaluating the usefulness of a website that many other students have found helpful. Contextualize the lesson using the *QUEST Inquiry Model* (Handout P-11) by pointing out that they are in the E phase of the QUEST, which includes deciding if a website is reliable (truthful) and has the info they want (useful).
2. Have students brainstorm why evaluating is useful in this class, in other classes, and outside of school. This can be done in pairs, in small groups, or as a whole class.
3. Generate excitement and get student buy-in on the purpose of the lesson before proceeding. Tell students that this strategy works in any web browser as well as in most other software programs (Word, PowerPoint, Publisher, etc.). It also works on hit lists.

Modeling

1. Tell the class that you already know that modern lacrosse originated with Native American tribes in Canada and the United States but that you want to know what the French had to do with it. Pull up Internet Explorer, go to *www.google.com*, and search for <lacrosse + history>.
2. Choose a site that looks promising (explain why you think it looks promising).
3. Check the site for reliability (look at URL and try to find author info).
4. Go to the toolbar at the top of the browser window. Click on Edit and then click on Find. Search for the word "French." If it's there, read the surrounding info and see if you find your answer. Click "Find Next" to see if it's mentioned again (on a Mac, go to Edit>Find Again multiple times). If not, quickly leave the site and try other sites until you find something about the French. Remark that this is a FASTER way to see if a website has the specific info you want than reading or skimming.

---

5. Now say that you want to verify the info about the French by fact-checking with another website.
6. Pull up Netscape Navigator and use *www.yahoo.com* to demonstrate that this feature works in any web browser and with any search engine. Search again for <lacrosse + history>.
7. Show that you can use Edit>Find on the search results list, too. Use Edit>Find to search for "origin" on the hit list. Click the "Find" button again to see if "origin" is listed elsewhere on the hit list.
8. Choose a site that looks promising.
9. Check the site for reliability.
10. Use Edit>Find to search for "French" again. Point out that you can also use the keyboard shortcut "Ctrl + F." Click the "Find" button again to see if the French are mentioned more than once.
11. See if everyone's satisfied that you've quickly found and verified the info you wanted (the French are credited with inventing the word "lacrosse").

Practice

1. If students are already involved in an inquiry project, have them try the Edit>Find and Ctrl + F feature on any hit list and website related to their topic.
2. If this is an isolated minilesson, have students quickly think of an interesting topic about which they have fairly strong prior knowledge. Then have them try the Edit>Find and Ctrl + F feature on any hit list and website related to this topic.

Scaffolding

Pair weaker students with stronger students. However, always be sure that the weaker student has control of the mouse and that the mentor student understands how to support a peer without taking over.

Feedback

1. Circulate around classroom or computer lab and ask students what they are doing and how it is helpful. If anyone seems unclear about the purpose of this lesson or how to implement it, remediate on the spot.
2. Praise students who are successfully using the Edit>Find feature.

Ticket Out the Door

Have each student tell you a fast method for finding specific words on a hit list or website (Edit>Find or Ctrl + F).

7 SYNTHESIZING

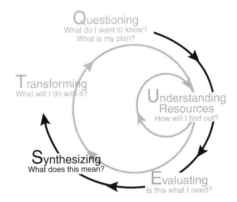

Questioning
What do I want to know?
What is my plan?

Transforming
What will I do with it?

Understanding
Resources
How will I find out?

Synthesizing
What does this mean?

Evaluating
Is this what I need?

KEY IDEAS

▶ Synthesis plays a role in our everyday lives when we make decisions.

▶ A reader forms a synthesis when mentally linking together kernels of ideas within a text or among texts.

▶ Synthesis is a complex strategy because it involves a combination of several different reading strategies, including activating prior knowledge, determining important ideas, and making inferences.

▶ Throughout the inquiry process, synthesis is necessary for readers to understand information gathered from a variety of sources, including text, graphics, and multimedia.

▶ Readers of varying skill levels benefit from models of synthesis through think-alouds and a gradual release of responsibility.

> Synthesis is about organizing the different pieces to create a mosaic, a meaning, a beauty, greater than the sum of each shiny piece. It is a complex process in which children, even the youngest, engage very naturally every day.
>
> —Keene and Zimmermann (1997, p. 28)

In this chapter we look at the process of synthesis, or the connecting of individual ideas to form an understanding. Finding and evaluating information is important, as described in the second and third steps of the QUEST model, but will not be enough unless a deep understanding of the information can be developed through a synthesis of ideas. Therefore, the guiding question for this chapter is, "What does this information mean?"

Why Is It Important to Synthesize?

Synthesizing is the pulling together of separate and unique ideas to form a new understanding, much in the way a detective links together clues to solve a mystery. Synthesis is the opportunity for learners to demonstrate the use of multiple reading strategies by pulling together various pieces of information to form an interpretation. As described in Chapter 2, synthesis is used by strategic readers to reach a higher level of understanding beyond just the recall of details. This higher level is reached when readers personalize the text by integrating words and ideas with their own thoughts and questions, thus creating new insights. Synthesis is not easy. While some students may not struggle to *find* quality information on the Internet, many are challenged to figure out what it *means* and what to do with it.

> "Not only does efficient searching have to produce websites, then we have the other whole area of reading and understanding those sites and being able to grab for later use exactly what suits your purpose."
> —Tracey, eighth-grade language arts teacher

The process of synthesizing requires readers to create a thread linking separate ideas from within a text or from multiple texts and then tie this thread to their own experiences by creating a new interpretation, or a way to view these ideas in a new light. Readers must not only understand the text, but must also be able to "own" the information. Even though synthesis is complex, this is a strategy that our students absolutely need in a world where they encounter massive amounts of information, whether in print or electronic form, and must make well-informed decisions about how to interpret and use this information.

 Language Arts Standard: Clarify concepts by summarizing information; synthesize material to be presented in written and/or oral form.

Although teachers may assume that students understand that the inquiry task involves synthesizing information from multiple sources, many students are unaware of this and/or are unable to carry it out (Bowler, Large, & Rejskind, 2001; Eagleton et al., 2003). The elementary school "copy it out of the encyclopedia" strategy perseveres right into middle and even high school; in fact, electronic resources make it even easier to copy information. One problem is the prevalent "one-stop-shopping" method, which is an outcome of the erroneous belief that one website should have all the information a student seeks. For example, one student felt trium-

Library Media Standard: Reorganize and synthesize information from a variety of sources and formats.

phant about his Internet inquiry project because, as he said, "I found that one webpage I needed to do my thing." This strategy, which may be acceptable in some library and encyclopedia research, is ill-advised in Web research because websites can, and do, report biased and/or incorrect information (see Chapter 6). To combat this problem, students should be taught to fact-check several sources before declaring "truth." Fact-checking can be enforced by asking students to visit a minimum number of websites during an inquiry project.

When Do We Synthesize?

Synthesis is a part of our everyday lives. Throughout the day, we pull together information from various sources to create our own interpretations. For example, one day Beth was preparing to go teach at the university. She wanted more information about the day's weather before deciding what to wear. First, she consulted both the forecast in the newspaper and the one on television. Next, she asked her son to call the local time and temperature number for the current temperature and the day's forecast. Then Beth asked her husband how the temperature felt when he went outside to get the newspaper. Finally, she tapped her prior knowledge of the type of weather that typically occurs during late winter in Kansas. Once she had integrated all of this information, Beth made an informed decision about what clothes would be comfortable for the day's weather.

Synthesis enables us to make both big and small decisions by relying on a combination of our prior experiences and new information gathered from what we read, what we see, and what we hear. We take those fragments, or bits of information, and make them our own. When children are young, their experiences and bits of information are few or may have gaps. For instance, when Beth's 10-year-old son was trying to decide which video game to purchase with his allowance, he relied on advice from friends, magazine advertisements, and his own experiences. What he neglected to determine was the cost of the video game, so at the checkout counter he realized that he did not have enough money. As children get older, their collection of experiences expands and they become better at selecting resources for gathering information.

> **Synthesis is the process of ordering, recalling, retelling, and recreating into a coherent whole the information with which our minds are bombarded every day. It is the uniquely human trait that permits us to sift through a myriad of details and focus on those pieces we need to know and remember.**
> —Keene and Zimmermann (1997, p. 169)

Another example: Beth's teenage daughter wanted to buy a cell phone. She knew that in order to convince her parents of this need, she had to first synthesize information from various sources, then form a clear and logical argument. She began by reading advertisements in the newspaper, watching commercials on television, and reading cell phone companies' websites. She also discussed cell phone plans and the pros and cons of various types of cell phones with friends and family. Throughout this process, she read text, interpreted charts, calculated figures, and listened to opinions. From these sources, she pulled together the most important ideas and synthesized them into an effective argument.

Synthesis during reading, whether in print or on the Web, bears a clear resemblance to the ways we synthesize information in our daily lives when we bring together bits of information collected from one source or among several. Synthesizing is an example of the real-world comprehension demands placed on readers when they are expected to summarize multiple texts and put this information into a new form, either oral or written. Synthesis begins with summarizing. Students must first be able to determine the important ideas and express these in a clear and concise way before they can then make these ideas their own. The terms "synthesize" and "summarize" are often used interchangeably, but they are actually quite different. A summarization is a brief presentation of the main points of a text. A synthesis takes a summary one step further by including the reader's personal response to the text in the form of connections to herself, other texts, and the world (Keene & Zimmermann, 1997).

As readers, we take individual pieces of information gathered for a summary and combine this information with our prior knowledge. A pattern or idea begins to emerge. This idea is then further developed by the collection of more information from reading and the refinement of a person's own thinking until a synthesis takes shape in the person's mind. Think of a stonemason building a stone wall by putting together oddly shaped pieces of stone and filling in the gaps with mortar. Like stonemasonry, the act of synthesizing cements the information from the text into a reader's mind and demonstrates how his thinking changes during the process of forming his unique mental stone wall.

 Math Standard: Integrate data to solve problems.

What Characterizes Synthesis?

Research in the area of synthesis mostly focuses on the step of summarization, which leads to a synthesis. Being able to clearly and concisely summarize ideas is crucial to creating a synthesis. Afflerbach and Johnston (1986) use the term "crunching" to describe the way a reader reduces text to more manageable kernels of important information. Skilled readers often begin by scanning a text for relevant words and ideas, then returning to the text for a more careful reading. Frequently, these readers pause during reading to mentally crunch new information into a kernel of an idea. These kernels form a summary of the text, and a synthesis is created when the reader uses her insights to link the kernels together. This process of crunching ideas into more manageable units becomes automatic in skilled readers, which makes the process difficult for teachers to observe, explain, and teach. Many studies have shown that summarization skills can be improved with explicit instruction, especially when the text is at the appropriate level for the reader. Young children are able to summa-

> **The ability to summarize information requires readers to sift through large units of text, differentiate important from unimportant ideas, then synthesize those ideas and create a new coherent text that stands for, by substantive criteria, the original. This sounds difficult, and the research demonstrates that, in fact, it is.**
>
> —Dole, Duffy, Roehler, and Pearson (1991, p. 244)

rize the plot in simple stories, such as folktales, but have greater difficulty with more complex analysis of text, such as comparing portions of the text to the theme (Brown & Smiley, 1977). Older students respond positively to instruction in summarizing, especially when the teaching and modeling are part of the total package, such as in the well-researched Reciprocal Teaching method (Palincsar & Brown, 1984; Rosenshine & Meister, 1994). In sum, research shows that instruction and practice in summarization improves students' ability to summarize and increases their overall comprehension of the text (Duke & Pearson, 2002).

Why Is Synthesis Difficult?

Synthesis is not an easily observable process, since it often occurs in a reader's head as she moves through texts (Figure 7.1). This complex skill is challenging to teach and learn, because learners must understand and apply various comprehension strategies, including activating prior knowledge, determining important ideas, making inferences, and asking questions, while also developing personal responses or connections to the text (see Chapter 2). In the book *Strategies That Work* (2000), Harvey and Goudvis attribute the complexities of synthesis to the challenge of using critical and creative thinking simultaneously. They describe a synthesis as an idea that evolves slowly over time and occurs only if the reader is focused on making meaning.

One reason synthesizing is so difficult is that much of the process is unseen. Afflerbach and Johnston (1986) describe summarizing as skimming, rereading, mentally listing important elements, and waiting for a new idea, or synthesis, to be automatically constructed. This last step of constructing an idea is one that research has not helped us clearly define. As this mental process is used more and more, it becomes automatic and even unconscious to the reader. A reader may be quite

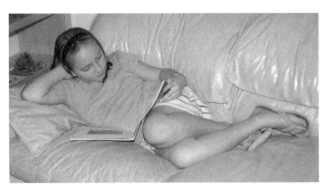

FIGURE 7.1. Synthesis occurs in the reader's head.

skilled at creating a synthesis but may have difficulty describing exactly what happens in his mind during this process. Without a clear description, it becomes difficult for a teacher to pass this information on to other students.

Synthesis and Reading on the Web

Internet readers face additional complexities when trying to pull together ideas for an inquiry project from various sources within a website or among several websites. The wide variety of text structures encountered in Web text are part of this complexity (see Chapter 2). Even before readers can apply their knowledge of synthesis, they must be skilled at navigating or deciding the path to follow in their Internet reading, based on knowledge of navigational tools and an evolving understanding of the text. There is so much information available on the Web that it is difficult to know where to focus one's attention. In Chapter 2, we described the process readers use during their transaction with Internet text. Skilled Internet readers demonstrate a complex weaving of navigation and reading strategies as they make decisions about where to read, what to read, and how carefully to read.

Skilled readers *expect* to read more than one entry within a website or more than one website to locate the answers to their questions, as described in Chapter 6. They understand that synthesizing information from the Internet relies heavily on skimming and scanning, along with navigating among various electronic formats such as webpages, e-mail, blogs, audio sources, interactive diagrams, instant messages, photographs, and discussion boards. Some readers even have several of these formats open on their computers at the same time and move back and forth among sources with a click of the mouse. Determining and integrating key ideas from these various electronic sources poses a challenge to both the student and the teacher, since the sources vary in the way information is presented and the type of information that is available. Finding the key idea in an e-mail message is quite different from finding the key idea in an interactive diagram. Internet readers must be able to collect and synthesize ideas from resources that present information in quite different ways.

 Social Studies Standard: Interpret and reconcile information in historical documents; describe the relationships in historical subject matter; identify principal conflicting ideas between competing narratives or interpretations of historical events.

Once a synthesis has been formed, or a connection made with these ideas, the learner's new way of looking at the synthesized idea is typically shared in a written or oral format. In the past, a synthesis was often shared through a research report, mural, poster, or other art media. Now, a synthesis of ideas gathered electronically often involves the use of technology to communicate ideas through the creation of a webpage, a PowerPoint presentation, or a video clip. To create a synthesis "outside the head," not only must the student be able to plan, locate, evaluate, and synthesize information, she must also be able to understand the various electronic formats for presenting this information. In this way, the complexities of synthesizing Web-

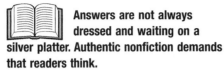 **Answers are not always dressed and waiting on a silver platter. Authentic nonfiction demands that readers think.**
                                    —Harvey (1998 p. 84)

based information continue to grow. In Chapter 8, we focus on the ways readers literally transform information into knowledge by creating an inquiry product.

How Do We Synthesize?

In order to teach synthesis, we must slow down the reading process and analyze the individual components. These components are among the comprehension strategies that form a proficient reader's toolbox (see Chapter 2). This slowing down of the process is somewhat artificial, because the strategies used to synthesize often occur simultaneously and intertwine among each other. Various comprehension strategies actually merge together as a synthesis is formed. One could think of synthesis as the culmination of the comprehension process and a chance to apply strategies that may have been learned or practiced individually.

While a synthesis is being created, a reader selects strategies from his mental toolbox that help most in forming a synthesis. Some strategies are in the background of the reader's mind, waiting for use whenever needed. Making connections, monitoring, and repairing comprehension are strategies the reader might call upon throughout the reading process as needed. However, during the creation of a synthesis, other strategies (described below) are brought to the forefront of the reader's mind and play a more significant role.

Activating Prior Knowledge

Before and during any informational reading task, the reader calls to mind what she knows about the topic of the text and the organizational structure found within the text, such as compare/contrast or sequential. When reading on the Internet, the reader also considers what she knows about using search engines, navigating, and reading within a website. These various types of prior knowledge are crucial for readers to make connections between what they read and what they know, and to use these connections for developing a deeper understanding of the text on a webpage. When synthesizing, prior knowledge helps a reader to both access information and determine what is important, which are the next two steps of the synthesizing process.

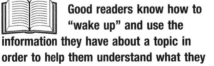 **Good readers know how to "wake up" and use the information they have about a topic in order to help them understand what they are reading.**   —Tovani (2000, p. 65)

Accessing and Evaluating Information

To be successful at synthesizing, Internet searchers must be able to locate information and make judgments about its reliability. A learner makes decisions about the text based on familiarity, convenience, time constraints, and his need for the most current information. In order to make these decisions, the reader may think through a series of questions such as:

- Which search engine best meets my needs?
- How do I form my question or keywords in order to get the most useful results?
- Which link is most useful for finding the information I want?
- Is the information I found credible?
- Where else can I look to confirm this information or find more?

Several of these questions may be answered early on in the inquiry process, during the Questioning, Understanding resources, and Evaluating phases; however, keep in mind that Internet inquiry is iterative, not linear. Answers to these questions help guide the reader into selecting the most appropriate website or links to other websites, providing the groundwork for identifying important ideas needed in the development of a synthesis.

Determining Important Ideas

Internet readers are inundated with information in the form of text, graphics, icons, multimedia resources, diagrams, photographs, and illustrations. Skilled readers must determine the most important ideas that deserve their attention and a place in their memory. A learner may begin by skimming the text to determine the gist, or main idea, recognizing that important points in Internet text may be found not only in the text but also in the visuals. At this point, he scans for titles, headings, bold words, or captions that hint at more information to come. If this perusal seems fruitful, the student returns for a more careful reading of the entire text, certain parts of the text, or visual displays. This rereading focuses on attention to details. Experienced readers pause at various places in the text to determine what is important by using the following mental process to sift through information (Brown & Day, 1983):

1. Mentally deleting unneeded information.
2. Creating a mental outline of ideas that are more important and less important.
3. Mentally constructing the kernel or main idea.

This process occurs subconsciously and seems to happen in the blink of an eye. The reader is constantly making mental decisions about which pieces of information are important and how best to whittle those down into a main idea. Sometimes this information comes directly from the words, and other times information is gathered from images that supplement or enhance the text.

Graphics and multimedia resources are valuable sources of information sometimes overlooked by the reader, whether in print or online. Visuals, such as charts, diagrams, and illustrations, are tools for the reader, if he knows how to harvest the information he needs. Video and audio clips can contain interesting and useful information. Encourage the reader to begin by previewing each resource as a whole. A reader should consider what the graphic means and possible questions that arise from this interpretation. Then suggest the reader take a more careful look by focusing in on the details. Stress the importance of identifying the information necessary for understanding the graphic. Next, model for students how to build a mental connection between the parts and the whole by thinking aloud. Describe the thought processes used to make sense of graphics and multimedia resources. As a class, discuss how these work together to convey an idea, then describe what must be done to put this idea into your own words.

When encountering multimedia resources, the learner must first know how to access a resource. Some sound or visual sources will pop open with a click on a link. Others require the downloading of software (often free) in order to view the clip. In our experience, students often view multimedia as something extra, rather than a primary source of information. For example, a fifth-grader was looking for information on Thomas Edison. When he encountered a video clip of Edison's family and life, he skipped the link, thinking it was about a different Thomas Edison. For various reasons, the student did not believe that this multimedia source could provide him with needed information. It may be that he lacked the skills to determine the important ideas from the video, and thought that watching would be a waste of time. In contrast, other students gravitate to multimedia, watching and listening to anything they can find even if it does not readily meet their informational needs.

> Although the intention of the assignment was to have students learn something of personal interest by doing research on the Web, there was little evidence that students thought that was the assignment. Students seemed to work on three other goals: finding a perfect Web page, getting a small number of hits, or finding a ready-made answer to their question.
> —Wallace et al. (2000, p. 84)

Determining what is important in a multimedia resource involves five steps. First the learner must identify her purpose by identifying the information she hopes to gain from the website. Next, she activates her prior knowledge about the topic of the multimedia resource. Then she watches or listens to the entire clip without stopping, focusing on a general impression of the meaning. Next, she watches or listens again, this time pausing two or three times to stop, think, and write about the important ideas. After finishing the clip, she takes time to summarize the important ideas and make a mental connection to other things she knows or has read. These strategies work hand-in-hand to encourage students to take full advantage of the multimedia sources that abound in an online environment.

Re-forming the Information into Your Own Idea

Determining important ideas is necessary but not sufficient for creating a synthesis. To move from summarizing to synthesizing, readers must personally interact with the text. Words and ideas from the text are integrated into the reader's personal questions, thoughts, and experiences. The integration provides the learner with the resources needed to create a new insight. Previously in this chapter, we used the analogy of a synthesis as a thread linking the kernels of important ideas together and tying into our prior knowledge. This thread is made stronger by our prior knowledge and influenced by our own experiences, beliefs, and values, or the sociocultural perspective we bring to our reading of the text (see Chapter 1). Re-forming the ideas into something new requires a higher level of thinking, including analysis, interpretation, and evaluation, in combination with an awareness of our own understandings as a reader. All of these mental tools enable the student to piece together ideas to form a unique view of what is being read.

 [When searching, students usually] try to find a concrete answer instead of collecting information from which they themselves can deduce an answer.
—Kuiper, Volman, and Terwel (2004, p. 7)

Demonstrating the Process of Synthesis

Because synthesis is so complex, we thought it would be helpful to explore the ways both skilled and less skilled readers demonstrate synthesis when reading on the Web. A group of 21 sixth-grade students were given the task of finding the answer to the question, "What is the difference between a landfill and a dump?" (Coiro & Dobler, in press). The question requires a synthesis of ideas from more than one website. The students possessed adequate knowledge of how to use the Internet to find information, based on an Internet survey. Each reader was asked to begin by using the search engine Yahooligans at *www.yahooligans.com.* Our observation of their Internet reading processes provided insights into the minds of these readers and the thought processes they used when creating a synthesis (Figure 7.2). What follows is a description of the skilled readers' approaches in contrast with the less skilled readers' approaches to the task.

FIGURE 7.2. Synthesizing information is an invisible process.

Skilled Readers' Approaches

The Internet reading process, as illustrated in the QUEST model, guided the search of all the skilled readers. These readers recognized that the answer to the landfill and dump question would likely involve the synthesis of more than one idea, and some of the readers determined that these different ideas would probably come from different websites. Most of the readers began by searching for <landfill + dump>. However, since this keyword combination returned no results, readers typically tried searching for <landfill> and <dump> separately. At this point, readers began to separate into those searching for a one-stop website with all the needed information and those who understood that the information would have to be gathered from more than one website.

Synthesizing is the most complex of comprehension strategies.
—Harvey and Goudvis (2000, p. 143)

Several of the skilled readers bypassed useful information for answering the question by scanning and skimming too quickly. For instance, one of the boys spent about 3 seconds on each webpage, hoping that the information he was looking for would just jump out at him—it never did. Luckily, his persistence kept him going, and after having little success, he began to slow down and read more carefully. In contrast, another student was a slow, careful reader. She read every word on each webpage because this was the same process she used for reading a book. This student seemed to believe that slow, careful reading was necessary so as not to miss any information. Understandably, her search for the similarities between a landfill and a dump was quite time-consuming. Internet readers typically do not have time to give such careful attention to every webpage encountered, nor is this attention necessary.

One insightful student determined quickly that the information she was seeking would not be found within a single website. When describing the process she used to locate the information, she explained how she first looked for information about landfills and then returned to the search engine to look for information about dumps. She joined together the ideas she had collected to describe a landfill as a modern dump. As is ideal, this student synthesized the ideas into a new perspective.

Less Skilled Readers' Approaches

Less skilled readers began the search with a limited understanding of how to pull ideas together from various websites to create a synthesis. This became apparent quite early on in their Internet searches. From the beginning, the less skilled readers had difficulty in identifying their search terms. Instead of typing the term "landfill" and "dump" into the search box, several of these readers typed in the entire search question. The addition of the extra, unneeded words, caused the search engine to give them no results. A second and third attempt

"Good readers could look at all the things first. Like, instead of just start reading, they could look at all the pictures and the captions and see if it has to do with what they want to read, and then start reading."
—Jessica, fifth-grader

involved rewording the search question and trying again. Some of the less skilled readers came to a halt at this point, unable to locate any useful information.

Other less skilled readers were able to locate at least one website that contained information about a landfill or a dump. These readers typically skimmed the page for an answer to their question, often hoping to find the *exact* answer. Much effort was needed to read and search in various locations and pull together pieces of information. Not surprisingly, these learners simply wanted to find the information and be finished with the task.

Readers in both groups demonstrated a need for the development of stronger reading and navigating skills in order to locate useful information quickly. The qualities of skilled Internet readers include being able to decode quickly and accurately, being persistent in their Internet search, being aware of when information does not seem to be accurate or to make sense, and having confidence in their ability to find the answer to the question.

How Do We Teach Synthesizing Strategies?

Of all the steps in the QUEST, Synthesizing may be one of the most challenging to teach. First, the act of synthesis involves the combination of several strategies, each one complex in its own right. Moreover, the process of mentally pulling together ideas is unseen by an observer and often inadequately described by the reader. In other words, it's difficult to explain exactly how a synthesis is formed within our own minds or in the minds of others, but we know one when we see one. How do we explain such complex thinking to a reader? How do we describe something that occurs in the mind? One place to begin is to focus on building a strong foundation in reading comprehension strategies, many of which are described in Chapter 2. Below, we highlight two models of instruction, teacher think-aloud and gradual release of responsibility (also described in Chapter 1), and present two classroom examples of synthesis in action.

Teacher Think-Aloud

As mentioned in Chapter 1, sharing our own thought processes through a think-aloud has been shown to be an effective way to model the process of synthesis for students. Some research supports the use of teacher modeling as a way to guide students into synthesizing ideas (Afflerbach & Johnston, 1986). Other research indicates that teacher modeling, as with a think-aloud, is most effective when the strategy explanation is explicit, leaving few opportunities for the reader to guess at the process (see Raphael, Wonnacott, & Pearson, 1983; Gordon & Pearson, 1983). After explanation, modeling demonstrates the way a reader flexibly uses strategies, depending on the reading purpose and the type of text.

A think-aloud gives the listener a bird's-eye view into the mind of the reader as he becomes privy to the thought processes a reader uses to gather information and make decisions about which website to select or where to read on the webpage. During the process, a teacher can share her purpose for reading, her interests, her choice of texts, and the sequence she used for creating her synthesis. Her students will have a better understanding of the process she will soon expect them to use in creating a synthesis.

> "If it sounds like the information on the website could help you, then keep it on your list, your little mental list. Because sometimes things pop up in a place that you don't think it would work because people think differently than you do, so they might organize the site differently than you do."
> —Mark, sixth-grader

Gradual Release of Responsibility

As discussed in Chapter 1, another effective way of teaching reading strategies is through the gradual release of responsibility as students move toward creating a synthesis on their own. Pearson and Gallagher (1983) refer to the gradual release of responsibility as the reader moves from listening and watching to demonstrating and creating. Early in the instructional sequence, the teacher assumes all of the responsibility for instruction, including direct instruction and modeling. Gradually, more responsibility is assumed by the reader through scaffolding and guided practice, until the student assumes all of

> "Good readers probably look for keywords and try to find those words in the paragraph, and they probably read the paragraph more carefully than I did. They probably look at different places to make sure they have the right answer also."   —Tenisha, sixth-grader

the responsibility for the use of a strategy while the teacher becomes a participant or facilitator. A teacher breaks down the synthesis process into smaller steps, describes each step, models each step, and gives students the opportunity for repeated practice until readers are able to create a synthesis independently.

Readers vary in skill and experience and may need different amounts of attention and practice at different stages along the way. Students who struggle with reading, who have physical or cognitive impairments, or who have emergent decoding skills may want to begin practicing synthesis through the use of text-to-speech software, as described in Chapter 3. Such software reduces the cognitive load of decoding so that readers can focus on developing strategies through listening comprehension.

In our work with less skilled Internet readers, we notice that if these students get stuck at one step of a synthesis process, they typically stop reading. If they cannot access useful information or find a website that connects to their prior knowledge, they never harvest enough information to create a synthesis. Young readers tend to struggle with the step of determining important ideas. When asked to create a summary of what they have read, some young readers tend to say too much. Everything seems as important as everything else. Alternately, they focus on the interesting and exotic ideas rather than the essential ideas. At other times, readers struggle with obtaining enough important information to create a summary. Still other readers are skilled at determining important ideas but are unsure of what to do with this information and how to make it their own. They may lack the prior knowledge and experiences needed for developing personal connections to the text. Another group of readers wants to stick with the literal, hoping to go right to one paragraph or one webpage, find the information, and be finished reading, seeming to lack the inner drive of inquiry that encour-

 The students we observed did not engage in information seeking as we define it, a process that includes multiple stages of question asking and refining, information gathering and evaluating, and finally synthesis and use of information.
—Wallace et al. (2000 p. 97)

ages them to keep searching and pulling together ideas from various websites in order to create a synthesis.

You can see how the process of the synthesis is fraught with possible difficulties. Synthesis can be characterized as mental aerobics, stretching your brain in different directions as you learn new ideas. For the rest of this chapter, we focus on ways to help students become more strategic about synthesizing.

Synthesis in Action: Guided Reading

The fourth-graders in Sandy Taylor's class are grouped by ability into guided reading groups. Sandy selects text appropriate for each group's reading ability and designs instructional activities to promote word study and comprehension based on the needs of the readers in each group. For the students in her middle-level ability group, Sandy selected text from A to Z Readers at *www.readinga-z.com*, entitled *Whales*. Sandy also obtained from the school library a text set of the book *Whales and Dolphins*, part of the Internet-linked series published by Usborne Discovery. From the Usborne Quicklinks website at *www. usborne-quicklinks.com*, the reader can link to various sources of information about whales, including downloadable pictures, an audio clip of humpback whales, directions for making a flip book of a whale swimming, an interactive quiz, and games about whale information.

[Synthesis] should go on throughout the process of reading—not just at the end. In a way it's a matter of bringing together different ideas and facts, from the text and from the reader's experience, and weaving them together into a tapestry, something larger, more complete than all the threads.
—Keene and Zimmermann (1997, p. 173)

Sandy's plan (see *Synthesizing Lesson Plan*, Handout S-16) for using these resources began with having the group read the A to Z Reader *Whales*, because the text was at their instructional level. She wanted to use *Whales and Dolphins* for accessing additional information, but found the text to be too difficult for this group of students. Therefore, she divided the text into manageable chunks and asked each student to read a section of interest. Students read and completed a *Text Map* (Handout S-1) as a way to visually display the information collected from the books. Next, the students accessed the Internet links to accompany *Whales and Dolphins*. These links provided additional information, which the students collected on their text map. After gathering information, they used the text map to help them create a poster about whales, and then presented the poster to the other guided reading groups. Sandy informally evaluated the text map, poster, and oral presentation to assess the students' ability to determine important ideas, summarize, and create a synthesis.

Synthesis in Action: Computer Lab

Kim Cunningham is an instructional technology facilitator at a K–6 school. As Valentine's Day was approaching, she planned a synthesis activity for each of the fourth- through sixth-grade classes' weekly computer time. The topic for the activity was chocolate, which she found motivating for even the most reluctant readers. As she prepared the activity, Kim located a website that was both useful and appropriate for this age group. The website *How Stuff Works* at *www.howstuffworks.com* has a link to a webpage entitled "How Chocolate Works." Based on this website, Kim designed a list of questions for students to answer and created a word processing document for recording answers. The questions were as follows:

- What tree provides the main ingredient in chocolate?
- What part of the seed is used?
- What ingredients are used to make milk chocolate?

While reading, students toggled back and forth between the Internet and the word processing program in order to read and record information. After locating answers, the students took their new-found information and used it to create individual PowerPoint presentations about chocolate. The presentation was a chance for students to apply electronic literacy skills such as creating a title card, changing backgrounds, using fill effects, importing clipart, incorporating animation, using slide transitions, and varying fonts. The fifth- and sixth-grade students were also taught how to create a hyperlink from a PowerPoint slide to a website. The individual chocolate presentations provided the students with an opportunity to demonstrate their skills in Synthesizing, as well as Transforming, the focus of Chapter 8.

Activities to Promote Synthesis

The most effective way to promote synthesis is to use reading materials—both print and electronic—at each reader's independent reading level. Using familiar texts that are easy to decode and understand will focus the instruction on the strategy rather than the other challenges a reader may face with the text. As your students become more skilled, increase the difficulty of the texts and pass on more responsibility to the students until they are able to form a synthesis on their own. This process will likely take time and practice, because synthesizing is a higher-level thinking skill—one with which some students may experience success only with much guidance and many opportunities to practice.

The *Text Map* (Handout S-1) referred to earlier helps students identify the features of a website that point out important information. The *Text Map Rubric*

(Handout S-2) helps you track student progress when used as a pre- and/or post-assessment. The *SQ3R Strategy* (Handout S-3), which has assisted readers of print text for years, is adapted here for Internet text. Handout S-4, *Before, During, and After*, is a great way to assist students in planning ways to collect information throughout the reading process. Because determining and summarizing important ideas from a website can be difficult, we offer the handout *Determining Important Ideas* (Handout S-5). Skills for synthesizing graphics and multimedia can be developed with *Worth a Thousand Words* (Handout S-6) and *What You See and Hear* (Handout S-7). The *Key Idea Synthesis Chart* (Handout S-8) not only helps students identify important ideas but asks them to justify their choices. The *Synthesis Map* (Handout S-9) provides a structure for pulling together ideas from several websites to form a synthesis, along with *Two-Column Web Journal* (Handout S-10) and *Design a Homepage* (Handout S-11). *Evidence For and Against* (Handout S-12) provides practice with synthesizing persuasive arguments. The *Synthesis Self-Checker* (Handout S-13) provides a format for evaluating the quality of a written synthesis. A *Synthesis Rubric* (Handout S-14) is provided for assessing a synthesis presented to the class or a small group, and students are encouraged to reflect on their own synthesizing abilities with the *Synthesis Self-Reflection* (Handout S-15). Finally, we offer a *Synthesizing Lesson Plan* (Handouts S-16 and S-17) for the elementary level and the middle level.

Summary

Synthesis facilitates the process of understanding what we see, hear, and read by creating a link between a collection of facts and ideas. At the heart of synthesis is determining what is important. Titles, headings, and visuals provide the Web reader with hints at important ideas, but valuable information can also be gained from a careful reading of longer texts, viewing a video, or listening to a sound clip. Once these important ideas are gathered and summarized, a reader forms a mental thread linking the ideas together. She makes the information her own through the creation of a personal interpretation or understanding.

After Synthesis, the next step in an Internet QUEST often involves the Transforming of this new-found knowledge into a format that can be shared with others through the creation of a final product. Chapter 8 is devoted to the idea of transformation, how it occurs, and ways to help students become more strategic when making notes, organizing information, citing sources, creating final products, and presenting what they've learned.

Handouts

All of the Chapter 7 handouts listed in the following chart can be used with both print and Internet texts; in fact, you may want to have students practice using some of them on easy informational texts before trying them with webpages, which are more complex owing to all the additional cueing systems (see Chapter 2). As with all of our handouts, choose a few that look promising and save the rest for another time.

Number	Name of handout	Purpose
S-1	Text Map	Identify features of a website
S-2	Text Map Assessment Rubric	Assess summarization of a website
S-3	SQ3R Strategy	Record the main points on a page
S-4	Before, During, and After	Engage in active reading strategies
S-5	Determining Important Ideas	Summarize important ideas
S-6	Worth a Thousand Words	Synthesize graphics
S-7	What You See and Hear	Synthesize multimedia
S-8	Key Idea Synthesis Chart	Identify ideas and justify choices
S-9	Synthesis Map	Synthesize from multiple sites
S-10	Two-Column Web Journal	Compare facts and responses
S-11	Design a Homepage	Synthesize information
S-12	Evidence For and Against	Synthesize persuasive arguments
S-13	Synthesis Self-Checker	Check your synthesis
S-14	Synthesis Rubric	Assess a synthesis
S-15	Synthesis Self-Reflection	Assess a synthesis
S-16	Synthesizing Lesson Plan—Elementary Level	Process of creating a synthesis from print and online sources
S-17	Synthesizing Lesson Plan—Middle Level	Process of creating a synthesis from print and online sources

HANDOUT S-1. Text Map

Name _____ Class _____ Date _____

Preview a website, focusing on Internet features.

URL: _____

Headings:	Subheadings:

Bolded or Italicized Words:	Graphics (pictures, icons, charts, maps, etc.). Describe:

Multimedia (audio, video, etc.). Describe:	Based on this information, what are the main ideas of this website?

HANDOUT S-2. Text Map Rubric

	STRONG	BASIC	EMERGING
Completeness	Text map reflects a complete viewing of the website. Each element is described in vivid detail.	Text map reflects an adequate viewing of the website. Each element is described, although some elements may contain limited information.	Text map reflects a limited viewing of the website. Appears that the student gave a quick glance and then described the website, leaving out several details.
Accuracy	Information shared in the text map accurately reflects the information found on the website.	Information shared in the text map is mostly accurate, but may contain some information the student has misinterpreted. Gaps in the information may also exist.	Key information from the website is missing or inaccurate. Unclear whether the student actually read the website.
Neatness	Ideas displayed on the text map are written clearly and are easy to interpret.	Ideas displayed on the text map are written somewhat clearly, but a few may be difficult to interpret.	Ideas displayed on the text map are messy, or written in a style such that the reader has trouble figuring out the words.

HANDOUT S-3. SQ3R Strategy

Name _____ Class _____ Date _____

SURVEY—QUESTION—READ—RECITE—REVIEW

URL: _____

SURVEY: Skim over the webpage, glancing at all the features (text, images, links, etc.) What do you think this page is going to cover?

QUESTION: Turn the titles and headings into questions. For example, if the site says "Panda Habitat" at the top, write the question, "What is the panda's habitat?"

READ: Read one section at a time. Write answers to the questions you wrote above.

RECITE: Summarize the main points without looking back at the webpage.

REVIEW: Reread your summary, checking the webpage for any main points you may have missed. Write any missing points here.

HANDOUT S-4. Before, During, and After

Name _____ Class _____ Date _____

Pick a website for your topic that you want to read closely and ask yourself the following questions.

URL: _____

BEFORE READING

1. What do I already know about this topic?

2. Why am I reading this?

3. How is this website organized?

DURING READING

1. What will the webpage talk about next? Use clues from text, links, and media.

2. What does it mean? (If you find something hard to understand.)

3. How does it connect with what I already know?

AFTER READING

1. What did I learn?

2. What did I miss? Reread to see if you missed anything important.

3. How can I use this info?

HANDOUT S-5. Determining Important Ideas

Name _____ Class _____ Date _____

Pick a website and use this chart to identify important ideas.

URL: _____

	Write your answers in this column
1. Skim the webpage. What is it about?	
2. Scan for five keywords from the webpage.	
3. Sketch or describe an illustration, icon, or chart on the webpage.	
4. What is the most important idea on the webpage?	
5. I know this idea is important because . . .	

Based on Harvey (1998). From *Reading the Web* by Maya B. Eagleton and Elizabeth Dobler. Copyright 2007 by The Guilford Press. Permission to photocopy this handout is granted to purchasers of this book for personal use only (see copyright page for details).

HANDOUT S-6. Worth a Thousand Words

Name _____ Class _____ Date _____

Much valuable information can be gained from a careful look at the graphics on a website, including photos, drawings, charts, graphs, and maps. Don't overlook these great resources, thinking that the answer to your question will be found only in the words. For this activity, select one graphic from a website to look at more closely.

URL: _____

Sketch the graphic here:

(1) OVERVIEW: Look over the whole picture. What does it make you think about? What does it make you wonder?	(2) FOCUS: Give careful attention to the details. Be sure to read the labels, captions, and description. What are three details you notice? What is one question you have?

(3) CONNECT: Build connections between the parts and the whole. How do the parts help you understand the graphic?

HANDOUT S-7. What You See and Hear

Name _____ Class _____ Date _____

Lots of information can be found in the multimedia options available on a website in the form of a slide show, movie, or sound clip. You might think you don't have time to watch or listen. Follow these easy steps for a better understanding of what you see and hear.

URL: _____

Circle the type of clip: VIDEO   AUDIO

____ Step 1: Identify your purpose. Think about why you are listening or watching. What do you hope to learn?

____ Step 2: Think about what you know. Before you begin listening or watching, jot down four or five things that you already know about the subject.

____ Step 3: Watch or listen to the clip straight through with no interruptions. What is your general impression?

____ Step 4: Watch or listen again. This time, use the pause button to stop two or three times while listening or watching. When you pause, first think about what you have seen or heard. Next, jot down two or three key ideas you want to remember. Then return to finish watching or listening.

Pause #1: What do you want to remember?

Pause #2: What do you want to remember?

Pause #3: What do you want to remember?

____ Step 5: Summarize. Write a sentence or two explaining the most important idea about what you saw or heard.

HANDOUT S-8. Key Idea Synthesis Chart

Name _____ Class _____ Date _____

Identify six of the most important ideas related to your inquiry question. Use at least two different websites to locate information about these ideas. Think about how you would explain the most important ideas to someone who had not read these websites.

Key Idea with URL	Put the Idea in Your Own Words	Explain Why the Idea is Important
1.		
2.		
3.		
4.		
5.		
6.		

HANDOUT S-9. Synthesis Map

Name _____ Class _____ Date _____

Find information on your topic from three different websites, summarize the info, then create a synthesis of all three.

URL#1 _____

Summary

URL#2 _____

Summary

URL#3 _____

Summary

Synthesis

HANDOUT S-10. Two-Column Web Journal

Name _____ Class _____ Date _____

Use this journal to record facts and your thinking as your read various websites. Feel free to use these sentence starters for your personal responses:

• I wonder . . .	• I am curious about . . .
• I can't believe . . .	• I doubt . . .
• I didn't realize . . .	• This reminds me of . . .
• Now I think . . .	• I still want to know . . .

URL #1: _____

Facts from the Website	Personal Response

URL #2: _____

Facts from the Website	Personal Response

URL #3: _____

Facts from the Website	Personal Response

HANDOUT S-11. Design a Homepage (page 1 of 2)

Name _____ Class _____ Date _____

After gathering information from two or more websites, synthesize your ideas by sketching a storyboard on paper. Decide what is important and how best to communicate these ideas to another reader. Use the model on page 2 if needed.

(1) Make up a URL that reflects your topic: http://www._____

(2) Make a banner that has the title of your page, a catchy phrase, and an icon or symbol for your topic.

(5) Draw buttons that would link to other places in your site.	(3) Write a Welcome Statement with the purpose of your site.
	(4) Make headings for key info. Put one to two sentences underneath each one.
	(6) Draw an image, chart, or graph here.

If needed, use this model to help you design your homepage storyboard.

My URL: http://www.whale-expert.com/homepage.html

Whale Expert Site
The Best Whale Info Center Ever!

Welcome to the Whale Expert Site!

Did you know that the blue whale is the biggest animal that ever lived? Did you know that the killer whale is actually a dolphin?

This site has everything you need to know about whales.
****

Baleen Whale
(Humpback)

Toothed Whale
(Killer Whale)

TYPES OF WHALES

Baleen Whales
Most baleen whales swim with their mouths open and strain food from the water. When they close their mouths, the water is forced out and food gets trapped in the fringe mat (baleen). After all the water is gone, the whale swallows its meal.

Toothed Whales
There are about 65 different species of toothed whales. Toothed whales, including all dolphins and porpoises, have teeth, only one blowhole (baleen whales have two) and are generally smaller than most baleen whales.

Types of Whales

About Us

Ask the Expert

Whale Links

Whale Diet

Whale Life Cycle

Whale Habitat

Whale Sounds

HANDOUT S-12. Evidence For and Against

Name _____ Class _____ Date _____

Identify two websites that display opposite views on an issue. Use this chart to list the evidence for and against the issue, then explain your personal opinion.

What's the issue? _____

URL #1: Evidence For	URL #2: Evidence Against	My Personal Opinion

HANDOUT S-13. Synthesis Self-Checker

Name _____ Class _____ Date _____

Synthesize info on your topic from two sites and use the self-checker to see how you did.

URL #1 _____

URL #2 _____

My Synthesis

- ☐ Is my synthesis short?
- ☐ Is my synthesis accurate?
- ☐ Is it in my own words?
- ☐ Does it include the most important ideas and info?
- ☐ Does it include some supporting details?
- ☐ Is there anything missing?
- ☐ Does the order make sense?

HANDOUT S-14. Synthesis Rubric

	STRONG	BASIC	EMERGING
Use of Supporting Details	Pertinent and complete supporting details demonstrate an integration of ideas.	The supporting details are adequate, but may be missing a key idea or two.	The supporting details are minimal and have left gaps in information.
Synthesis of Ideas	Ideas are integrated into prior knowledge, reflecting a deep understanding of the topic.	Some new or unique ideas are presented, but limited connections are made between the new and the known, reflecting an adequate understanding.	Basic facts are restated from the text, and few new or unique ideas are presented, reflecting little understanding of the topic.
Presentation of Synthesis	Shares ideas from the visual display that indicate comprehension and synthesis. Speaks clearly and loudly and is comfortable with the material.	When sharing ideas, the visual display is used as a reference, but most of the information comes directly from the presenter. Speaks clearly and loudly, but is not fully comfortable with the material.	Shares information mostly by reading from the poster. May not articulate clearly or may be difficult to understand. Not comfortable with the material.

HANDOUT S-15. Synthesis Self-Reflection (use with Handout S-17)

Name _____ Class _____ Date _____

Think about the following questions as they relate to your synthesis activity. Be honest!

1. How would I rate the quality of my activity between 1 and 5? _____
   Why did I give it this rating?

2. What is the best part of my synthesis activity?

3. What do I wish I had done differently during this activity?

4. How well did I use sticky notes and a *Text Map* (Handout S-1) during this activity?

5. How well did my partner and I work together? If you worked alone, write N/A.

6. What did I learn about creating a synthesis?

Objectives

1. To determine important ideas from text and websites.
2. To create a synthesis of important ideas.

Time

Three or four class periods

Materials

1. *QUEST Inquiry Model* (Handout P-11)
2. A to Z Readers at *www.readinga-z.com*, entitled *Whales*
3. *Whales and Dolphins* published by Usborne Discovery
4. Usborne Quicklinks website at *www.usborne-quicklinks.com*
5. *Text Map* (Handout S-1)
6. Sticky notes

Assessment Options

1. *Text Map Rubric* (Handout S-2)
2. *Synthesis Rubric* (Handout S-14)

Introduction

1. Tell students you will be teaching them a strategy for synthesizing that many other students have found useful. Contextualize the lesson, using the *QUEST Inquiry Model* (Handout P-11), by pointing out that they are in the <u>S</u> phase of the QUEST, which includes synthesizing information.
2. Explain that a synthesis is a way to bring together the ideas you learn from reading books, magazines, and websites. Say, "We can take these ideas and explain them to someone else, such as a teacher, other students, and parents, by writing, making a poster or other display, or simply telling the ideas to someone. We are going to do a little of all three."
3. Activate prior knowledge about whales and dolphins by creating a group list of facts.
4. Have the group read the A to Z Reader *Whales*. Listen to individual students read a page or two and note fluency.
5. Provide the students with the text *Whales and Dolphins*. Divide the text into manageable chunks and invite students to select a section to read; include the first chunk for the teacher.
6. Pass out sticky notes.

Modeling

1. Think aloud while reading from *Whales and Dolphins*.
2. Model for students how you will determine an important idea. Then write the idea on a sticky note and place the note near the idea in the book. Complete this step three times.

Practice

1. Have students get in small groupts to read their text chunks and identify three important ideas. Place these on sticky notes.
2. Invite students to locate additional information from the websites provided in the text.
3. Complete the *Text Map* (Handout S-1) as a group, gathering additional information from the websites to add to the ideas on the sticky notes.
4. Move from the text map to creating a poster displaying the most important information.
5. Use headings, graphics, and some text to convey ideas.
6. Give an oral presentation of posters to the class.

Scaffolding

1. If anyone is struggling to decode their text, have a proficient reader read it aloud.
2. Allow weaker writers to dictate ideas to stronger writers.
3. Group shy students with brave ones for oral presentations.

Feedback

1. Have students provide feedback to each other following each presentation, including compliments and suggestions.
2. Give students a copy of the *Synthesis Rubric* (Handout S-14) prior to your evaluating their text map, poster, and presentation.

Ticket Out the Door

Have students name two characteristics of a good synthesis based on the rubric (i.e., completeness and accuracy).

HANDOUT S-17. Synthesizing Lesson Plan—Middle Level (page 1 of 2)

Objectives

1. To determine important ideas from text and websites.
2. To create a synthesis of important ideas.

Time

Three or four class periods

Materials

1. *QUEST Inquiry Model* (Handout P-11)
2. Access to a variety of print and online resources related to the topic of oceanic life
3. An overhead copy of a page of informational text about an ocean animal
4. *Text Map* (Handout S-1)
5. *Synthesis Self-Reflection* (Handout S-15)
6. Sticky notes

Assessment Options

1. *Text Map Rubric* (Handout S-2)
2. *Synthesis Rubric* (Handout S-14)

Introduction

1. Tell students you will be teaching them a strategy for synthesizing that many other students have found useful. Contextualize the lesson, using the *QUEST Inquiry Model* (Handout P-11), by pointing out that they are in the S̲ phase of the QUEST, which includes synthesizing information.
2. Explain that a synthesis occurs when we bring together information found in various sources and then present it to others in a new way. Have students brainstorm why synthesizing is useful in this class, in other classes, and outside of school. This can be done in pairs, in small groups, or as a whole class.
3. Activate prior knowledge about oceanic life. Brainstorm a list of animals that live in the ocean, and have pairs of students select an ocean animal to study further.
4. Have students locate resources from the library or in the classroom with information about their selected ocean animal.
5. Pass out sticky notes.

Modeling

1. Think aloud while reading from an overhead copy of a page of informational text about an ocean animal.
2. Model for students how you will determine an important idea. Then write the idea on a sticky note and place near the idea on the page. Complete this step three times.

Practice

1. Have students read their texts in partners and identify three important ideas for each. Place these on sticky notes.
2. Invite students to use a search engine to locate a website with additional information about their chosen animal.
3. Have the students complete the *Text Map* (Handout S-1) in partners, based on the information found on the website.
4. Move from the text map to creating a visual displaying the most important information (poster, chart, PowerPoint slide show).
5. Use headings, graphics, and some text to convey ideas.
6. Give an oral presentation of the displays to the class.
7. Have students complete a *Synthesis Self-Reflection* (Handout S-15).

Scaffolding

1. If anyone is struggling to decode their text, have a proficient reader read it aloud.
2. Allow weaker writers to dictate ideas to stronger writers.
3. Group shy students with brave ones for oral presentations.

Feedback

1. Have students provide feedback to each other following each presentation, including compliments and suggestions.
2. Give students a copy of the *Synthesis Rubric* (Handout S-14) prior to your evaluating their text map, display, and presentation.

Ticket Out the Door

Have students name two characteristics of a good synthesis based on the rubric (i.e., completeness and accuracy).

8 TRANSFORMING

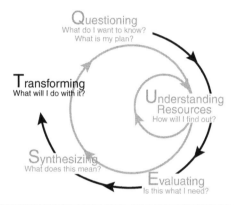

KEY IDEAS

▶ Information by itself is not knowledge. Since many students struggle with Transforming information into knowledge, we must provide instruction and scaffolding in this important skill.

▶ The key question that guides the T phase of the inquiry process is, "What will I do with this information?"

▶ Since a large majority of learners do not know how to make notes in their own words, they need to be taught specific strategies for notemaking, whether it be from books or from electronic resources.

▶ When queried, most students are not able to articulate an organizational strategy for how to manage all the information they collect during inquiry.

▶ Citing sources has traditionally been an area of challenge for students, and the ease of copying information and media from the Internet has made this task even more challenging.

▶ In an effort to move beyond the traditional research report, we like to offer students the opportunity to demonstrate what they've learned in various formats, such as webpages, slide shows, and posters.

▶ While not all inquiry projects must eventually be presented orally, this is a frequently used method for sharing knowledge products.

> **Taking information and converting it into knowledge is like spinning straw into gold. Through students' independent thoughts, they are able to produce and contribute knowledge, a significant accomplishment in the present and an important skill for the future.**
> **—Guinee and Eagleton (2006, p. 52)**

A pile of information is not very useful unless it is internalized as knowledge and eventually transformed into something new. In this chapter, we draw from years of classroom-based research to investigate the strategies involved in Transforming information into knowledge. Since this phase of the QUEST is similar for traditional library research and Internet inquiry, we focus specifically on the technological aspects because these are the ones that have been least explored. Successful Transformation necessitates that students have strategies for notemaking, organizing information, citing sources, creating a product, and presenting final products to others.

Why Is It Important to Transform Information?

Just as with the writing process, in which not all rough drafts are selected for a final polish, not all inquiries lead to a final product. For example, a simple search for an isolated fact on the Internet may satisfy a practical information need, such as obtaining directions for driving to a friend's house. However, full-scale classroom inquiry often requires transforming various pieces of information into an original product. Information by itself is not power; rather, knowledge is power (Perkins, 1986). Students who can convert information into useful knowledge, perhaps even derive solutions to real problems, and then share it with others are well on their way to success in school and in life (Leu, Kinzer, Coiro, & Cammack, 2004).

 **Information is not power in the digital age. More information than could possibly be useful in a hundred lifetimes is already immediately available to us. Power is what can be done with information: making arguments, connecting different data, perceiving themes, reaching new understandings, providing services that are useful in the real world.**
—Wilhelm and Friedemann (1998 p. 162)

Regrettably, many students are not able to transform information into knowledge (Guinee & Eagleton, 2006). Often, students' final products simply mirror what they happen to find on the Web, with no real synthesis or formation of a new idea, as described in Chapter 7. For example, one eighth-grade student found a time line on the Web, so she recreated it on a poster covering the same information. Students' final products are often a simple recall of facts rather than a synthesized, compelling perspective on a topic. Students need guidance on appropriate use of media formats, such as placing captions under pictures on posters and using large fonts with minimal text on slide show presentations. They must resist the temptation to become so enamored with multimedia features that their products lack

 Summarizing the results, we conclude that most researchers agree on two points. Firstly, children must acquire search skills as well as skills to use the information they find effectively. Both aspects require much training and support.
—Kuiper, Volman, and Terwel (2004, p. 14)

substantive content. Toward this end, Kajder (2003) recommends that in order to avoid "visual assault," multimedia products should contain 80% content and 20% glitz.

Many teachers with whom we've worked have remarked that while some of their students are facile at *finding* information, most lack strategies for *doing* something with it. Students also have difficulty knowing when they have "enough" information to begin constructing a final product. These skills do not come naturally to all learners, so they must be taught and practiced.

 Language Arts Standard: Participate in shared reading and writing activities; understand and present more than one point of view on an issue; write coherently about specific topics.

When Do We Transform Information?

We transform information in our daily lives every time we have an "aha!" moment, when seemingly random pieces of information suddenly meld into a coherent whole. Transformation can also happen more intentionally, as when a teacher looks over a few different lesson plan ideas and then creates his own plan to suit his objectives and the needs of his students. Transformation occurs every time we write, draw, make up a song or dance, invent a recipe, or use a novel metaphor to explain an abstract concept.

Transformation is at the core of a constructivist philosophy of learning (see Chapter 1). In classrooms where creativity and originality are applauded (as opposed to environments that promote rote memorization, correct answers, and "psyching out" the teacher so as to conform to a certain point of view), transformation takes place all the time. It is impressive to observe what happens when students are given freedom to express themselves using any format they wish and participate in determining how they will be assessed (see Chapter 4). With the proper scaffolding, most students thrive when given the freedom to create. These are the times when kids forget they are even "learning" and beg to be given extra time during recess, lunch, and after school to *work* on projects. Researchers have found

 Science Standard: Share findings and ideas for critical review by colleagues and other scientists; provide explanations to investigated problems or questions; communicate about science in different formats.

that many students are especially motivated when designing multimedia projects (Eagleton, 1999, 2002; Finkelman & McMunn, 1995; Lehrer, Erickson, & Connell, 1994; Tierney et al., 1997).

What Characterizes Information Transformation?

Information transformation is analogous to the concept of transmediation. Transmediation means taking content from one form of representation (such as print) and recreating it in another (such as art). In the context of Internet inquiry, transformation means synthesizing content from various resources (namely, websites) and then creating something original (such as new webpages, posters, or essays) based on a personally meaningful research question. To be successful with the Transformation phase of the QUEST, students must have strategies for notemaking, organizing information, citing sources, designing a product, and presenting it to others, topics which we address in turn.

 Social Studies Standard: Develop written narratives and short interpretive essays, as well as other appropriate presentations, from investigations of source materials.

Notemaking

Taking notes, or as our colleague Dr. Judi Moreillon aptly terms it, "note*making*," is crucial to information transformation, because it is impossible to remember everything that is found in the course of an Internet QUEST. Unfortunately, very few students make notes in their own words (Guinee & Eagleton, 2006). For instance, one eighth-grader admitted, "I don't take down notes, I just print and highlight, that's how I get my info." When using computers, students make heavy use of the copy/paste feature and the print button, which results in final projects that contain large volumes of plagiarized information. Even though most middle schoolers can parrot back a definition of "plagiarism," many don't seem to know how to avoid it and don't appear to realize when they've done it (Guinee & Eagleton, 2006).

In general, stronger students type their own notes and weaker students copy large chunks of text, though this is not always the case—it can be a strategic choice to paste a big chunk of Web-based information for later digestion. The question is, how often is a big chunk of copied text transformed into a student's own words? The answer: *Rarely*. Figure 8.1 shows one seventh-grader's final text as compared to the website text from which she got the information. Do you notice any similarities? Not only did the student submit the text unaltered, but she did not even understand what it meant. When she presented her project to the class and the teacher innocently asked for clarification on the "dun factor" information, the student was unable to define it, much less expand upon the concept.

In a pilot study of 36 eighth-graders, Guinee and Eagleton (2006) found that the students used four types of notemaking strategies during Web inquiry: (1) copy and paste large chunk; (2) copy small chunk (3) paraphrase; and (4) note to self. In this study, students saved an average of only *five* notes during an Internet inquiry

Website Text	Student's Final Text
A description of the Kiger Mustang would begin with their coloration which is known as the "dun factor." The dun factor colours are dun (which resembles a buckskin but is genetically different), red dun, grulla and claybank. There are also a few bays, blacks, and sorrels present in the Kiger Mustang herds.	A description of the Kiger Mustang would begin with their coloration which is known as the "dun factor." The dun factor colours are dun (which resembles a buckskin but is genetically different), red dun, grulla and claybank. There are also a few bays, blacks, and sorrels present in the Kiger Mustang herds.

Source: *www.horseweb.com/hw_articles/breeds/kiger.htm*

FIGURE 8.1. Information without transformation.

project in which 2 weeks were devoted to searching and notemaking. This begs the question, "How did they complete final products based on only five notes?" On average, only 16% of students' notes were paraphrased; in contrast, nearly 77% of their notes were copied verbatim. Most of these verbatim notes were then included in final projects without substantial changes.

Copy and Paste Large Chunk

In the pilot study, 45% of the students' notes involved highlighting gigantic portions of webpages and copying the unfiltered contents into word processing documents, a strategy we call copying large text chunks (Guinee & Eagleton, 2006). Some students pasted more than 1,000 words of text, and although this can save time up front, it simply postpones the inevitable chore of extracting key information. The challenge for teachers is to make sure students eventually do evaluate and synthesize this material.

Copy Small Chunk

Copying small chunks is a strategy we define as copying less than four lines of text, or about 50 words. Unlike the previous approach, this strategy requires that the reader selectively identify target information for copying. In this study, students copied small chunks for an average 32% of their notemaking. For example, in addition to collecting short quotations by Martin Luther King, Jr., one student copied the following information on his family life:

> Four children were born to Dr. and Mrs. King: Yolanda Denise (November 17, 1955 Montgomery, Alabama) Martin Luther III (October 23, 1957 Montgomery, Alabama) Dexter Scott (January 30, 1961 Atlanta, Georgia) Bernice Albertine (March 28, 1963 Atlanta, Georgia).

Paraphrase

Paraphrasing key ideas is the optimal notemaking strategy from a teacher's perspective. One learner described it thus: "I look at a certain paragraph and pick out whatever useful it has and put it down in my own words." In his search for information on Vivaldi's family, this student's notes read, "Vivaldi had four brothers and four sisters, He and his father were the two musisions [*sic*] of the family." Similarly, in an investigation of George Harrison's personality, one girl wrote, "George was the easy going on [one] in the beatles group." Unfortunately, only 16% of the notes saved by these students fell into this category.

Note to Self

The strategy of writing a metacognitive note to oneself was evidenced in only 4% of the notes analyzed, and can be attributed to only two students; however, this strategy is worthy of mention. Examples of (unedited) metacognitive notes are as follows:

- Gotta come here again!!!!!!!!!!!!!!!! I mean it!!!!!!!!!!!!!!! This is and exelent site!!!!!
- Keep in mind. This is a really informative site, one that should be used as a good resorce.
- Need this for future ref.

The relatively few notes collected by the eighth-graders and the lack of synthesis present in the notes they did make led researcher Kathleen Guinee to look more closely at notemaking practices in the upper elementary level. In a fifth-grade class, she observed that during the short Web-based research assignments, the students tended not to make *any* notes, with only a third of the fifth-graders reporting that they made notes during their research task. When asked, the students explained that they didn't make notes because they didn't feel the need. Typical reasons included "because I could keep the info in my mind" and because the information source and writing tool were both on the computer. It seems that these students considered notemaking exclusively as a tool for reducing cognitive load (Guinee & Eagleton, 2006). However, the CHoMP notemaking strategy described below accentuates that making notes is useful for more than simply helping students remember what they've read.

CHoMP Notemaking Strategy

Clearly, students are in serious need of notemaking strategies. Notemaking is not only useful during Web inquiries but also when writing down directions, studying textbooks, conducting interviews, and listening to lectures. Based on a compilation of the literature on summarization (e.g., Brown & Day, 1983; Hare & Borchardt, 1984; Winograd, 1984), Maya developed an original strategy for notemaking called "CHoMP" (Guinee & Eagleton, 2006). The verb "chomp" serves as an effective metaphor for the concept that notemaking involves selectively biting off small pieces of information. With CHoMP, students learn to:

- Cross out small words, such as prepositions and conjunctions;
- Highlight important information in the remaining text;
- o (Since this is just a placeholder, students have fun substituting other vowels);
- Make notes based on the highlighted information by abbreviating, truncating, making lists, using symbols, and drawing instead of writing full sentences;
- Put the notes in their own words.

The CHoMP strategy not only stresses the importance of making notes, but also helps students to create useful paraphrased notes for transforming information they've gathered into their own words. Before teaching CHoMP, we recommend administering a pretest of students' existing notemaking strategies. Using a one-page expository text, such as an Informal Reading Inventory for your grade level, instruct students to "show how you normally make notes." Ask them to make notes using pens and highlighters, and then write a summary based on their notes. In our experiences during this pretest, students highlight far too much information, write verbatim notes, and generate a mostly verbatim summary. Use this same procedure for a posttest after the instructional unit to observe changes in your students' notemaking. We've observed dramatic change by our students, even those with learning disabilities who struggle with print.

Introduce CHoMP as a generalizable strategy for notemaking that will help students not only in your class, but also in other classes and in the future. We've had students brainstorm the uses of notemaking at this point to ensure they understand the purpose of the lesson and the potential for transfer. After discussing the purpose, model the first step of CHoMP (Cross out) on the overhead with a single paragraph, such as the one shown in Figure 8.2. It is especially powerful to use sample sentences and paragraphs from websites that students have actually encountered in mini-inquiries prior to a notemaking unit. Provide additional paragraphs for guided and independent practice, and for homework, if desired. Most students find this first step easy; in fact, Figure 8.2 was produced by a seventh-grader with severe learning disabilities.

For CHoMP Step 2 (Highlight), repeat the modeling, guided practice, and independent practice procedure used with Step 1. This time, demonstrate the process of highlighting important information. This is generally the most difficult step for students, because it's hard for many of them to discern what is *important* versus merely interesting or unusual. We found it extremely helpful to model this decision-making process using a teacher think-aloud at the overhead. Figure 8.3 shows a different student's highlighted text.

The Siberian tiger spends a lot of time hunting because only about one in ten of its hunting trips is successful. It preys mainly on deer and wild pig, but it also eats fish. Creeping to within 30 to 80 feet of its victim, the tiger pounces and grabs the prey by the nape of the neck with its back feet still planted firmly on the ground. If the tiger misses its prey on the pounce, it may chase it for up to 650 feet but rarely catches it.

FIGURE 8.2. CHoMP Step 1: Cross out.

The Siberian tiger spends a lot of time hunting because only about one in ten of its hunting trips is successful. It preys mainly on deer and wild pig, but it also eats fish. Creeping to within 30 to 80 feet of its victim, the tiger pounces and grabs the prey by the nape of the neck with its back feet still planted firmly on the ground. If the tiger misses its prey on the pounce, it may chase it for up to 650 feet but rarely catches it.

FIGURE 8.3. CHoMP Step 2: Highlight.

In preparation for CHoMP Step 3 (Make notes), model a variety of notemaking methods, such as abbreviating, truncating, making lists, using symbols, and drawing. Then return to the texts with which the students have been working to model and practice making notes. Figures 8.4 and 8.5 show two students' different approaches to making notes about the Siberian tiger text.

Finally, for CHoMP Step 4 (Put in your own words), have the students use their notes to write an original summary. This step is most effective when students do not refer to the original text. Figure 8.6 shows one student's final notes, which were creatively and accurately paraphrased from the original text. As evidence of CHoMP's promise as a notemaking strategy, this summary was produced by the same student whose verbatim notes were shown earlier in Figure 8.1.

Once students have transformed texts using CHoMP, the likelihood of plagiarism is greatly diminished and students are in a much better position to construct

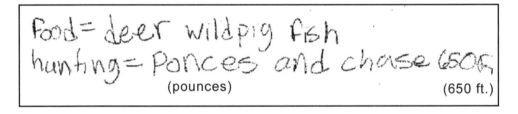

FIGURE 8.4. CHoMP Step 3: Make notes (using truncation and lists).

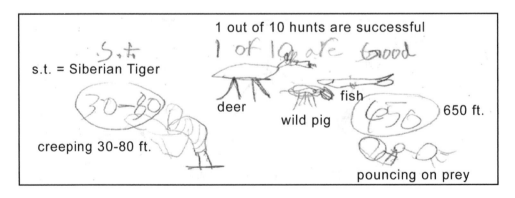

FIGURE 8.5. CHoMP Step 3: Make notes (abbreviating and drawing).

Original Text	Final Text Using CHoMP
The Siberian tiger spends a lot of time hunting because only about one in ten of its hunting trips are successful. It preys mainly on deer and wild pig, but it also eats fish. Creeping to within 30 to 80 feet of its victim, the tiger pounces and grabs the prey by the nape of the neck with its back feet still planted firmly in the ground. If the tiger misses its prey on the pounce, it may chase it for up to 650 feet but rarely catches it.	The Siberian tiger can hunt very well, here is how it hunts. The tiger awaits its prey 30 or 80 feet away and ponces [*sic*] on its prey with feet clenched in the soil. If it misses it, it will run 650 feet or more. But otherwise, it's bye-bye lunch.

FIGURE 8.6. CHoMP Step 4: Put in own words.

their own knowledge. We will share lesson plans and handouts for teaching the CHoMP notemaking strategy at the end of this chapter.

Organizing Information

After asking dozens of students to describe their strategies for organizing information, we've come to the conclusion that organizing information is not an area of strength for many elementary and middle school students, especially those with learning disabilities. We have all witnessed the hapless student with a binder stuffed full of wrinkled papers from all his classes, the inevitable dropping of the binder, the hasty restuffing, and well, you know the rest. Then there's the daily frantic search for homework in the backpack or desk full of who-knows-what (Figure 8.7). Add these images to classic excuses such as "my dog ate it," and you have a fairly accurate picture of the level of organization on which many students operate.

Figure 8.8 shows typical responses by students in grades 5–8 to the question, "How do you usually organize the information you find about a research topic?," sorted by no evidence of strategies, weak strategies, somewhat strong strategies, and strong strategies. After interviewing dozens of students, note that there was only *one* student who was able to articulate a strong organizational strategy.

> [Students can't] organize their own locker[s], much less something as abstract and complex as information!
> —Wilhelm and Friedemann (1998, p. 97)

One of the most striking aspects of these students' responses is the way in which computers can both help and hinder the organizational process. Computers can help when students are taught to create separate digital folders for each research project and to create separate files to save notes for each research question. Computers can also be helpful in reducing the volume of "scrap paper" notes that are easily lost. However, computers can also hinder the organizational process because students may forget where they saved files, lose disks, or simply copy, paste, and print without any clear plan for what to do with all the unprocessed information.

FIGURE 8.7. The ubiquitous backpack search.

	TYPICAL STUDENT RESPONSES
No Strategies	• I don't have a strategy. • Well, since I usually do it on the last day, my mom helps me look at stuff, so I don't need to keep it. [*laughter*] • Usually you try to save it, at least that's what the teachers tell you to do.
Weak Strategies	• I usually write it down on a scrap paper. • I just copy it, I mean just print it. Yeah. • I print 'em and put them in a folder. • I usually copy and paste it to Word. And after that I print it and read it over. Or I just print it from the webpage. • I usually cut and paste to a file so that I could just have all my stuff together and then after that I would print.
Somewhat Strong Strategies	• I'd print it out and lay it out in a stack. Maybe put one pack of paper sideways, to keep track of each section. • I'd organize it and collect the useful information out of it and then probably trash the rest. • I'll copy it and put it on a word processor because then I could just copy that sentence or two that I think would really go good with my topic.
Strong Strategies	• On the same computer I open up Word and I minimize it and then when I find important information then I type it into my Word document and I paraphrase it.

FIGURE 8.8. Students' typical organizational strategies.

Helping students learn stronger organizational strategies is beneficial in school and in life. For inquiry projects, the age-old 3×5 notecard method is still viable, and despite all the conveniences of modern technology, we often find ourselves suggesting to students that they print out their notes, cut them up with scissors, and rearrange them on a large, flat surface (Figure 8.9). For some students (and adults), reordering information on a screen is too visually and cognitively demanding, especially if scrolling is involved. Organizational skills developed in the elementary and middle school years can be useful through one's time in school and even beyond. We have both worked with undergraduate and even graduate students who could benefit from improving their strategies for organizing information.

Another effective strategy for organizing information and ideas is concept mapping (see Bromley, Irwin-DeVitis, & Modlo, 1995, for ideas). The classic example is a bubble map depicting a topic in the center, with subtopics and sub-subtopics linked to the center bubble (similar to Handout Q-3 in Chapter 4). A popular software tool for concept mapping is *Inspiration* (2006) (or *Kidspiration*, designed for grades K–5). Not only does it relieve the chore of handwriting, but it is infinitely flexible, allowing instant movement of text, clipart, and student-generated graphics into multiple linked relationships. A handy feature of *Inspiration* is the ability to toggle between the map view (Figure 8.10) and the outline view (Figure 8.11). The outline view displays the contents of the concept map in a traditional hierarchical outline that can then be used to organize a final product.

Citing Sources

To produce responsible research products, it is necessary to cite sources. The ability to consistently and accurately document sources is challenging for most learners up through the middle grades (Bowler et al., 2001; Eagleton et al., 2003; McNabb et al., 2002). The Internet complicates this process, because many students jump from website to website so quickly that they can't remember where their information was gleaned. We need to teach younger students and retrain older students to SLOW DOWN on the information highway and be more metacognitively aware. Probably

FIGURE 8.9. Rearranging inquiry notes.

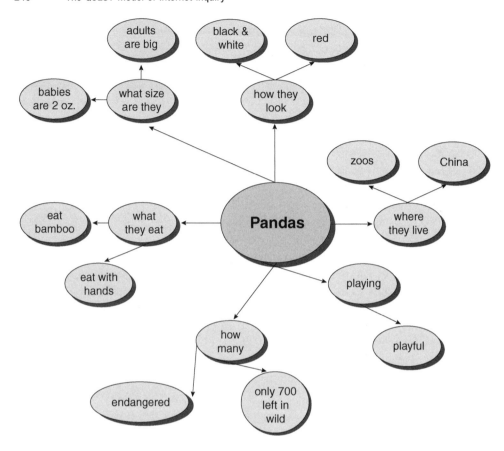

FIGURE 8.10. Fourth-graders' concept map (graphic view).

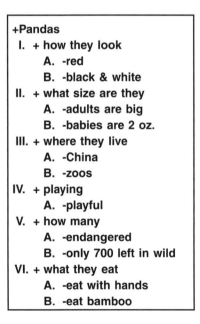

+Pandas
  I. **+ how they look**
       A. **-red**
       B. **-black & white**
 II. **+ what size are they**
       A. **-adults are big**
       B. **-babies are 2 oz.**
III. **+ where they live**
       A. **-China**
       B. **-zoos**
IV. **+ playing**
       A. **-playful**
 V. **+ how many**
       A. **-endangered**
       B. **-only 700 left in wild**
VI. **+ what they eat**
       A. **-eat with hands**
       B. **-eat bamboo**

FIGURE 8.11. Fourth-graders' concept map (outline view).

every one of us, at one time or another, has forgotten where we found something really cool on the Internet, so just imagine how hard it must be for our students.

To help with remembering and citing sources, a handy browser feature is the "history" button, which tracks all the websites you've visited recently. Unfortunately, since students usually share computers at school, this feature may not be useful for them. Another trick is to use the "bookmark" or "favorites" feature in the web browser to save sites for return visits; however, since some school districts disallow bookmarking or erase bookmarks overnight, this may not be of help to your students either. Therefore, our best advice is to train students to get in the habit of copying and pasting URLs (web addresses) adjacent to their notes, so they'll have a permanent record of where the information was obtained and can return to sites easily. This has the added benefit of reminding students that we expect them to make notes rather than try to hold all the information in their heads. To build this habit, have your students regularly submit their notes throughout an inquiry project, and do not accept notes without URLs. We do not recommend having students handwrite URLs on paper, because it is too laborious and often leads to typographical errors.

Teachers always ask us how to handle copyrighted images gathered from the Web. It's hard enough to get kids to cite where they found information, much less the multitudes of images they collect. The best option is free clipart, which can be found online by searching for <clipart + free>. If free clipart is unavailable for their purposes, we ask students to get in the habit of saving the URL where they found the image, and paste the URL next to the picture in whatever software they're using to create their final format. Because our students do not publish commercial products, we have not felt the need to contact book or website publishers for permission to use images in student projects; however, if your school is planning a large production, you may need to shepherd students through this important process.

Library Media Standard: Demonstrate strategies for communicating ideas.

Creating a Product

As we discussed in Chapter 4, some students have difficulty envisioning a final product for their inquiries and often create final products that don't do justice to the knowledge that was gained. In some cases, students don't plan their time well and are rushed when they get to the final product. In other cases, students don't actually have enough information to make a decent final product. Many students simply don't know how to represent knowledge, especially in formats other than a traditional research report. We try to encourage them to be creative without loosing sight of the goal of answering their original research question(s).

Through actively engaging in their own hypermedia or hypertext productions, students learn to investigate, discuss, and reflect on the meanings of texts in their lives.
—Beach and Bruce (2002, p. 162)

A helpful tactic for keeping students on track toward a final product is to co-develop benchmarks for each part of the process (see Chapter 4). For example, we always require rough drafts of notes and products before polished drafts. We also read students' Reflection Logs on a daily basis so that we can address concerns immediately. We give frequent assessments and grading rubrics to ensure that students understand our instructional objectives and so that we can provide timely feedback. We reserve time for students to share their ideas, strategies, and processes with each other while engaged in inquiry, rather than at the end when it is too late to change course.

Researcher: "What are your strategies for writing up your research?"

Student: "I just kinda grab a little bit of notes and stretch it out as far as I can with word fillers and stuff like that."

Examples of former students' projects (both weak and strong) are the best models for creating a final product. Teacher-designed templates can also help scaffold learners who need guidance. One teacher we know asks her students to pursue two focus areas within their chosen topics, choosing one final format that is familiar (e.g., a poem) and one that will stretch them a little (e.g., a website). We have also done projects in which we ask the kids to choose one format that showcases their writing and one that showcases their creativity. Here are some common pitfalls to avoid with respect to inquiry products:

- Large chunks of information that are copied straight from a source.
- Multimedia products that have more glitz than content.
- Posters that have pictures without captions or any other descriptive text.
- Art projects that don't include any actual information (remember the Jerry Garcia bust in Chapter 4?).
- Poems, crossword puzzles, and acrostics that don't contain sufficient information.
- Any product that doesn't show evidence of extensive research and information transformation.

Presenting

The final step in the QUEST process often involves communicating what's been learned to interested others. This doesn't always need to take the form of an oral presentation, but we usually require several oral presentations per year so that students gain experience and comfort with presenting in front of peers, teachers, school staff, parents, and even the community. Even shy students feel pride in presenting inquiry projects because it is exciting to share their passions and creations with others and even more thrilling if the audience actually learns something valuable. Students who like to "ham it up" really shine during oral presentations, as did one older learner who surprised everyone by wearing a white T-shirt for his presentation and standing directly in front of the LCD projector so that his website on Hummers (military Humvee vehicles designed for consumers) appeared on his shirt instead of on the screen (Figure 8.12). He was animated and extremely funny, evidencing none of the print literacy challenges that had hampered him throughout the project.

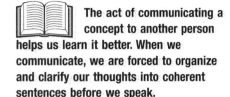 The act of communicating a concept to another person helps us learn it better. When we communicate, we are forced to organize and clarify our thoughts into coherent sentences before we speak.
—Zwiers (2004, p. 20)

However, unlike our Humvee enthusiast, many students have weak oral presentation skills. For example, in one classroom, although the teacher required an introduction and a conclusion to each oral presentation, many of her students neglected to mention key contextual information or state why they had selected their topics. The teacher later reflected:

"A student presented this morning on Jackie Robinson. She had a fabulous Inspiration document, which was a bubble map that she used to talk about his family. She had a PowerPoint that traced his career, and she had a fabulous skit in two scenes, which showed Jackie Robinson attempting to get a meal at a restaurant and being denied because of his color. However, in the introduction she didn't tell the class that he was the first African American baseball player and it was before the Civil Rights Act in 1964, so he encountered a lot of discrimination."

Besides expecting students to share accurate and complete information as presenters, we also expect certain behavior of those students receiving the information. Being an effective presenter and being a polite audience member go hand in hand. Share your expectations with students before presentations begin. Encourage presenters to be aware of posture, voice, and

 Math Standard: Communicate and connect varied kinds of numerical information; develop, analyze, and explain procedures; use patterns and relationships to solve problems.

FIGURE 8.12. Creative presentation technique.

content of their presentations. Ask audience members to be considerate and polite. Students will often rise to our expectations.

How Do We Teach Transformation Strategies?

As with all the other QUEST strategies, we recommend the teaching approach described in Chapter 1 that includes modeling, scaffolding, practice, and feedback. Modeling information transformation via teacher think-alouds is very helpful to students. If you have been following our advice and conducting inquiry alongside your students, this is the time to project your research questions and notes on the screen and talk through how you intend to go about transforming the information you've gathered into something original that demonstrates what you've learned.

Notemaking

Prior to starting a unit focused on notemaking, we recommend that you administer a pretest in order to assess your students' current notemaking strategies. Short passages from Informal Reading Inventories or basal readers are good sources of expository text for this purpose. Give each student a passage that best matches his independent reading level and have him follow the instructions on the *Notemaking Assessment* (Handout T-1). Encourage the use of highlighters or pens so you can better compare how your students perform on the posttest at the end of the unit. After the pretest, have students share their notemaking strategies and record similarities and differences. Have students look for the following characteristics of effective notemaking strategies:

- Highlighting of key ideas (not too much, not too little)
- Highlighting words and phrases instead of whole sentences
- Reasonable number of notes (fewer words than in the original passage)
- Notes that use different wording than the original passage
- Notes that are not in full sentences
- Use of abbreviations, symbols, lists, and pictures
- Summaries that provide a synthesis of the notes rather than a mirror image of the notes or the original passage
- Summaries that are shorter than the original passages
- Summaries that are primarily in students' own words

We have had great success teaching the four-step CHoMP notemaking strategy (discussed above) by teaching each step individually. You may wish to print out the *CHoMP Notemaking Poster* (Handout T-2) on colorful paper and/or on an overhead transparency. Although your lessons may be more effective if you use text that is familiar to the students (perhaps drawn from their textbooks or websites that they've visited during mini-inquiries), we provide practice activities for *Two-Step Notemaking* (Handout T-3), *Three-Step Notemaking* (Handout T-4), and *Four-Step Notemaking* (Handout T-5). Each has several passages to use for guided practice, independent practice, and homework, with the passages increasing in length for each additional step of the process. Because notemaking can be very tedious for some learners, continue to emphasize the value of notemaking strategies in and out of school. You can also have students work together on notemaking exercises (Figure 8.13).

Inquiry Products

As reiterated throughout this book, we like to offer as much student choice as possible when conducting inquiry projects. Not only is it critical to allow students to choose their own topics, but most students will devote additional effort if they are also given some latitude to demonstrate what they've learned in a format of their own choosing. However, since many students do not know how to effectively show what they've learned, they need to be taught strategies for creating a variety of types of inquiry products. If you don't have prior student projects to use as models, we provide samples and criteria for common formats at the end of this chapter, including a *Sample Webpage* (Handout T-6), *Sample Slide Show* (Handout T-7), *Sample News Article* (Handout T-8), *Sample Acrostic Poem* (Handout T-9), *Sample Flier* (Handout T-10), and *Sample Q&A* (Handout T-11). We also have examples of a *Basic Webliography* (just URLs) for younger students (Handout T-12) and a *Standard Bibliography* for older students (Handout T-13). *Presentation Guidelines* (Handout T-14) help scaffold the final challenge of the QUEST. See the *Notemaking Lesson Plans* for Elementary and Middle School Levels (Handouts T-15 and T-16) for ideas on how to begin.

Summary

This chapter on Transforming provided research and classroom examples of the process of transforming information into knowledge. We discussed strategies for notemaking, organizing information, citing sources, creating a product, and presenting final products to others. Since this phase of the QUEST is similar for traditional

FIGURE 8.13. Notemaking collaboration.

inquiry and Internet inquiry, we have emphasized the areas in which technology can either help or hinder the process.

The final chapter of this book briefly presents some thoughts and ideas for reflecting on the QUEST. Although students are expected to self-reflect during inquiry, it is also advisable to set aside some time to debrief the experience at the end. In addition to being evaluated by traditional measures such as posttests and interviews, students can evaluate their progress by rereading their Reflection Logs and by reenacting the inquiry process. Teachers can also engage in self-reflection and share their insights with the class.

Handouts

The following chart lists the activities and templates that were discussed in this chapter on Transforming. Because notemaking is such a crucial skill for gathering, synthesizing (Chapter 7), and transforming information into something original, we offer quite a few handouts that can be used in a notemaking unit. Similarly, since many students, from the early grades through high school, struggle with envisioning and designing final formats that showcase their knowledge of an inquiry topic, we've included six sample formats along with the criteria that were determined by the class in advance. These examples are genuine student artifacts that can serve as reasonable models for students in grades 3–8.

Number	Name of Handout	Purpose
T-1	Notemaking Assessment	Assess notemaking strategies
T-2	CHoMP Notemaking Poster	Poster for wall or overhead
T-3	Two-Step Notemaking	Teach CHoMP strategy
T-4	Three-Step Notemaking	Teach CHoMP strategy
T-5	Four-Step Notemaking	Teach CHoMP strategy
T-6	Sample Webpage	Sample final format
T-7	Sample Slide Show	Sample final format
T-8	Sample News Article	Sample final format
T-9	Sample Acrostic Poem	Sample final format
T-10	Sample Flier	Sample final format
T-11	Sample Q&A	Sample final format
T-12	Basic Webliography	Template for citations
T-13	Standard Bibliography	Template for citations
T-14	Presentation Guidelines	Scaffold presentation
T-15	Notemaking Lesson Plan—Elementary Level	Teach notemaking strategies
T-16	Notemaking Lesson Plan—Middle Level	Teach notemaking strategies

HANDOUT T-1. Notemaking Assessment (page 1 of 2)

Name _____ Class _____ Date _____

☐ Pretest   ☐ Posttest

Please show your best notemaking strategies. You have 15 minutes to complete the test after the passage is read aloud to you.

DIRECTIONS:

1. Review the passage.

2. Use a highlighter pen and/or pencil to make marks on the passage.

3. Make notes on this page.

4. Write a summary, based on your notes, on the next page.

MY NOTES:

_____

_____

_____

_____

_____

_____

_____

_____

_____

_____

_____

_____

_____

_____

_____

_____

_____

_____

_____

_____

MY SUMMARY:

_____

_____

_____

_____

_____

_____

_____

_____

_____

_____

_____

_____

_____

_____

_____

_____

_____

_____

_____

_____

_____

_____

_____

_____

_____

_____

_____

_____

_____

_____

_____

_____

_____

_____

_____

_____

_____

_____

_____

STEP 1: Cross out small words.

STEP 2: Highlight important info.

o

STEP 3: Make notes (shorten, change words, make lists, use symbols, draw).

STEP 4: Put in your own words.

HANDOUT T-3. Two-Step Notemaking

Name _____ Class _____ Date _____

Read each sentence, then practice notemaking by doing these two steps:

STEP 1: Cross out small words
STEP 2: Highlight important info

I. GUIDED PRACTICE

   1. Boa constrictors have poor vision, so they have to sense their prey by smelling the air with their tongues.

   2. Peacocks are among the easiest birds to raise, but they must be kept in pens so they don't run away.

   3. Guinea pigs communicate with each other using lots of different sounds, which shows how important their hearing is to them.

   4. One reason Siberian tigers are endangered is that some people believe that almost every part of the tiger can be used for medicine or to cure diseases.

II. INDEPENDENT PRACTICE

   5. Rockhopper penguins live in rocky areas with high grasses, where they make burrows and nests.

   6. The Kiger mustang is more than just another wild horse on the range of the American West; it is a descendant of horses brought to the New World by the Spaniards.

   7. Fat bears in winter coats overheat quickly and may run slower than 30 mph, whereas slim bears can run faster than 30 mph.

   8. The platypus's large front feet can be used as powerful paddles for swimming as well as for digging a burrow in a riverbank.

Name _____ Class _____ Date _____

I. GUIDED PRACTICE

Read each paragraph, then practice notemaking by doing these three steps:

STEP 1: Cross out small words
STEP 2: Highlight important info
     o
STEP 3: Make notes (shorten, change words, make lists, use symbols, draw)

---

1. Siberian tigers are among the most endangered animals in the world. Fewer than 200 are believed to still live in the wild. Their range includes eastern Russian, northern Korea, and northeastern China.

2. The platypus is a small egg-laying mammal with webbed feet, a tail like a beaver's, and a horny beak resembling the bill of a duck. It has a thick covering of waterproof hair. The bill is a blue-gray, blackish color, and the lower bill is smaller than the upper bill.

3. Boas' sharp teeth help them to get a good grip on their prey, but unlike some snakes, they do not have fangs or venom. Instead, the boa constrictor kills its prey by suffocating it. The boa tightens its coils each time the prey exhales until the animal can no longer breathe in.

II. INDEPENDENT PRACTICE

STEP 1: Cross out small words
STEP 2: Highlight important info
    o
STEP 3: Make notes (shorten, change words, make lists, use symbols, draw)

---

 4. Grizzly bears are found in river valleys, mountain forests, and open meadows all over the world. They range in North America, Western and Central Europe, some parts of Japan, and Russia, and can be found as far north as the tundra region.

 5. The Kiger mustang is smaller than some of today's breeds of horses, averaging 14–15 hands and 800–1,000 pounds. They are of medium size with heavy shoulders and necks. Their feet are small and black. Their legs are long and have rounded bones.

 6. Rockhopper penguins gather in very large, noisy colonies when they breed, all gabbling away at once. The male sits on the egg for 4 months until it hatches. When trying to attract a mate, a Rockhopper shakes its head back and forth, tossing and showing off its yellow feathers.

Name _____ Class _____ Date _____

Read each paragraph, then practice notemaking by doing these four steps:

I. GUIDED PRACTICE

STEP 1: Cross out small words
STEP 2: Highlight important info
     o
STEP 3: Make notes (shorten, change words, make lists, use symbols, draw)
STEP 4: Put in your own words

---

1. Boa constrictors are snakes that can grow to 3–14 feet long and can weigh over 100 pounds. Their bodies can have different patterns, such as oval, diamond, or bat-shaped, in colors of reddish brown outlined in black, on a background of cream, pale tan, or gray.

MY NOTES:

MY SUMMARY:

_____

_____

_____

_____

_____

_____

_____

I. GUIDED PRACTICE

STEP 1: Cross out small words
STEP 2: Highlight important info
      o
STEP 3: Make notes (shorten, change words, make lists, use symbols, draw)
STEP 4: Put in your own words

---

 2. The grizzly bear is one type of brown bear. The bears' color ranges from light brown (almost blonde) to black. They have a sturdy, stocky build and a noticeable hump behind the head. They get their name from the silver color that appears on the tips of their fur as they get older.

MY NOTES:

MY SUMMARY:

_____
_____
_____
_____
_____
_____
_____
_____
_____
_____

II. INDEPENDENT PRACTICE

STEP 1: Cross out small words
STEP 2: Highlight important info
    o
STEP 3: Make notes (shorten, change words, make lists, use symbols, draw)
STEP 4: Put in your own words

---

 3. Even though it is a strange-looking creature, the platypus is an excellent underwater hunter. It catches crayfish and worms on the bottoms of muddy rivers where visibility is low. It is able to search for food in darkness using its special, beak-like snout, which is filled with sensors and can detect any movement in the murky water.

MY NOTES:

MY SUMMARY:

II. INDEPENDENT PRACTICE

STEP 1: Cross out small words
STEP 2: Highlight important info
      o
STEP 3: Make notes (shorten, change words, make lists, use symbols, draw)
STEP 4: Put in your own words

---

 4. No other horse in America is quite like the Kiger mustang found on Steens Mountain in Central Oregon. The Spanish mustang was a part of early American history, having roots in Native American culture, and is the horse that helped settle the West. At one time, it was thought to be extinct in the wild. Since the Kiger mustangs might be the best remaining examples of the Spanish mustang, it is very important to preserve them.

MY NOTES:

MY SUMMARY:

_____

_____

_____

_____

_____

_____

_____

_____

_____

Arnold Shwarzenegger - Microsoft Internet Explorer

File   Edit   View   Favorites   Tools   Help

Arnold Shwarzenegger

"I'm Gonna Pump You Up!"

Childhood

Arnold was born July 30, 1947 in Graz, Austria. He grew up in a small village. When he was 15, he started weightlifting. When he was 20, he won the Mr. Universe title because he was the strongest man in the world. He made 13 bodybuilding records. He became a U.S. citizen in 1983. He went to the University of Wisconsin and got his Bachelor's degree in Business and Economics.

Career

Arnold is an actor, a writer, and a politician. He has been in Terminator and Batman. He fights the bad guys in movies, like an action hero. He wrote a book called "The New Encyclopedia of Modern Bodybuilding." Now he is the Governer of California.

Webliography

http://www.actorarchives.com/arnold/biography.html

http://www.facts1.com/general/recent.htm

http://www.fasbnet.com/T3/arnold1.htm

My Computer

Web page Criteria:

- Theme: Famous person
- Topic: Arnold Schwarzenegger
- Focus areas: Childhood and career
- Number of images: At least 2
- Sources: At least 3
- Software: Netscape Composer

Diana,
Princess of Wales

1961-1997

Diana's Family

- July 1, 1961, Diana was born in Norfolk, England.
- Lady Diana had two sisters and one brother. Sarah and Jane were her sisters.
- When she was 16 years old she went to West Heath boarding school.

Charles and Diana

- Diana and Charles got married on July 29, 1981 at St. Paul's Cathedral.
- Over 750 million people watched the wedding on TV.

William and Harry

June 21, 1982 Prince William (Arthur Philip Louis) was born.

September 15, 1984 Prince Harry (Henry Charles Albert David) was born.

Separation

In July of 1996, just before their 15th wedding anniversary, Prince Charles and Princess Diana decided to end their marriage with divorce.

Tragedy

- In the early morning of August 31,1997 Diana was involved in a car accident.
- The car accident took her life at age 37.
- Diana's death shocked the world and spread sadness and disbelief everywhere.

Slide Show Criteria:

- Theme: Hero
- Topic: Princess Diana
- Focus area: Family
- Number of slides: Minimum of 4
- Images: Minimum of 4
- Sources: Minimum of 3
- Software: Microsoft PowerPoint

Princess Diana

Date: 1/12/2002

Diana, Princess of Wales, Makes Many Contributions to Society

Princess Diana

Contributes to

society

She helps:

Breast cancer

HIV/AIDS

Domestic abuse

Drug addiction

The banning of land mines

Princess Diana supported many charities throughout her career. At one time, she supported as many as 110. These charities included HIV/AIDS, domestic abuse, drug addiction, breast cancer, and the banning of land mines.

After her separation and divorce, she cut back to supporting only six charities. Her schedule was hectic, including travel and public appearances. She traveled thousands of miles a year to support

her favorite charities. She often took her sons with her to visit hospitals and homeless shelters.

In June 1997 she auctioned off seventy-nine of her evening gowns. This was part of an event held at Christie's in New York. This event raised more than $ 5.7 million for AIDS and Cancer funds.

In 1997, she received the Nobel Peace Prize. She worked to increase public awareness

about the dangers of land mines. She traveled to far off areas such as Angela and the former Yugoslavia. She represented the International Campaign to ban Land mines.

Had Princess Diana's life not been cut short by the tragic car accident on August 31, 1997. She would have continued her charity work. During her short lived career, she made many contribution to society.

Diana with Mother Teresa during a visit at a convent in the Bronx borough of New York on June 18, 1997

News Article Criteria:

- Theme: Hero
- Topic: Princess Diana
- Focus area: Contributions to society
- Images: Minimum of 2
- Sources: Minimum of 3
- Software: Microsoft Publisher

Little Women was the title of one of her most popular books

On November 29, 1832, Louisa was born.

Under her father's supervision, Louisa was taught everything she needed to know.

It was in concord, MA, that Louisa was mainly raised.

She read a lot of books and even tutored a girl named Ellen.

At the age of twelve, Louisa got a job to help support her family.

May, Elizabeth, and Anna, were Louisa's sisters.

Amos Bronson Alcott was Louisa's Dad.

Years of writing, helped to improve every one of her books.

Abigail May was Louisa's Mom.

Louisa died after working in a hospital and catching Typhoid Fever.

Contrast between the storyline of Little Women and her family, was very similar.

Often trying to help her family with finances, Louisa was inspired to write many thrillers.

To Louisa's horror, her sister Elizabeth died in 1858.

The whole family supported many causes like women's right's and the abolition of slavery.

Acrostic Poem Criteria:
- Theme: Hero
- Topic: Louisa May Alcott
- Focus area: Family life
- Sources: Minimum of 3
- Software: Microsoft Word

BACK TO THE MAT

FREESTYLE WRESTLING

Summer Camp for Beginners

Lowest Price Camp Anywhere, only $17 for one week!

Featuring **Live Demos** by Famous Wrestlers, such as:

Bobby Douglas,	Daniel Lgali	John Goodbody
Head coach for Iowa	2nd World Cup 1998	Bouncer in the meanest bar

You will learn these basic moves in **Only One Week!**

- **Takedown:** Getting the opponent from a standing position down to the mat. You have to have control to get a point for a takedown.
- **Breakdown:** Getting the opponent from hands and knees to flat on the mat.
- **Crotch Lift:** From flat on his face, put arm around his leg and lift! Then flip him over.
- **Gut Wrench:** When you have him flat on the mat face down, lock arms around his waist. Lift and roll him onto his back.
- **Pin:** When opponent's shoulders are flat on the mat and you are in control for 3 seconds.
- **Headlock:** Get the back of his head into the crook of your arm, lift his head up so he can't bridge. Wait for ref to call a pin!
- **Arm Bar:** Thread your forearm behind his elbow and over his back then apply the pressure!
- **Half Nelson:** Put arm under opponent's armpit, wrap hand behind his head, make a fist, drive fist down toward the mat.
- **Cradle:** Wrap one arm around opponent's head and one arm around the back of his knee, lock hands together take him to his back.

We're located at 321 North Pole Drive 12938

We're open from 1:00 pm to 8:00 pm

Call now to register!

677-766-7667

Flier Criteria:

- Theme: Sports
- Topic: Wrestling
- Focus area: Wrestling techniques
- Images: Minimum of 2
- Software: Microsoft Word

History of the Stanley Cup

Q: When was the Stanley Cup introduced?
A: Lord Stanley and his seven sons from England came to Canada in March of 1892.because Lord Stanley was going to become the governer general of Canada. It was originally called the Dominion Hockey Challenge Cup.

Q: How much did the original cup cost?
A: Lord Stanley sent his assistant to buy the cup for ten Guineas, which was about $50 back then.

Q: Does the Stanley Cup still look the same today?
A: No, the Stanley cup now is bigger and it is all silver with the names of the teams who won the Stanley Cup game and the dates when they won it. The original cup is now in a museum because it got too big.

Q: What is the meaning of the rings around the cup?
A: On the old Cup they added a new ring for every year that a team won. The new Stanley Cup has rings, but they don't keep adding rings, now they just carve the teams' names.

Q: Does the winning team get to keep the cup?
A: They get to keep the cup until the next season begins. One time one of the teams got so drunk they threw the Stanley Cup into a river. It was a deep river and the Cup sank to the bottom, so someone had to go get it.

Q: Why was hockey created?
A: Because the people who played an Irish field game called "Hurley," which was like hockey, but it was played on grass. The thought in the winter, why not try to play it on ice. Hockey was originally called "ice hurley."

Q: Why is the Stanley Cup a cup?
A: That one is still a mystery!

Original Dominion Challenge Cup	Modern Day Stanley Cup
nhl.com/hockeyu/history/ cup/cup.html?clk=001	nhl.com/columns/picarello/ pic_hall071901.html

Q&A Criteria:

- Theme: Sports
- Topic: Hockey/Stanley Cup
- Focus area: History
- Images: Minimum of 2
- Software: Microsoft Word

HANDOUT T-12. Basic Webliography

When citing sources from the Internet, list the websites in alphabetical order, as follows:

animaldiversity.ummz.umich.edu/accounts/dacelo/d._novaeguineae$narrative.html

home.mira.net/~areadman/king.htm

theaviary.com/bd-051097.shtml

www.calm.wa.gov.au/plants_animals/odd_kookaburra.html

www.honoluluzoo.org/kookaburra.htm

www.netspace.net.au/~fcfhsp/chooks.htm

HANDOUT T-13. Standard Bibliography

When citing sources, use the following format.

BOOKS

Hollands, D. (2000). *Kingfishers and kookaburras: Jewels of the Australian bush.* New South Wales, Australia: New Holland.

Page, R., & Jenkins, S. (2005). *I see a kookaburra: Discovering animal habitats around the world.* Boston: Houghton Mifflin.

ARTICLES

Legge, S. (2000). Kookaburra feeding habits: It's no laughing matter. *Animal Behaviour, 59*(5), 1009–1018.

WEBSITES

Department of Conservation and Land Management. (2004). Laughing kookaburra. *Nature Base.* Retrieved November 23, 2006, from *www.calm.wa.gov.au/plants_animals/odd_kookaburra.html.*

Sholits, L. (2001). Laughing kookaburra: *Dacelo novaeguineae. Animal Diversity Web.* Retrieved November 23, 2006, from *animaldiversity.ummz.umich.edu.*

HANDOUT T-14. Presentation Guidelines

Name _____ Class _____ Date _____

Use this outline for your oral presentation.

1. Hello, my name is _____

2. I did my inquiry project on the _____ and _____
                                (focus area 1)   **(focus area 2)**

   of _____.
          (topic)

3. I chose these focus areas because _____

   _____

   _____

4. Some interesting facts about this topic are _____

   _____

   _____

5. I will show you what I've learned by presenting my _____
                                               (formats)

6. SHOW PROJECT NOW

7. Some things I've learned about this topic are _____

   _____

   _____

8. Some things I've learned about _____ are _____
                              (instructional focus of unit)

   _____

   _____

9. I hope you enjoyed my presentation. Are there any questions?

Objective

Students will learn an effective strategy for notemaking, which involves crossing out little words and highlighting important words.

Time

One or two class periods

Materials

1. *QUEST Inquiry Model* (Handout P-11)
2. *CHoMP Notemaking Poster* (Handout T-2)
3. *Two-Step Notemaking* (Handout T-3)
4. Transparency of Handout T-3
5. Overhead projector
6. Highlighter pen and pencil for each student

Assessment Options

Notemaking Assessment (Handout T-1), along with short passages that students can easily decode.

Introduction

1. Share notemaking strategies from the *Notemaking Assessment* (Handout T-1) as a group.
2. Tell students you will be teaching them a strategy for notemaking that many other students have found useful. Contextualize the lesson, using the *QUEST Inquiry Model* (Handout P-11), by pointing out that they are in the T̲ phase of the QUEST, which includes putting info in their own words.
3. Have students brainstorm why notemaking can be useful in your class, in other classes, and outside of school (Examples: doing research, taking down directions, making shopping lists, writing in calendars, etc.). This can be done in pairs, in small groups, or as a whole class.
4. Generate excitement and get student buy-in on the purpose of the lesson before proceeding. Tell students that effective notemaking strategies will help them now and in the future when they get into middle school and beyond.

Modeling

1. Tell the class you are going to teach them an easy notemaking strategy called "CHoMP" and that today's lesson will focus on the first two steps.
2. Model crossing out and highlighting on the overhead while thinking aloud about your choices.

Practice

1. Pass out *Two-Step Notemaking* (Handout T-3) and pens/pencils.
2. Read each passage aloud before having anyone start crossing out or highlighting.
3. Conduct guided practice on CHoMP Steps 1 and 2 (crossing out and highlighting).
4. Have students carry out independent practice and/or homework activities.

Scaffolding

1. Create a new handout with easier text for weaker readers.
2. Reduce the number of passages for younger children and struggling learners.
3. Do more guided practice and less independent practice and homework for students who are having difficulty.
4. Increase font size for students with visual impairments.

Feedback

1. Go over independent practice passages with the class. Compare strategies.
2. Look over the homework to see who gets the idea and who needs additional practice.
3. Let students know how they are doing. If they're struggling, try to isolate the problem—are they having trouble decoding or comprehending the passages, or are they having trouble with one of the first two steps of the CHoMP strategy?

Ticket Out the Door

Have each student tell you what the "C" and the "H" stand for in CHoMP.

Objective

Students will learn an effective strategy for notemaking, which involves eliminating unnecessary info, identifying important info, and making short notes.

Time

One or two class periods

Materials

1. *QUEST Inquiry Model* (Handout P-11)
2. *CHoMP Notemaking Poster* (Handout T-2)
3. *Three-Step Notemaking* (Handout T-3)
4. Transparency of Handout T-3
5. Overhead projector
6. Highlighter pen and pencil for each student

Assessment Options

Notemaking Assessment (Handout T-1), along with short passages that students can easily decode.

Introduction

1. Share notemaking strategies from the *Notemaking Assessment* (Handout T-1) as a group.
2. Tell students you will be teaching them a transferable strategy for notemaking that many other students have found useful. Contextualize the lesson, using the *QUEST Inquiry Model* (Handout P-11), by pointing out that they are in the T̲ phase of the QUEST, which includes making notes without plagiarizing.
3. Have students brainstorm why notemaking is useful in this class, in other classes, and outside of school (Examples: doing research, taking down directions, making shopping lists, writing in calendars, taking notes from textbooks or lectures, etc.). This can be done in pairs, in small groups, or as a whole class.
4. Generate excitement and get student buy-in on the purpose of the lesson before proceeding. Tell them that effective notemaking strategies will help them now and in the future when they get into high school and college.

Modeling

1. Tell the class you are going to teach them an easy notemaking strategy called "CHoMP" and that today's lesson will focus on the first three steps.
2. Emphasize that notes are NOT complete sentences; rather, they are a type of shorthand. Describe and model five notemaking styles:
   a. shortening (abbreviating)
   b. changing words (converting "big" words into small words)
   c. making lists (items that go together)
   d. using symbols (=, +, ?)
   e. drawing

Practice

1. Pass out *Three-Step Notemaking* (Handout T-4) and pens/pencils.
2. Read each passage aloud.
3. Conduct guided practice on CHoMP Steps 1 through 3 (crossing out, highlighting, and making notes).
4. Have students carry out independent practice and/or homework activities.

Scaffolding

1. Create a new handout with easier text for weaker readers.
2. Reduce the number of passages for struggling learners.
3. Do more guided practice and less independent practice and homework for students who are having difficulty.
4. Increase font size for students with visual impairments.

Feedback

1. Go over independent practice passages with the class. Compare strategies.
2. Look over the homework to see who gets the idea and who needs additional practice.
3. Let students know how they are doing. If they're struggling, try to isolate the problem—are they having trouble decoding or comprehending the passages, or are they having trouble with some aspect(s) of CHoMP: crossing out, highlighting important info, or making notes?

Ticket Out the Door

Have each student tell you what the three letters (C, H, & M) stand for in CHoMP.

9 ▼ REFLECTING ON THE QUEST

KEY IDEAS

▶ Although students should engage in self-reflection throughout an Internet inquiry QUEST, it is also valuable to reflect on the process at the end.

▶ Student progress can be measured with posttests, interviews, surveys, and self-reflection.

▶ Reenacting an inquiry project can be an effective method of solidifying the QUEST process for students.

▶ When teachers engage in self-reflection, it is beneficial to share their discoveries with their students.

> **Changes in the strategic knowledge required to navigate traditional text environments have been glacial; changes in the strategic knowledge required to navigate Internet environments are meteoric.**
> **—Leu (1997, p. 65)**

In this chapter we will share some thoughts on teacher and student self-reflection by encouraging you to ask yourself, "What have I learned as a teacher?" and "What have my students learned?" A first step in our own self-reflection is to call to mind what information we have gained that influences our learning. In Part I of this book, we focused on developing an understanding of learning and reading, with both print and Web text, to serve as a foundation and rationale for our instruction. Part II presented the QUEST model as a systematic way to teach the inquiry process, emphasizing essential literacy strategies that our students need to be successful. This final chapter is written with the goal of bringing together the ideas from both sections into a cohesive overall view of learning, reading, the Web, and the QUEST model. We conclude with our own self-reflections as authors of this book.

What Have I Learned as a Teacher?

Master teachers engage in ongoing self-reflection. The familiar adage "monitor and adjust" is always a good mantra for teachers. As we reach the end of our journey together in this book, we encourage you to ask yourself what new knowledge and strategies *you've* gained and then to share this with your students. Students appreciate it when we present ourselves as lifelong learners rather than all-knowing dispensers of information. If you are relatively new to computers, you've probably come a long way in your understanding of how to teach with technology. If you are new to literacy, then you've probably made headway in both areas. If you are trying out an inquiry-based curriculum for the first time, then, we hope, you've found a comfortable place at the intersection of technology, literacy, and inquiry, which is the heart and soul of this book.

Figure 9.1 contrasts two remarks from Deborah, who, as a seventh-grade special educator, had a strong grasp of literacy instruction but was less experienced with inquiry and technology before she worked with us. She, like the other teachers with whom we've collaborated, really appreciated being mentored during Internet inquiry instruction. Since we cannot visit all your classrooms, our intent is that this book will serve as a guide and model for your teaching.

We sincerely hope that, like Deborah, you have gained confidence in your ability to both navigate the Internet and use it as a tool for your own learning and that of your students. The QUEST model provides a framework to support and encourage both teachers and students to gather information and transform this information into new ideas. We hope you have recognized the important and valuable literacy skills needed to locate, understand, and use information from the Internet, and the strong need our students have to be literate in many different ways.

BEFORE QUEST	AFTER QUEST
"In all the years I've taught I've always dreaded doing research projects with my students because I'm terrified to do it! You end up doing all the work for the kids, and they're frustrated and you're frustrated, and it's a nightmare boat that you're all rowing down the same river."	"I gained the satisfaction of knowing that research projects don't have to be a big dinosaur—that big scary thing that is overwhelming because no one can do it. That fear's been diminished for me because now I know how to break down the process and teach it to my students."

FIGURE 9.1. Teacher reflection—before and after.

What Have My Students Learned?

As is obvious, posttests, postinterviews, surveys, and even casual conversation and observation are some ways to determine what your students have learned (see Chapter 3). A good time to administer posttests is after a long-term inquiry project that focused on one major strategy, such as keyword selection or notemaking. However, to see growth on posttests, there has to have been effective modeling, appropriate scaffolding, sustained practice, and timely feedback. As stated in Chapter 1, true learning takes time, so don't be disappointed if your students (especially computer novices, students with learning disabilities, and older students who have to "unlearn" previous habits) don't demonstrate a complete overhaul in their approaches to inquiry. Keep your eye out for small gains. For example, when evaluating a student's understanding of the inquiry process (Chapter 3, Handouts P-2 to P-6), look for indicators of growth in areas such as "think about your topic before you start searching," "use topic + focus keywords," "decide if this website has the info you need," or "make notes in your own words." These small but significant improvements are cause for great joy on your part.

> **Web Strategies Oral Posttest:** "Pick out two keywords that relate to your topic. Then put them on the little searchy-ma-bobby with a plus sign, and if there isn't any good info, just click on any of those website thingies or try new keywords."
> —Haley, seventh-grade student with learning disabilities

Similarly, if you ask students to draw a picture of the Internet (Chapter 3, Handout P-8) at the end of the year, do they accurately depict it as a network of computers? If not, then encourage next year's teacher(s) to pick up where you left off in order to continue helping students construct a deeper understanding of this essential information resource. Maybe you can even lend your colleagues this book and point them to our companion website, *www.ReadingTheWeb.net*.

> **The World Wide Web is a uniquely rich resource for authentic inquiry, but students must learn to orchestrate sophisticated strategies to become literate in this complex environment.** —Eagleton (2002, online)

Formal assessments are not the only means of evaluating student learning. You will also want to provide opportunities for your students to engage in frequent self-reflection (Figure 9.2). If your students have been keeping Reflection Logs during inquiry projects (which we highly recommend), provide opportunities for them to reread their logs, comparing their entries at the beginning, middle, and end. Sample Reflection Log prompts are as follows:

- This is how things are going with my research project:
- Today, we learned:
- My project would be going so much better if:
- Today, I was working on these parts of my project:
- This is how I feel about what I've done so far:
- Something new I've learned about finding information on the Web is:

FIGURE 9.2. Student self-reflection.

- Something I am still having trouble with is:
- Things I want to remember to work on tomorrow are:
- These things were easy that I did today:
- These things were hard that I did today:
- Some things I still want to know about searching on the Web are:
- I think a good topic for a minilesson would be:
- Some things I learned about inquiry are:
- Some things I learned about the Web are:
- Some things I learned about choosing research topics are:
- Some things I learned about choosing research questions are:
- Some things I learned about choosing focus areas are:
- Some things I learned about choosing keywords are:

There are several activities you can do to promote self-reflection (see Rankin, 1999, for more ideas). One is to have the students prepare a Help Manual for another class or for next year's students. Another is to have them teach another class one or more of the strategies that they've learned. A nice extension activity is to have students teach someone at home how to be a more effective Internet QUESTer and then report back to you. It is empowering for students to take on the role of teacher, especially students who are traditionally "at the margins" of the peer group (Meyer & Rose, 1998).

A powerful method of self-reflection is to have students re-enact the inquiry process from beginning to end. This can be done in less than one class period. Figure 9.3 shows a group of fourth- and fifth-grade students' reenactment of their cartoon inquiry project, with photos and captions to illustrate each step of the process. You can imagine how effective this activity is in solidifying students' understanding of what the process of inquiry entails. To illustrate the lasting impression of inquiry-based projects: Maya bumped into one of the fourth-grade girls from the cartoon project *five years later* when she was in high school, whereupon the teen instantly recognized Maya and recalled the cartoon inquiry project with great enthusiasm and nostalgia.

First, we brainstormed the topic. We agreed on cartoons.

Then, we got cartoon books from the library.

We wrote cartoon scripts in two teams.

We interviewed adults and kids about cartoons.

We organized our information on note cards.

Then we typed our information on the laptop and created a website.

Ta-ta-ta-daaaaah!   Th-th-th-that's all folks!

FIGURE 9.3. Inquiry project reenactment.

To truly determine whether your students have internalized new strategies for reading and learning on the Web, be on the lookout for evidence of generalization and transfer. In other words, do your students independently and automatically apply the skills and strategies they've been learning in their next inquiry project? In their next reading project? In their next writing project? Do they apply synthesis and transformation strategies while studying for a test or when working across the content areas? If so, this is when you know that real learning has taken place.

> "Those four things—reading ability, organizational skills, nonprocrastination, and writing—are the major stumbling blocks for my kids, they are the Great Wall of China. These kids don't get it the first or second or even the third time around. In general, this population has difficulty with transferring knowledge.
>
> —Deborah, seventh-grade special educator

What Have We Learned as Authors?

Our work with Internet readers and their teachers is both enlightening and inspiring. Students often amaze us with their insights and creativity. When given strategic instructions and choices about their learning, students usually rise to our high expectations. We have also been impressed by teachers who take risks and choose to be learners alongside their students. These teachers often find themselves out of their comfort zone when dealing with technology, but continue to return day after day, ready to tackle the next step of the process. Though it is a cliché, we feel that we have learned as much, if not more, from the students and teachers with whom we've worked as they have from us. We hope that we have painted a true picture of these learners, and that they have inspired you as much as they inspire us.

Final Thoughts

Throughout this book, we have set out to capture the essence of Internet inquiry by describing the process through the QUEST model. We have included detailed explanations, vivid descriptions, and illustrative graphics with the intent of bringing the inquiry process to life. We have built on what we as educators already know about learning, reading, and the quest for finding and making use of information.

When you encourage your students to ask deep questions, to critically evaluate information, and to transform ideas, you are embarking on a learning adventure for both yourself and your students. As teachers, we are asking students to generate questions that are often not answered as easily as the multiple choice or true/false questions commonly found in traditional curricula. Rather, we are asking students to think deeply about topics and ideas, expecting them to transform information through various formats requiring expertise we may not have yet developed ourselves. No lesson plan, teacher's guide, or staff development workshop can truly prepare you for the unexpected things that occur. Our best advice is to keep your focus on the inquiry *process* through the QUEST model, and go with the flow. The process of learning is more important than the end product, and students will watch for your cues about what is important and how to proceed.

This book has described authentic teaching and learning and presents the process of inquiry our students will face in their future as working professionals in the real world. Being a lifelong learner is about asking the questions burning in our hearts and minds and having the strategies needed to find and use the answers. We are preparing students to internalize those habits. In doing so, we are letting go of some control in the learning process by stepping aside to be a mentor or guide rather than a person who delivers information. This change may feel uncomfortable at first, and may cause us to question whether to continue down this path, but on we must go. The convergence of literacy and technology is ubiquitous in the world of work, in our personal inquiries, and in the lives of our students. We would be doing students a disservice by not preparing them to apply the inquiry process to the world's most massive source of information, one that will impact their future daily lives in ways we cannot even imagine. We don't take this responsibility lightly. In fact, wanting to help teachers become more comfortable with locating, using, and understanding information from the Web is the sole purpose of this book. When we approach Internet inquiry as both teachers and learners, we join our students on the journey of inquiry—and what an adventure it will be!

REFERENCES

Afflerbach, P. P. (2002). Teaching reading self-assessment strategies. In C. C. Block & M. Pressley (Eds.), *Comprehension instruction: Research-based best practices* (pp. 96–111). New York: Guilford Press.

Afflerbach, P. P., & Johnston, P. H. (1986). What do experts do when the main idea is not explicit? In J. F. Bauman (Ed.), *Teaching main idea comprehension* (pp. 49–72). Newark, DE: International Reading Association.

American School Library Association. (1998). *Information literacy standards for student learning.* American Association of School Librarians and Association for Educational Communications and Technology. Retrieved June 27, 2006, from *www.ala.org/ala/aasl/aaslproftools/ informationpower/InformationLiteracyStandards_final.pdf.*

Armbruster, B. B. (1984). The problem of "inconsiderate texts." In G. G. Duffy, L. R. Roehler, & J. Mason (Eds.), *Comprehension instruction: Perspectives and suggestions* (pp. 202–217). New York: Longman.

Armstrong, T. (2000). *Information transformation: Teaching strategies for authentic research, projects, and activities.* Ontario: Pembroke.

Baker, L., & Brown, A. L. (1984). Metacognitive skills and reading. In P. D. Pearson, R. Barr, M. L. Kamil, & P. Mosenthal (Eds.), *Handbook of reading research* (pp. 353–394). New York: Longman.

BBC News. (2002, February 20). *Web rage hits the Internet.* Retrieved October 21, 2006, from *http://news.bbc.co.uk/1/hi/sci/tech/1829944.stm.*

Beach, R., & Bruce, B. C. (2002). Using digital tools to foster critical inquiry. In D. E. Alvermann (Ed.), *Adolescents and literacies in a digital world* (pp. 147–163). New York: Peter Lang.

Beers, K. (2004). Equality and the digital divide. *Voices from the Middle, 11*(3), 4–5.

Berghel, H. (1997). Cyberspace 2000: Dealing with information overload. *Communications of the ACM, 40*(2), 19–24.

Bilal, D. (2002). Perspectives on children's navigation of the World Wide Web: Does the type of search task make a difference? *Online Information Review, 26*(2), 108–117.

Blachowicz, C. L., & Fisher, P. J. (2003). Best practices in vocabulary instruction: What effective teachers do. In L. M. Morrow, L. B. Gambrell, & M. Pressley (Eds.), *Best practices in literacy instruction* (2nd ed., pp. 87–110). New York: Guilford Press.

Block, C., & Pressley, M. (Eds.). (2002). *Comprehension instruction: Research-based best practices.* New York: Guilford Press.

Bolter, J. D. (1991). *Writing space: The computer, hypertext and the history of writing.* Hillsdale, NJ: Erlbaum.

Bowler, L., Large, A., & Rejskind, G. (2001). Primary school students, information literacy and the Web. *Education for Information, 19,* 201–223.

Broch, E. (2000). Children's search engines from an information search process perspective. *School Library Media Research, 3.* Retrieved October 25, 2006, from *www.ala.org/ala/aasl/aaslpubsandjournals/slmrb/slmrcontents/volume32000/childrens.htm.*

Bromley, K., Irwin-DeVitis, L., & Modlo, M. (1995). *Graphic organizers.* New York: Scholastic.

Brown, A. L., & Day, J. (1983). Macrorules for summarizing texts: The development of expertise. *Journal of Verbal Learning and Verbal Behavior, 22,* 1–15.

Brown, A. L., Palincsar, A. S., & Armbruster, B. B. (2004). Instructing comprehension-fostering activities in interactive learning situations. In R. B. Ruddell & N. J. Unrau (Eds.), *Theoretical models and processes of reading* (5th ed., pp. 780–809). Newark, DE: International Reading Association.

Brown, A. L., & Smiley, S. S. (1977). Rating the importance of structural units of prose passages: A problem of metacognitive development. *Child Development, 48,* 1–8.

Bruce, B. C. (2002). Diversity and critical social engagement: How changing technologies enable new modes of literacy in changing circumstances. In D. E. Alvermann (Ed.), *Adolescents and literacies in a digital world* (pp. 1–18). New York: Peter Lang.

Bruner, J. (1986). *Actual minds, possible worlds.* Cambridge, MA: Harvard University Press.

Burbules, N. C. (1997). Rhetorics of the Web: Hyperreading and critical literacy. In I. Snyder (Ed.), *Page to screen: Taking literacy into the electronic era.* (pp. 102–122). New York: Routledge.

Calkins, L. M. (1994). *The art of teaching writing.* Portsmouth, NH: Heinemann.

Carroll, M. (2004). *Cartwheels on the keyboard: Computer-based literacy instruction in an elementary classroom.* Newark, DE: International Reading Association.

CAST AspireREADER [Computer software]. (2006) Wakefield, MA: CAST, Inc. Retrieved September, 2006 from *www.cast.org/products/ereader/index.html.*

Castek, J., Bevans-Mangleson, J. (2006). Reading adventures online: Five ways to introduce the new literacies of the Internet through children's literature. *The Reading Teacher, 59,* 714–728.

Chandler-Olcott, K., & Mahar, D. (2001). A framework for choosing topics for, with and by adolescent writers. *Voices from the Middle, 9*(1), 40–47.

Clay, M. (1991). *Becoming literate: The construction of inner control.* Portsmouth, NH: Heinemann.

Cohen, M., & Riel, M. (1989). The effect of distant audiences on students' writing. *American Educational Research Journal, 26*(2), 143–159.

Coiro, J. (2003). Reading comprehension on the Internet: Expanding our understanding of reading comprehension to encompass new literacies. *Reading Teacher, 56*(5), 458–464.

Coiro, J., & Dobler, E. (in press). Reading comprehension on the Internet: Exploring the online comprehension strategies used by sixth-grade skilled readers to search for and locate information on the Internet. *Reading Research Quarterly.*

Connecticut State Department of Education. (1998). *The Connecticut framework K–12 curricular goals and standards: Social studies.* Retrieved October 25, 2006, from *www.state.ct.us/sde/dtl/curriculum/frsocst.pdf.*

Connecticut State Department of Education. (2005). *Core science curriculum framework.* Retrieved October 25, 2005, from *www.state.ct.us/sde/dtl/curriculum/science/framework/ScienceCoreFramework2005v2.doc.*

de Argaez, E. (2006, January). *Internet world stats news, 14*. Retrieved October 10, 2006, from *www.internetworldstats.com/pr/edi014.htm#3*.

Dennis, S., Bruza, P., & McArthur, R. (2002). Web searching: A process-oriented experimental study of three interactive search paradigms. *Journal of the American Society for Information Science and Technology, 53*(2), 120–133.

Dewey, J. (1938). *Experience and education*. New York: Macmillan.

Dickson, W. P. (1985). Thought-provoking software: Juxtaposing symbol systems. *Educational Researcher, 14*(5), 30–38.

Dobler, E. (2003, December). *Informational text and Internet text: Similarities and differences among text features*. Paper presented at the National Reading Conference, Scottsdale, AZ.

Dole, J. A., Duffy, G. G., Roehler, L. R., & Pearson, P. D. (1991). Moving from the old to the new: Research on reading comprehension. *Review of Educational Research, 61*, 239–264.

Downes, T., & Fatouros, C. (1995). *Learning in an electronic world: Computers and the language arts classroom*. Portsmouth, NH: Heinemann.

Duffy, G. G. (2002). The case for direct explanation of strategies. In C. C. Block & M. Pressley (Eds.), *Comprehension instruction: Research-based best practices* (pp. 28–41). New York: Guilford Press.

Duke, N. K., & Pearson, P. D. (2002). Effective practices for developing reading comprehension. In A. E. Farstrup & S. J. Samuels (Eds.), *What research has to say about reading instruction* (pp. 205–242). Newark, DE: International Reading Association.

Dyson, A. H. (1993). A sociocultural perspective on symbolic development in primary grade classrooms. *New Directions for Child Development, 61*, 25–39.

Eagleton, M. B. (1999, April). The benefits and challenges of a student-designed school website. *Reading Online*. Retrieved October 25, 2006, from *www.readingonline.org/articles/art_index.asp?HREF=eagleton/index.html*.

Eagleton, M. B. (2002, July/August). Making text come to life on the computer: Toward an understanding of hypermedia literacy. *Reading Online, 6*(1). Retrieved October 25, 2006, from *www.readingonline.org/articles/art_index.asp?HREF=eagleton2/index.html*.

Eagleton, M. B., & Guinee, K. (2002). Strategies for supporting student Internet inquiry. *New England Reading Association Journal, 38*(2), 39–47.

Eagleton, M. B., Guinee, K., & Langlais, K. (2003). Teaching Internet literacy strategies: The hero inquiry project. *Voices from the Middle, 10*(3), 28–35.

Eagleton, M. B., & Hamilton, M. D. (2002). Using technology to address language arts standards. *New England Reading Association Journal, 38*(1), 38–43.

Eisenberg, M., & Berkowitz, B. (2001). *Big6: An information problem-solving process*. Retrieved October 25, 2006, from *www.big6.com*

Eisner, E. W. (1991). Rethinking literacy. *Educational Horizons, 69*(3), 120–128.

Eisner, E. W. (1994). *Cognition and curriculum reconsidered*. New York: Teachers College Press.

Eisner, E. W. (1997). Cognition and representation. *Phi Delta Kappan, 78*(5), 349–353.

Fidel, R., Davies, R. K., Douglass, M. H., Holder, J. K., Hopkins, C. J., Kushner, E. J., et al. (1999). A visit to the information mall: Web searching behavior of high school students. *Journal of the American Society for Information Science and Technology, 50*, 24–37.

Finkelman, K., & McMunn, C. (1995). *Microworlds as a publishing tool for cooperative groups: An affective study* [Report No. 143]. East Lansing, MI: National Center for Research on Teacher Learning. (ERIC Document Reproduction Service No. ED 384 344).

Gardner, H. (1983). *Frames of mind: The theory of multiple intelligences*. New York: Basic Books.

Garner, R. (1987). *Metacognition and reading comprehension*. Norwood, NJ: Ablex.

Garner, R., & Gillingham, M. G. (1998). The Internet in the classroom: Is it the end of transmission-oriented pedagogy? In D. Reinking, M. McKenna, L. Labbo, & R. Keiffer (Eds.), *Handbook of literacy and technology: Transformations in a post-typographic world* (pp. 221–231). Mahwah, NJ: Erlbaum.

Gee, J. P. (2001). Reading as situated practice: A new literacy studies perspective. *Journal of Adolescent and Adult Literacy, 43*(5), 412–423.

Gee, J. P. (2003). *What video games have to teach us about learning and literacy.* New York: Palgrave Macmillan.

Gibson, M. R., & Mazur, J. (2001). "It's funner now!" Where online guidance stops and mentoring starts: Fifth graders' perceptions of doing research with the research buddy. In R. M. Branch & M. A. Fitzgerald (Eds.), *Educational media and technology yearbook* (Vol. 6, pp. 93–114). Englewood, CO: Libraries Unlimited.

Glasgow, J. N. (1997). It's my turn: Motivating young readers using CD-ROM storybooks. *Learning and Leading with Technology, 24*(4), 18–22.

Goodman, K. S. (1982). *Language and literacy: The selected writings of Kenneth S. Goodman* (G. V. Gollasch, Ed.). Boston: Routledge & Kegan Paul.

Goodman, K. S. (1994). Reading, writing and written texts: A transactional sociopsycholinguistic view. In R. B. Ruddell, M. R., Ruddell, & H. Singer (Eds.), *Theoretical models and processes of reading* (4th ed., pp. 1093–1130). Newark, DE: International Reading Association.

Goodman, K. S. (1996). *On reading.* Portsmouth, NH: Heinemann.

Gordon, C. J., & Pearson, P. D. (1983). *The effects of instruction in metacomprehension and inferencing on children's comprehension abilities* [Tech. Rep. No. 277]. Urbana, IL: University of Illinois, Center for the Study of Reading.

Graves, D. H. (1983). *Writing teachers and children at work.* Portsmouth, NH: Heinemann.

Grisham, D. L. (2001, April). Technology and media literacy: What do teachers need to know? *Reading Online, 4*(9). Retrieved October 25, 2006, from *www.readingonline.org/editorial/edit_index.asp?HREF=/editorial/april2001/index.html.*

Guinee, K. (2005a, April). *Open-ended research vs. fact finding: Differences in fifth graders' Internet search string construction.* Paper presented at the 86th Annual Meeting of the American Educational Research Association, Montreal, Canada.

Guinee, K. (2005b, December). *Lighting the path: Scaffolding fifth-graders' subject knowledge during Internet inquiry.* Paper presented at the 55th Annual Meeting of the National Reading Conference, Miami, Florida.

Guinee, K., & Eagleton, M. B. (2006). Spinning straw into gold: Transforming information into knowledge during Web-based research. *English Journal, 95*(4), 46–52.

Guinee, K., & Eagleton, M. B. (unpublished manuscript). *Children and young adolescents' mental models of the Internet.*

Guinee, K., Eagleton, M., & Hall, T. E. (2003). Adolescents' Internet search strategies: Drawing upon familiar cognitive paradigms when accessing electronic information sources. *Journal of Educational Computing Research, 29*(3), 363–374.

Gunn, H., & Hepburn, G. (2003). Seeking information for school purposes on the Internet. *Canadian Journal of Learning and Technology, 29*(1). Retrieved October 25, 2006, from *www.cjlt.ca/content/vol29.1/04_gunn_hepburn.html.*

Hafner, K. (2004, June 21). Old search engine, the library, tries to fit into a Google world. *New York Times,* pp. Retrieved July 3, 2006, from *www.nytimes.com/2004/06/21/technology/21LIBR.html?ex=140315.400&en=19bc49100fbfccba&ei=5007&partner=USERLAND.*

Hagood, M. C., Stevens, L. P., & Reinking, D. (2002). What do THEY have to teach US? Talkin' 'cross generations! In D. E. Alvermann (Ed.), *Adolescents and literacies in a digital world* (pp. 68–83). New York: Peter Lang.

Hansen, J. (1981). The effects of inference training and practice on young children's reading comprehension. *Reading Research Quarterly, 16,* 391–417.

Hare, V. C., & Borchardt, K. M. (1984). Direct instruction of summarization skills. *Reading Research Quarterly, 20,* 62–78.

Hargittai, E. (2002, April 1). Second-level digital divide: Differences in people's online skills.

First Monday, 7(4). Retrieved October 25, 2006, from *www.firstmonday.dk/issues/issue7_4/ hargittai/index.html.*

Harste, J. C. (1994). Literacy as curricular conversations about knowledge, inquiry and morality. In R. Ruddell, M. Ruddell, & H. Singer (Eds.), *Theoretical models and processes of reading* (4th ed., pp. 1220–1242). Newark, DE: International Reading Association.

Harvey, S. (1998). *Nonfiction matters.* York, ME: Stenhouse.

Harvey, S., & Goudvis, A. (2000). *Strategies that work.* York, ME: Stenhouse.

Henry, L. A. (2006). SEARCHing for an answer: The critical role of new literacies while reading on the Internet. *Reading Teacher, 59*(7), 614–627.

Hill, J. R., & Hannafin, M. J. (1997). Cognitive strategies and learning from the World Wide Web. *Educational Technology Research and Development, 45*(4), 37–64.

Hoffman, J. L., Wu, H., Krajcik, J. S., & Soloway, E. (2003). The nature of middle school learners' science content understandings with the use of online resources. *Journal of Research in Science Teaching, 40*(3), 323–346.

Hoyt, L., & Therriault, T. (2003). Understanding text structures. In L. Hoyt, M. Mooney, & B. Parkes (Eds.), *Exploring informational texts: From theory to practice* (pp. 52–58). Portsmouth, NH: Heinemann.

Inspiration [Computer software]. (2006). Portland, OR: Inspiration Software. Retrieved October 25, 2006, from *www.inspiration.com/productinfo/inspiration/index.cfm.*

International ICT Literacy Panel. (2001). *Digital transformation: A framework for ICT literacy.* Princeton, NJ: Educational Testing Service. Retrieved October 10, 2006, from *www.ets.org/ Media/Tests/Information_and_Communication_Technology_Literacy/ictreport.pdf.*

International Reading Association. (2001). *Integrating literacy and technology in the curriculum: A position statement.* Retrieved October 25, 2006, from *www.reading.org/resources/issues/positions_technology.html.*

Jacobs, G. E. (in press). People, purposes, and practices: Insights from cross-disciplinary research into instant messaging. In J. Coiro, M. Knobel, C. Lankshear, & D. Leu (Eds.), *Handbook of research on new literacies.* Mahwah, NJ: Erlbaum.

Jakes, D. S., Pennington, M. E., & Knodle, H. A. (2002). *Using the Internet to promote inquiry based learning.* Retrieved October 25, 2006, from *www.biopoint.com/inquiry/ibr.html.*

Jansen, B. J., & Pooch, U. (2001). A review of Web searching studies and a framework for future research. *Journal of the American Society for Information Science and Technology, 52*(3), 235–246.

Jansen, B. J., Spink, A., & Pfaff, A. (2000). Linguistic aspects of Web queries. *Proceedings of the American Society for Information Science Annual Meeting, 37,* 169–176.

Jansen, B. J., Spink, A., & Saracevic, T. (2000). Real life, real users, and real needs: A study and analysis of user queries on the Web. *Information Processing and Management, 36*(2), 207–227.

Jonassen, D. H. (2000). *Computers as mindtools for schools: Engaging critical thinking.* Upper Saddle River, NJ: Prentice-Hall.

Kafai, Y., & Bates, M. J. (1997). Internet Web-searching instruction in the elementary classroom: Building a foundation for information literacy. *School Library Media Quarterly, 25*(2), 103–111.

Kajder, S. B. (2003). *The tech-savvy English classroom.* Portland, ME: Stenhouse.

Kamil, M. L., & Lane, D. M. (1998). Researching the relationship between technology and literacy: An agenda for the 21st century. In D. Reinking, M. McKenna, L. Labbo, & R. Keiffer (Eds.), *Handbook of literacy and technology: Transformations in a post-typographic world* (pp. 323–341). Mahwah, NJ: Erlbaum.

Keatley, C. (1999). Elementary language immersion students: Changes in reading comprehension strategies across grades. *NCLRC Language Resource, 3*(1). Retrieved October 25, 2006 from *nclrc.org/readings/hottopics/elemlangimmersion.html.*

Keene, E. O., & Zimmermann, S. (1997). *Mosaic of thought*. Portsmouth, NH: Heinemann.

Kehoe, L. (1993, November 30). Casting the net worldwide. *Financial Times*, p. 11.

Kinzer, C. K., Gabella, M. S., & Rieth, H. J. (1994). An argument for using multimedia and anchored instruction to facilitate mildly disabled students' learning of literacy and social studies. *Technology and Disability, 3*(2), 117–128.

Kinzer, C. K., & Leu, D. J. (1997). The challenge of change: Exploring literacy and learning in electronic environments. *Language Arts, 74*(2), 126–136.

Kozma, R. B. (1991). Learning with media. *Review of Educational Research, 61*(2), 179–211.

Kress, G. (1998). Visual and verbal modes of representation in electronically mediated communication: The potentials of new forms of text. In I. Snyder (Ed.), *Page to screen: Taking literacy into the electronic era* (pp. 53–79). New York: Routledge.

Kress, G. (2003). *Literacy in the new media age*. London: Routledge.

Kucer, S. B. (2001). *Dimensions of literacy: A conceptual base of teaching reading and writing in school settings*. Mahwah, NJ: Erlbaum.

Kuhlthau, C. C. (1993). *Seeking meaning: A process approach to library and information services*. Norwood, NJ: Ablex.

Kuiper, E., Volman, M., & Terwel, J. (2004, April 12). *The Internet as an information resource in education: A review of the literature*. Paper presented at the Annual Meeting of the American Educational Research Association 2004, San Diego.

Kymes, A. (2005, March). Teaching online comprehension strategies using think-alouds. *Journal of Adolescent & Adult Literacy, 48*(6), 492–500.

Labbo, L. D. (1996). A semiotic analysis of young children's symbol making in a classroom computer center. *Reading Research Quarterly, 31*(4), 356–383.

Ladewig, B. (2005). Key concept synthesis. Greece Central School District. Retrieved July 3, 2006 from *www.greece.k12.ny.us/instruction/ela/6-12/Reading/Reading%20Strategies/keyconceptsynthesis.htm*.

Langford, L. (2001). A building block: Towards the information literate school community. *Teacher Librarian. 28*(5), 18–21.

Lankshear, C., & Knobel, M. (2003). *New literacies: Changing knowledge and classroom learning*. Buckingham, UK: Open University Press.

Large, A., & Beheshti, J. (2000). The Web as a classroom resource: Reactions from the users. *Journal of the American Society for Information Science, 51*(12), 1069–1080.

Large, A., Beheshti, J., & Moukdad, H. (1999). Information seeking on the Web: Navigational skills of grade-six primary school students. *Proceedings of the American Society for Information Science Annual Meeting, 36*, 84–97.

Lawless, K. A., Brown, S. W., Mills, R., & Mayall, H. J. (2003). Knowledge, interest, recall and navigation: A look at hypertext processing. *Journal of Literacy Research, 35*(3), 911–934.

Lebo, H. (2003). *The UCLA Internet report: Surveying the digital future, year three*. Los Angeles: UCLA Center for Communication Policy. Retrieved October 25, 2006, from *www.digitalcenter.org/pdf/InternetReportYearThree.pdf*.

Lehrer, R., Erickson, J., & Connell, T. (1994). Learning by designing hypermedia documents. *Computers in the Schools, 10*(1/2), 227–254.

Lemke, J. L. (1993). Education, cyberspace and change. *Electronic Journal on Virtual Culture, 1*(1). Retrieved October 25, 2006, from *http://infomotions.com/serials/aejvc/aejvc-v1n01-lemke-education.txt*.

Lenhart, A., Simon, M., & Graziano, M. (2001). *The Internet and education: Findings of the Pew Internet and American Life Project*. Washington, DC: Pew Internet and American Life Project. Retrieved October 25, 2006, from *www.pewinternet.org/pdfs/PIP_Schools_Report.pdf*.

Leu, D. J. (1997). Caity's question: Literacy as deixis on the Internet. *Reading Teacher, 51*(1), 62–67.

Leu, D. J., Jr. (2000, February). Our children's future: Changing the focus of literacy and literacy instruction. *Reading Online.* Retrieved October 25, 2006, from *readingonline.org/electronic/ elec_index.asp?HREF=/electronic/RT/focus/index.html.*

Leu, D. J., Jr. (2002). The new literacies: Research on reading instruction with the Internet. In S. J. Samuels and A. E. Farstrup (Eds.), *What research has to say about reading instruction* (pp. 310–336). Newark, DE: International Reading Association.

Leu, D. J., Kinzer, C. K., Coiro, J., & Cammack, D. (2004). Toward a theory of new literacies emerging from the Internet and other ICT. In R. B. Ruddell & N. Unrau (Eds.), *Theoretical models and processes of reading* (5th ed., pp. 1568–1611). Newark, DE: International Reading Association.

Leu, D. J., Leu, D. D., & Coiro, J. (2004). *Teaching with the Internet K–12: New literacies for new times* (4th ed.) Norwood, MA: Christopher-Gordon.

Lonsdale, M., & McCurry, D. (2004). Literacy in the new millenium. *Report for the Australian Council for Educational Research.* Retrieved October 25, 2006, from *www.ncver.edu.au/ research/proj/nr2L02.pdf?PHPSESSID=9e837f133741ad7aaffe110eb42627fb.*

Lorenzen, M. (2001). The land of confusion? High school students and their use of the World Wide Web for research. *Research Strategies, 18*(2), 151–156.

Lubans, J. (1999, March 5). *Key findings on Internet use among students.* Retrieved October 25, 2006 from *lubans.org/docs/key/key.html.*

Luke, C. (2002). Re-crafting media and other ICT literacies. In D. E. Alvermann (Ed.), *Adolescents and literacies in a digital world* (pp. 132–146). New York: Peter Lang.

Mackey, M. (2003). Researching new forms of literacy. *Reading Research Quarterly, 38*(3), 403–407.

Macrorie, K. (1988). *The I-search paper.* Portsmouth, NH: Boynton/Cook.

Marchionini, G. (1995). *Information seeking in electronic environments.* Cambridge, MA: Cambridge University Press.

McEneaney, J. E. (1998). Are less able readers disadvantaged by reading in electronic environments? *Proceedings of the 1998 annual conference of the Society for the Social Implications of Technology* (pp. 28–32). New York: Institute for Electronic and Electrical Engineers.

McEneaney, J. E. (2000, January). Learning on the Web: A content literacy perspective. *Reading Online.* Retrieved October 25, 2006, from *www.readingonline.org/articles/art_index.asp? HREF=mceneaney/index.html.*

McEneaney, J. E. (2003). A transactional theory of hypertext structure. In C. M. Fairbanks, J. Worthy, B. Malock, J. V. Hoffman, & D. L. Schallert (Eds.), *Yearbook of the National Reading Conference* (pp. 272–284). Oak Creek, WI: National Reading Conference.

McKenzie, J. (1999). The research cycle. *From Now On: The Educational Technology Journal, 9*(4). Retrieved October 25, 2006, from *questioning.org/rcycle.html.*

McMackin, M., & Siegel, B. (2001, February). Integrating research projects with focused writing instruction. *Reading Online, 4*(7). Retrieved October 25, 2006, from *readingonline.org/articles/ art_index.asp?HREF=/articles/mcmackin/index.html.*

McNabb, M. L., Hassel, B., & Steiner, L. (2002). Literacy learning on the Net: An exploratory study. *Reading Online, 5*(10). Retrieved October 25, 2006, from *www.readingonline.org/articles/art_index.asp?HREF=mcnabb/index.html.*

Meyer, A., & Rose, D. H. (1998). *Learning to read in the computer age.* Cambridge, MA: Brookline Books.

Mortensen, T. E. (in press). Of a divided mind: Weblog literacy. In J. Coiro, M. Knobel, C. Lankshear, & D. Leu (Eds.), *Handbook of research on new literacies.* Mahwah, NJ: Erlbaum.

Moukdad, H., & Large, A. (2001). Users' perceptions of the Web as revealed by transaction log analysis. *Online Information Review, 25*(6), 349–358.

Murray, J. H. (1999). *Hamlet on the holodeck: The future of narrative in cyberspace.* Cambridge, MA: MIT Press.

Nachmias, R., & Gilad, A. (2002). Needle in a hyperstack: Searching for information on the World Wide Web. *Journal of Research on Technology in Education, 34,* 475–486.

Nahl, D., & Harada, D. V. (1996). Composing Boolean search statements: Self-confidence, concept analysis, search logic, and errors. *School Library Media Quarterly, 24*(2), 199–207.

National Center for Education Statistics. (2005). *Internet access in U.S. public schools and classrooms: 2000-2003.* Retrieved October 21, 2006, from *http://nces.ed.gov/surveys/frss/publications/2005015/tables.asp.*

National Institute of Child Health and Human Development (NICHD). (2000). Report of the National Reading Panel. *Teaching children to read: An evidence-based assessment of the scientific research literature on reading and its implications for reading instruction* (NIH Publication NO. 00-4769). Washington, DC: U.S. Government Printing Office.

New London Group. (1996). A pedagogy of multiliteracies: Designing social futures. *Harvard Educational Review, 66,* 60–92.

Nielsen/NETRatings. (2004, March 18). *Three out of four Americans have access to the Internet.* Retrieved October 25, 2006, from *www.nielsen-netratings.com/pr/pr_040318.pdf.*

Ogle, D. (1986). K-W-L: A teaching model that develops active reading of expository text. *Reading Teacher, 39,* 564-570.

Palincsar, A. S., & Brown, A. L. (1984). Reciprocal teaching of comprehension-fostering and comprehension monitoring activities. *Cognition and Instruction, 1,* 117–175.

Palmquist, R. A., & Kim, K. S. (2000). The effect of cognitive style and online search experience on Web search performance. *Journal of the American Society of Information Science, 51,* 558–567.

Papert, S. (1996). *The connected family.* Atlanta: Longstreet Press.

Pappas, M. L., & Tepe, A. E. (1997). *Pathways to knowledge®: Follett's information skills model* (3rd ed.). McHenry, IL: Follett. Retrieved October 25, 2006, from *www.sparkfactor.com/clients/follett/home.html.*

Pardo, L. S. (2004). What every teacher needs to know about comprehension. *Reading Teacher* 58(3), 272–280.

Paris, S. G., Lipson, M. Y., & Wixson, K. K. (1983). Becoming a strategic reader. *Contemporary Educational Psychology, 8,* 293–316.

Pearson, P. D., & Gallagher, M. C. (1983). The instruction of reading comprehension. *Contemporary Educational Psychology, 8,* 317–344.

Pearson, P. D., Roehler, L. R., Dole, J. A., & Duffy, G. G. (1992). Developing expertise in reading comprehension. In S. J. Samuels & A. E. Farstrup (Eds.), *What research has to say about reading instruction* (pp. 145–199). Newark, DE: International Reading Association.

Perkins, D. N. (1986). *Knowledge as design.* Hillsdale, NJ: Erlbaum.

Pikulski, J. J., & Chard, D. J. (2005). Fluency: Bridge between decoding and reading comprehension. *Reading Teacher, 58*(6), 510–519.

Pressley, M. (2001, September). Comprehension instruction: What makes sense now, what might make sense soon. *Reading Online, 5*(2). Retrieved October 25, 2006, from *www.readingonline.org/articles/art_index.asp?HREF=/articles/handbook/pressley/index.html.*

Pressley, M. (2002). Metacognition and self-regulated comprehension. In A. E. Farstrup & S. J. Samuels (Eds.), *What research has to say about reading instruction* (3rd ed., pp. 291–309). Newark, DE: International Reading Association.

Pressley, M., & Afflerbach, P. (1995). *Verbal protocols of reading: The nature of constructively responsive reading.* Hillsdale, NJ: Erlbaum.

RAND Reading Study Group [RRSG]. (2002). *Reading for understanding: Towards an R&D program in reading comprehension.* Santa Monica, CA: RAND. Retrieved October 25, 2006, from *www.rand.org/multi/achievementforall/reading/readreport.html.*

RAND Reading Study Group [RRSG]. (2004). A research agenda for improving reading comprehension. In R. Ruddell & N. Unrau (Eds.), *Theoretical models and processes of reading* (5th ed., pp. 720–754). Newark, DE: International Reading Association.

Rankin, V. (1999). *The thoughtful researcher: Teaching the research process to middle school students.* Englewood, CO: Libraries Unlimited.

Raphael, T. E., & Pearson, P. D. (1985). Increasing students' awareness of sources of information for answering questions. *American Educational Research Journal, 22*, 217–236.

Raphael, T. E., Wonnacott, C. A., & Pearson, P. D. (1983). *Increasing students' sensitivity to sources of information: An instructional study in question–answer relationships* (Technical Report No. 284). Urbana, IL: University of Illinois, Center for the Study of Reading.

Reinking, D. (1994). *Electronic literacy.* (Perspectives in Reading Research No. 4). Athens, GA: National Reading Research Center.

Reinking, D. (1997). Me and my hypertext: A multiple digression analysis of technology and literacy (*sic*). *Reading Teacher, 50*(8), 626–643.

Reinking, D. (1998). Introduction: Synthesizing technological transformations of literacy in a post-typographic world. In D. Reinking, M. McKenna, L. Labbo, & R. Keiffer (Eds.), *Handbook of literacy and technology: Transformations in a post-typographic world* (pp. xi–xxx). Mahwah, NJ: Erlbaum.

Rose, D. H., & Meyer, A. (2002). *Teaching every student in the digital age: Universal design for learning.* Alexandria, VA: Association for Supervision and Curriculum Development.

Rosenblatt, L. R. (1978). *The reader, the text, the poem: The transactional theory of the literary work.* Carbondale: Southern Illinois University Press.

Rosenblatt, L. R. (1985). Viewpoints: Transaction versus interaction: A terminological rescue operation. *Research in the Teaching of English 19*, 96–107.

Rosenblatt, L. R. (1994). The transactional theory of reading and writing. In R. Ruddell, M. Ruddell, & H. Singer (Eds.), *Theoretical models and processes of reading* (4th ed., pp. 1057–1092). Newark, DE: International Reading Association.

Rosenshine, B., & Meister, C. (1994). Reciprocal teaching: A review of the research. *Review of Educational Research, 64*(4), 479–530.

Rouet, J. (2003). What was I looking for? The influence of task specificity and prior knowledge on students' search strategies in hypertext. *Interacting with Computers, 15*(3), 409–428.

Roush, W. (2004, March). Search beyond Google. *Technology Review.* Retrieved October 25, 2006, from *www.technologyreview.com/articles/04/03/roush0304.asp?p=1.*

Salomon, G. (1997). Of mind and media: How culture's symbolic forms affect learning and thinking. *Phi Delta Kappan, 78*(5), 375–380.

Schachter, J., Chung, G. K. W. K., & Dorr, A. (1998). Children's Internet searching on complex problems: Performance and process analyses. *Journal of the American Society for Information Science, 49*(9), 840–849.

Schmar-Dobler, E. (2003). Reading on the Internet: The link between literacy and technology. *Journal of Adolescent and Adult Literacy, 47*(1), 80–85.

Sharp, D. L., Bransford, J. D., Goldman, S. R., Risko, V. J., Kinzer, C. K., & Vye, N. J. (1995). Dynamic visual support for story comprehension and mental model building by young, at-risk children. *Educational Technology Research and Development, 43*(4), 25–42.

Short, K. G., & Burke, C. (1991). *Creating curriculum: Teachers and students as a community of learners.* Portsmouth, NH: Heinemann.

Short, K. G., Kauffman, G., & Kahn, L. (2000). "I just *need* to draw": Responding to literature across multiple sign systems. *Reading Teacher, 54*(2), 160–171.

Short, K. G., Schroeder, J., Laird, J., Kauffman, G., Ferguson, M., & Crawford, K. (1996). *Learning together through inquiry: From Columbus to integrated curriculum.* York, ME: Stenhouse.

Siegel, M. (1995). More than words: The generative power of transmediation for learning. *Canadian Journal of Education, 20*(4), 455–475.

Smith, F. (1997). *Reading without nonsense.* New York: Teachers College Press.

Smolin, L. I., & Lawless, K. A. (2003). Becoming literate in the technological age: New responsibilities and tools for teachers. *Reading Teacher 56*(6): 570–578.

Snyder, I. (1996). *Hypertext: The electronic labyrinth.* New York: New York University Press.

Sorapure, M., Inglesby, P., & Yatchisin, G. (1998). Web literacy. *Computers and Composition, 15*(3), 409–424.

Street, B. (Ed.). (1993). *Cross-cultural approaches to literacy.* Cambridge, UK: Cambridge University Press.

Suhor, C. (1984). Towards a semiotics-based curriculum. *Journal of Curriculum Studies, 16*(3), 247–257.

Sutherland-Smith, W. (2002). Weaving the literacy web: Changes in reading from page to screen. *Reading Teacher, 55,* 662–669.

Tao, L., & Reinking, D. (2000). Issues in technology: E-mail and literacy education. *Reading and Writing Quarterly, 16,* 169–174.

Teale, W. (1997). Dear readers. *Language Arts, 74*(2), 80–82.

Thinking Reader [Computer Software]. (2005). Tom Snyder Productions, Scholastic. Retrieved October 25, 2006, from *www.tomsnyder.com/Products/product.asp?sku=THITHI.*

Thomas, A. (in press). Cyberspace, cybercommunity, cyberculture, cybercitizenship. In J. Coiro, M. Knobel, C. Lankshear, D. Leu (Eds.), *Handbook of research on new literacies.* Mahwah, NJ: Erlbaum.

Tierney, R. J., Kieffer, R., Whalin, K., Desai, L., Moss, A. G., Harris, J. E., et al. (1997). Assessing the impact of hypertext on learners' architecture of literacy learning spaces in different disciplines: Follow-up studies. *Reading Online.* Retrieved October 25, 2006, from *www.readingonline.org/research/impact.*

Todd, R. (1998). From net surfers to net seekers: WWW, critical literacies and learning outcomes. *Teacher Librarian 26*(2) 16–21.

Tovani, C. (2000). *I read it, but I don't get it.* Portland, ME: Stenhouse.

Vygotsky, L. (1978). *Mind in society: The development of higher psychological processes.* Cambridge, MA: Harvard University Press.

Wallace, R. M., Kupperman, J., Krajcik, J., & Soloway, E. (2000). Science on the Web: Students online in a sixth-grade classroom. *Journal of the Learning Sciences, 9*(1), 75–104.

Watson, J. S. (1998). "If you don't have it, you can't find it." A close look at students' perceptions of using technology. *Journal of the American Society for Information Science, 49*(11), 1024–1036.

Wilhelm, J. (2004). Inquiring minds use technology. *Voices from the Middle, 11*(3), 45–46.

Wilhelm, J. D., & Friedemann, P. D. (1998). *Hyperlearning: Where projects, inquiry, and technology meet.* York, ME: Stenhouse.

Windsor Public Schools. (2001). *Curriculum summary for language arts K–8.* Windsor, CT: Author.

Windsor Public Schools. (2002a). *Curriculum summary for mathematics K–8.* Windsor, CT: Author.

Windsor Public Schools. (2002b). *Library media curriculum performance standards, grades K–12.* Windsor, CT: Author.

Windsor Public Schools. (2004). *K–12 District literacy benchmarks.* Windsor, CT: Author.

Winograd, P. N. (1984). Strategic difficulties in summarizing texts. *Reading Research Quarterly, 19,* 404–425.

Zwiers, J. (2004). *Building reading comprehension habits in grades 6–12: A toolkit of classroom activities.* Newark, DE: International Reading Association.

INDEX